Cataclysms, Crises, and Catastrophes:

Psychology in Action

Master Lecturers

Andrew Baum

Calvin Jeff Frederick

Irene Hanson Frieze

Edwin S. Shneidman

Camille B. Wortman

Edited by
Gary R. VandenBos
and Brenda K. Bryant

AMERICAN PSYCHOLOGICAL ASSOCIATION
WASHINGTON, DC 20036

0708563

Library of Congress Cataloging-in-Publication Data

Cataclysms, crises, and catastrophes.

  (The master lectures ; v. 6)
  Lectures presented at the 1986 APA Convention in
    Washington, D.C.
  Includes bibliographies.
  1. Disaster victims—Psychology. 2. Disasters—
Psychological aspects. 3. Stress (Psychology)
4. Victims of crime—Psychology. 5. Victims—Psychology.
I. Baum, Andrew. II. VandenBos, Gary R. III. Bryant,
Brenda K., 1948–   . IV. American Psychological
Association. Convention (1986 : Washington, D.C.)
V. Series: The Master lectures series ; v. 6)

[DNLM: 1. Disasters—congresses. 2. Stress, Psycholog-
ical—congresses. W1 MA9309V v.6 / WM 172 C357 1986]
HV553.C27 1987   363.3′4   87-19134
ISBN 0-912704-77-2

Copies may be ordered from:
Order Department
P.O. Box 2710
Hyattsville, MD 20784

Published by the American Psychological Association, Inc.
1200 Seventeenth Street, N.W., Washington, DC 20036
Copyright © 1987 by the American Psychological Association.

Printed in the United States of America.

CONTENTS

MASTER LECTURES

Self-Study Instrument

Each year the Master Lectures are presented at the APA Convention, and attendees have an opportunity to receive credit. If you were unable to attend the Master Lectures, you may obtain Continuing Education Credit through a self-study instrument (SSI) developed to accompany each volume of this series, beginning with Volume 2. For further information about this or previous years' SSI, please write or phone:

MLS-SSI
CE Program Office
American Psychological Association
1200 Seventeenth St., N.W.
Washington, DC 20036
(202) 955-7719

PREFACE

Psychologists neither live nor work in a vacuum. Each day, students of psychology learn concepts and techniques that will affect their interactions with other people, whether as clients, co-workers, or companions, for the rest of their lives. Each day, instructors face the responsibility of teaching those students. Each day, researchers gather data and draw conclusions upon which both the knowledge of psychology and its application are based. And, each day, clinical practitioners must apply the concepts and techniques they were taught in graduate school, as well as newly developed theories and applications that they later learn, in order to assist to the greatest extent possible the individuals and families that they serve. At the same time, psychologist practitioners in many fields also reach outside of their offices, beyond the immediate needs of a limited group of clients—into their communities and nation.

The chapters in this volume illustrate why this interaction between theory and practice, between a firm foundation in knowledge and basic human understanding, is so vital. They also illustrate how psychologists help individuals under stress confront, understand, and grow beyond not only the ordinary stresses they must face each day, but also the extraordinary stresses that today arise so often and so suddenly as a result of both natural disasters (such as volcanoes, floods, and fires) and humanmade disasters (such as toxic spills and acts of violence, crime, and terrorism).

Regardless of the nature of the disaster or whether it involves many people or only a few (or even only one), the immediacy of such concerns can be easily demonstrated. Even as the 1986 Master Lectures, upon which the chapters in this volume are based, were being presented—between August 22 and August 26, 1986—events occurred that affected not just individuals, but communities and nations as well. In that one week:

• A mail carrier in Oklahoma killed 14 co-workers and then took his own life.
• 2,000 people were forced to flee while fires burned out of control along the Cote d'Azur.
• Severe storms struck Britain and 11 people were killed.
• Hundreds of villagers were killed by an outpouring of volcanic gas in Cameroon.
• Terrorist bombs killed 4 people in France.
• Gunmen attempted to assassinate a Zulu leader, but killed his wife instead.
• Hostages continued to be held in Lebanon, as street fighting continued in Beirut.

Regardless of the environment in which psychologists work, whether they are involved in basic research or education or applied psychology or clinical practice, they are seeking out *real* world issues and functional methods for understanding the impact of those issues on individuals. At the same time, psychologists must identify possible resolutions for the stresses and trauma that result for individuals and entire communities. Natural disaster, violence in its many forms, terrorism, death—all are harsh realities that must be endured, and psychologists make substantial contributions to the effectiveness with which individuals meet and cope with these stresses that all of us face.

Psychologists are explorers and discoverers. They explore the reactions of human beings to small frustrations and great successes, to pleasing colors and the aftermath of disaster, always looking for answers to how and why people think, feel, and behave as they do. What psychologists gain through this exploration is a greater understanding of the reality of experience, of how those experiences can alter the expectations and methods of coping of the people who live through them, as well as of those who only hear about them. The psychologist, regardless of where he or she may work, is always applying what is known in an effort to resolve the unknown. The psychologist, no matter how small the question being asked may appear to be, is looking for the larger answer.

Although by no means definitive, the information that clinical practitioners, community psychologists, applied social psychologists, health psychologists, and others will find in these chapters will provide a broad view of current understandings of how catastrophic events affect individuals and groups and of how human beings adapt and can be helped to adapt to the resulting stresses. The chapters in this volume provide insight into the effects of disasters resulting from technological accidents as well as natural disasters (Andrew Baum), crime and terrorism (Calvin Jeff Frederick), violence against women (Irene Hanson Frieze), suicide (Edwin S. Shneidman), and irrevocable losses resulting from death, illness, and other life events (Camille B. Wortman and Roxane Cohen Silver).

The very nature of the kinds of crises experienced by the victims of such events emphasizes the fact that there is still much to be learned. The full implications, both short-term and long-term, of some events for victims are still unclear. The mechanisms human beings employ during and after such crises are still being discovered. Some processes and methods of coping that may be "healthy" at one moment in an individual's life may, 6 months, a year, or 5 years later, be less effective as a coping strategy—perhaps even be self-destructive. Psychologists—who are as intensely concerned with generating new knowledge about human reaction and interaction as they are with helping others—have a vital, day-to-day role to play in identifying, assessing, and treating those individuals faced with personal and shared life crises.

Gary R. VandenBos
Brenda K. Bryant

The topic and lecturers for the 1986 Master Lectures were selected by the APA Continuing Education Committee in 1985. The committee making the selections included: Deanna Chitayat (Chair), Clyde A. Crego, Charles Swencionis, Helen Farmer, and Mary L. Tenopyr. The lectures were presented at the 1986 APA Convention. Barbara Hammonds of the APA Continuing Education Office and Vivian Makosky, Associate Executive Director for Governance Affairs, handled the operational components of the Master Lectures. Other staff who contributed to the preparation of the manuscripts for publication were Deanna D'Errico, Donna Stewart, and Kathy Gutwillig of the APA Special Publications Office.

ANDREW BAUM

TOXINS, TECHNOLOGY, AND NATURAL DISASTERS

A ndrew Baum is Professor and Director of Graduate Studies in the Department of Medical Psychology at the Uniformed Services University of the Health Sciences (USUHS) in Bethesda, MD. He is also co-director of the Military Stress Studies Center at USUHS. He is editor of the *Journal of Applied Social Psychology* and has coauthored three text-books: *Introduction to Health Psychology* (with Robert J. Gatchel), *Environmental Psychology* (with Jeffrey D. Fisher and Paul A. Bell), and *Social Psychology* (with Jerome E. Singer and Jeffrey D. Fisher). He is also coeditor (with Jerome E. Singer) of two series of books: *Advances in Environmental Psychology* and *Handbook of Psychology and Health.*

Baum belongs to numerous professional societies, including the Academy of Behavioral Medicine Research (of which he is the secretary-treasurer), the American Psychological Association (Divisions 8 and 34, and Fellow of 34 and 38), and the Society for Behavioral Medicine. He was the 1985 recipient of an APA Division of Health Psychology award for Outstanding Contribution to Health Psychology. His research interests include stress, control, learned helplessness, synergistic effects of stress and licit drug use, and architecture.

TOXINS, TECHNOLOGY, AND NATURAL DISASTERS

R esearch on disasters has been uneven. One reason for this is that the study of disasters is complicated by methodological problems associated with field research that are exacerbated, in part, by the nature of disaster events. Baseline data are rarely available; because disasters are unpredictable and infrequent in any one locale, assessment of preimpact behavior and health is difficult. Large prospective study of an area that subsequently experiences a disaster can provide predisaster data when circumstances permit, but this is unusual (e.g., Robins, Fischbach, Smith, Cotler, & Solomon, 1986). Assessments of predisaster mental and physical health can be made by assessing subjects' medical records, but data in these files are often incomplete and difficult to use (Baum, Schaeffer, Lake, Fleming, & Collins, 1986). Lack of preimpact data increases the need for adequate control groups, but this too can be problematic. Finding individuals who are comparable to victims but unaffected by the disaster can be difficult, and more often researchers must settle for com-

The opinions or assertions contained herein are those of the author and are not to be construed as official or reflecting the views of the Department of Defense or the Uniformed Services University of the Health Sciences. Because the author is a federal employee, this chapter is in the public domain.

The author would like to thank India Fleming, Martha M. Gisriel, and Joan Ballard for their help in preparing this chapter.

parisons of victimized and less affected groups. Selection of subjects is also difficult, because many traditional methods of sampling to ensure representativeness or eliminate potential biases are often inappropriate or impossible (Drabek, 1970).

When acute response is of interest, it is necessary to begin data collection soon after the event occurs. Funding structures typically do not allow for rapid funding of research, and maintenance of quick-response research teams that can get to an affected area quickly requires conditional funding or strong institutional support. When researchers arrive in disaster areas, they may find a chaotic environment in which normal amenities are not available. Telephone surveys are not effective when large numbers of victims are made homeless and have no access to a phone, and face-to-face interviews must be conducted under conditions of disruption and ongoing activity. In addition, temporary "removal" of subjects from a disaster for the purposes of data collection will alter their experience of the disaster, resulting in potential misinterpretation of findings.

Most studies of disaster have relied on descriptive data, and the study of response was begun soon after the event (Drabek, 1970). Problems with sampling, numbers of subjects, consistency of measures, and inclusion of appropriate control groups are common. Many studies have focused on organizational or social group effects; fewer have considered individual response or both together. Research has taken (a) the approach of clinical–descriptive studies, documenting the nature of symptoms of disaster victims; (b) an epidemiological orientation in which rates of impairment and disasters following a disaster are measured; and (c) a quasi-experimental field research approach focusing on psychological variables as mediators of response and subsequent effects. The first and second approaches do not typically consider individual differences in stress and experience (Gleser, Green, & Winget, 1981). Some laboratory simulations of "disaster exercises" have been reported but have not been frequent (Drabek, 1970). Studies of long-term response following a disaster and investigations of chronic physical and mental health effects of disasters are less common than are examinations of short-term effects and mental health consequences (e.g., Trainer & Bolin, 1976). Follow-up and longitudinal studies of disaster impact have not been reported very often, and when they have been done, their results have often been difficult to interpret.

In this chapter, methodological problems and limitations will not specifically be considered. Almost all of the studies reported suffer from one or more of the problems already noted, and this accounts for some inconsistencies among studies and for limits on conclusions from the extant literature (see Green, 1982). Regardless, much can be learned about responses to extreme stress and victimization by evaluating this literature and relating it to research on related issues or stressors.

In this chapter, I will discuss issues concerning definition and characterization of disasters, typical responses to such disasters, and short- and long-term effects of victimization by disaster. I will also briefly examine differences across disasters that allow prediction of trauma or health consequences, including whether a disaster is caused by natural or human acts.

Space limitations do not permit a complete examination of victimization by disaster. Consequently, a number of variables that mediate disaster response will not be considered. Children, who are often affected by disaster, will not be discussed in detail, and sex differences in response, for which findings are inconsistent, will not be systematically considered either. Similarly, the role of adult age, predisposition to distress, and other demographic factors will not be discussed. Recognizing that these factors are important personal determinants of disaster response, I will emphasize psychological variables and factors related to individuals' responses and victimization and mood, behavior, and health outcomes. Other characteristics and levels of analysis that will not be covered here are not necessarily less important or meaningful but rather are not central to my focus here.

The Nature of Disaster

Disasters may be viewed and analyzed on several levels. On the one hand, they are events that vary with the medium in which they occur. Geophysical events, climatic or meteorological events, technological events, or biological events all may be distinguished one from another (e.g., earthquakes from drought, tornadoes from nuclear accidents or plague, and so on). On the other hand, disasters may also be political or economic events, influencing hierarchical organization and upsetting economic balances. As social events, they may cause social disruption, disorganization, and massive migration. As psychological events, they may produce trauma, fear, stress, and shock. The nature of disaster includes all of these levels of analysis, each interacting with the others to produce an event and its impact.

Because of this complexity, disasters are hard to define. There are essential characteristics, but the precise mix of these factors that make an event a disaster are hard to pin down. This is particularly frustrating because most of us know well what is a disaster and what is not. Most cases can clearly be called either disasters or not; the close calls or difficult distinctions are events where there are enough reasons to call something a disaster although it does not easily fit into one or another category.

For the most part, laypeople and scientists alike define disasters in terms of the peculiar nature of an event, the impact of the event, and the way in which victims respond. Earthquakes and tornadoes are almost automatically termed disasters, even though the destructiveness and scope of their impacts may vary tremendously. On the other hand, contamination of drinking water or release of radiation may not be as readily labeled as a disaster. If an event is destructive, it is often called a disaster, although events that cause no destruction may be disastrous as well. In addition, responses to disasters are as numerous as types of disaster events, ranging from shock and dazed disbelief to purposive and heroic activity.

The key to understanding disasters, including events and their impact, is to identify the conditions under which different responses occur. In this section of this chapter I discuss definitions, characteristics, and responses to disasters, to provide a basis for understanding psychological implications of disaster and predicting its short- and long-term consequences.

Defining Disaster

The concept of *disaster* includes many attributions or assumptions, almost all of which are negative. Defining it has proved difficult. Some people seemingly have equated it with its effects on individuals, including death, damage, loss, disruption, loss of control, and trauma. In addition, the nature of the event is often part of the picture—sudden, enormously powerful, and overwhelming events are often part of defining a disaster. Lastly, patterns of response to disaster are often included in concepts of disaster, including panic and dazed behavior of some victims, and social coalescence and heroic responses by other victims. However, the lack of preciseness of definitions of disaster is highlighted by the difficulty one might have in determining whether something is a disaster or not. How much damage is needed to make a storm a disaster? Is a hurricane necessarily a disaster, even if its impact is limited? Was the accident at Three Mile Island a disaster, even though little physical damage occurred?

Several approaches to these definitional problems have been taken. Some researchers (e.g., McLuckie, 1975) separate the disaster agent or event from the disaster itself, considering the former to be the physical event and the latter to be its impact. Emergency periods following an event and its immediate impact have been distinguished from the disaster events or impact. Greater emphasis appears to be on the effects of the disaster event, as reflected by the Federal Emergency Management Agency's (1984) definition of disaster:

> A major disaster is defined . . . as any hurricane, tornado, storm, flood, high water, wind-driven water, tidal wave, tsunami, earthquake, volcanic eruption, landslide, mudslide, snowstorm, drought, fire, explosion, or other catastrophe . . . which, in the determination of the President, causes damage of sufficient severity and magnitude to warrant major disaster assistance above and beyond . . . available

resources of States, local governments, and private relief organizations in alleviating the damage, loss, hardship or suffering caused by
a disaster. (p. 1)

In other words, a disaster is defined in terms of the damage it causes.
Of course, this definition is constrained by its purpose; to regulate federal
disaster assistance, the government must provide guidelines for granting
aid rather than trying to distinguish and explain various aspects of these
events. However, the emphasis on damage—the effects of the disaster—is
not simply a matter of economics and the law; it reflects a pervasive
social expectation or definition and emphasis on the immediate havoc
associated with a disaster. What makes a disaster a disaster is the extent
of damage done.

Perhaps the most obvious way to define a disaster is to equate it with
particular events or physical agents. Hurricanes, fires, tornadoes, and the
like are disasters that fall under such a scheme, equating disaster with
their potential destructiveness and disruptions. Dynes (1970) called these
events *disaster agents,* separating them from the effects of the event, such
as social disruption, loss, or terror. Defining a disaster in terms of its agent,
however, seems shortsighted; without considering the impact, such a
definition becomes hard to defend. What characteristics of a potential
event make it a disaster? What about a storm that ravages an area where
nothing can be or is damaged? Clearly, something more is needed.

One solution is to consider the impact of an event, that is, if the event
is sufficient to produce widespread destruction, disruption, or loss of life.
Thus, a rainstorm can become a disaster if it causes flooding that, in turn,
causes great destruction. Under normal conditions, however, it is simply a
rainstorm. What criteria are to be used and how much destruction or
death is necessary before something becomes a disaster? Though some
models use benchmarks for such a determination, the complexity of assessing impact suggests that this will not be adequate. Is an event that
causes great social disruption or individual fear and stress a disaster even
if there is no visible damage? Barkun (1974) suggests that the answer is
yes: "Disaster means damage—physical, social, and psychological" (p. 72).

If one considers impact alone—that is, whether there is damage of
one sort or another—one runs the risk of including so many different
events and situations that classification as a disaster loses some of its
meaning. The nature of the agent must also be considered, but not exclusively. Thus, damage caused by any sudden, powerful event that is beyond the realm of everyday experience could be considered a disaster,
although this would include rape, assault, and other individual stressors,
as well as cataclysmic events that are clearly not what most people mean
by disaster. To this definition, then, one might add the idea of scope; to be
a disaster, a situation must involve a substantial proportion of the people
in a community or area. Quarantelli (1985) has suggested that the degree
of social disruption can be used to define disasters. Magnitude of impact

is still the crucial parameter, but instead of focusing on loss of life or property, this approach considers effects on group and community functioning.

> Thus, if there is considerable destruction of material goods and/or a relatively large number of deaths or injuries, the event is viewed as a disaster. It is a disaster not because of the physical impact per se, but because of the assumed social consequences of the physical happenings. (p. 46)

This criterion adds teeth to previous definitions, because it includes only those events and impacts that are sufficient to produce social dysfunction whether or not physical damage occurs.

Quarantelli (1985) raises another interesting issue: What about events that cause little disruption but great disfigurement of the environment or those that engender social disorganization in the absence of any physical impact at all? For example, he points out that the major New Madrid earthquake of 1811–1812 had "massive physical effects on the topography of the region" (p. 47), but it is not often considered a disaster because few people lived in the region and relatively few were affected. Or, alternatively, what about an event that never materializes but causes social disorganization anyway? False rumors about a dam failure and impending flood produced social effects that were comparable to those associated with an actual dam break (Danzig, Thayer, & Galanter, 1958; Golec, 1980). These instances challenge formal definitions of disaster and suggest that, at some point, the search for specific and distinctive conceptualizations may cease to be useful.

Another approach to the definition of disasters is to consider disaster as a subordinate event, one of a type of events similar to Lazarus and Cohen's (1978) inclusion of disaster in their description of cataclysmic events. Disaster may also be viewed as a special case of crisis or collective stress situation (e.g., Barton, 1970; Drabek & Haas, 1970). In this mode, disaster is seen as an instance in which demands posed by a crisis situation exceed the resources, capabilities, and preparations for a response (Quarantelli, 1985). This type of definition avoids anchoring a definition in any one or a combination of disaster characteristics; it matters little whether the event is sudden or occurs gradually, whether it is acute or chronic, or whether it causes loss or not, if it poses threats or demands beyond the individual's or group's ability to cope. These characteristics may affect the overall level of demand posed by a crisis, because sudden or long-term conditions may be more likely to overwhelm immediate resistance capabilities. By focusing on psychological, behavioral, and social responses, this conceptualization is more sensitive to varying perceptions of events and crises. Furthermore, because crises are consensual events, this concept eliminates events that are more open to debate or conflict, such as civil disturbances (Quarantelli, 1985).

Lazarus and Cohen (1978) included disasters as one of several cataclysmic events—stressors characterized by great power, sudden onset, excessive demands on individual coping, and large scope (affecting many people). These events are generally outside the realm of normal, everyday experience, beyond the immediate control of victims, and considered to be as close to universally stressful as events generally can be. Also included in this class of stressors are humanmade catastrophes such as war, bombings, imprisonment, and relocation. Though not explicitly addressed in this definition, events such as the Three Mile Island accident would probably fall in this class because the scope, impact on local and worldwide communities, suddenness, unique nature, and lack of controllability are comparable with other cataclysmic events.

Cataclysmic events, then, are defined in terms of a number of characteristics; if an event exhibits enough of these characteristics, it may be considered cataclysmic, and expectations are affected accordingly. The effects of the event are only part of this conceptualization, because the nature of the event and its interpretation by potential victims are also crucial. Disasters share certain characteristics with these other events.

Characterization of disasters as stressful events has been a theme in several recent discussions of disaster (e.g., Baum & Davidson, 1985; Warheit, 1985). By viewing disasters in this context, one can use research and theory on stress to understand and predict the effects of disasters. The degree to which the characteristics of a disaster cause stress may be used as an index of impact or a predictor of mental health consequences, and the nature of the victimized population may be used as a mediator of stress that is produced in individuals. Thus, stress levels may increase if an event occurs suddenly, but if a community is prepared in advance, the stressful impact may be blunted. Similarly, stress levels may be higher when an event poses serious and immediate threats to life and property than when it does not, but if clear evacuation orders are issued and followed, this may not actually occur. The stressfulness of a disaster and, hence, its potential mental health effects are determined by an array of characteristics of the disaster event, the victimized population, and the individuals involved.

Disaster Characteristics

Much research has focused on identifying characteristics of the event or impact that predict mood and behavior change. In a paper relating disaster characteristics to trauma potential, Bolin (1985) listed several parameters that together define disaster impact. Some are related to the effects of the disaster event rather than the event itself: The degree to which victims are exposed to terror and horror is an important determinant of disaster impact. Terror is thought to be related to the proximity of victims to the "raw physical effects" of the disaster—the destruction of homes, collapse of buildings or bridges, or destruction of roads or fields by a flash flood. Horror, defined as witnessing death or dealing with dead or dying victims, is possible whenever death, injury, or disfigurement is involved.

Bolin (1985) discussed the duration of the event as a characteristic that also defines outcomes. He noted that the duration of the event impact must also be considered, and he suggested that longer duration of impact is associated with more severe consequences. Intensity must also be considered, as events of shorter duration are often more intense and, therefore, may have major effects as well. The unexpectedness of a disaster event, a joint function of the nature of the event and the community's preparedness and prediction capabilities, reflects an interaction of event and situational characteristics. Similarly, the degree of the threat posed, affected by physical conditions and subjective risk assessments, may be seen as a product of enduring and more transient conditions. Generally speaking, the greater the degree to which these characteristics are present in a disaster, the greater the acute and chronic psychological effects.

Davidson and I (1985) presented a similar discussion of disaster characteristics, describing them in terms of potential for stress experience, independent of destruction and loss of life or property. Duration of the event or impact, the speed with which the event subsides and recovery can proceed, the extent of impact, and the predictability and controllability of the event and its impact are seen as contributing to stress and consequences of a disaster. Quarantelli (1985) also lists a number of characteristics of disasters that help to define them. They include the proportion of the involved population that is victimized, the duration of impact, suddenness, predictability, unfamiliarity, depth of involvement of the victimized population, and the likelihood of recurrence.

Warning is another characteristic of a disaster situation that appears to mediate its impact. Fritz and Marks (1954) suggested that a lack of warning can increase the impact of a disaster. However, being warned of an impending disaster does not ensure minimization of consequences. The effectiveness of the warning system, the preparedness of a community, and other factors intervene between the issuance and benefits of alerting news.

This was made clear in a study of response to warnings of a flood (Drabek & Stephenson, 1971). The effectiveness of repeated warnings in getting people to evacuate was undermined by several factors. If families were separated at the time of warning, they tended to be more concerned with finding each other than with evacuation. In addition, unless a direct order to evacuate was heard, people sought confirmation of the danger and the need to leave. Some simply continued what they were doing, and overall, there was a great deal of skepticism reported. Family and friends were important sources of confirmation or denial of the threat. Although the media actually notified the most people, it was the least effective in producing appropriate responses. Warnings from friends and relatives were far more effective. Similarly, response to hurricane warnings about several different hurricanes was affected by a number of variables; the source of the warning had less effect on response than did expectations of damage, confidence in weather forecasting, and site characteristics (Baker, 1979).

Fritz and Marks (1954) also discussed two characteristics of a disaster situation that appeared to be associated with emotional disturbances. Consistent with other studies suggesting the primacy of concern for family members, Fritz and Marks suggested that separation of family members during a disaster engendered acute anxiety about each other's welfare. In addition, they found that horror, the trauma of witnessing death or exposure to the dead and badly injured, exacerbated emotional problems.

The analysis of disasters for trauma potential and their classification as stressful events, whether on an individual or collective basis, have identified a number of event and victim characteristics that may be associated with subsequent disruption and pathology. The extent of the horror or terror experienced appears to contribute to trauma, as do the suddenness, scope, and intensity of the event, the preparedness of the victims, the extent of warnings, and the familiarity of victims with the type of disaster event. Low points, when the worst has passed, appear to be important; if there is no clear low point, consequences may become chronic or may increase. Those characteristics that carry some psychological meaning appear to be more important than those with less experiential relevance; whether the event was a hurricane or a tornado appears to be less important in determining social and psychophysiological effects than are characteristics relating more directly to how individuals experience these events. Thus, Trainer and Bolin (1976) defined disasters almost exclusively in terms of psychologically relevant characteristics: Disasters are abrupt, unanticipated events that produce severe disruption and a need for relocation.

Acute Response to Disasters

Research has produced varying findings with respect to effects of disasters on behavior and mental health. Some studies suggest that disasters result in profound disorganization and stress that may lead to continuing disturbance, whereas other studies suggest that psychological effects are acute and dissipate rapidly after the danger has passed. In such cases, chronic stress or psychiatric impairment is rare and may be limited to those victims with prior histories of psychological vulnerability or disturbance (e.g., Kardiner, Linton, DuBois, & West, 1945). At a larger community level, some studies have found that overall effects of disaster may be positive, because the acute response includes increased social cohesiveness within local groups and consequent social stability over the recovery period. Clearly, these findings are inconsistent and require explanation. Why do some studies find pervasive negative effects of victimization by disaster whereas others find only benefits?

Warheit (1985) argued that the lack of clear conceptual frameworks to guide research is partly responsible for such findings. The events that are classified as disasters are very different, ranging from natural calamities associated with earthquakes and storms to humanmade events such as nuclear and toxic waste accidents, fires, and aircraft disasters. By attempting to group all of these events together without adequate understanding of the different demands and threats they pose, researchers have almost assured some degree of inconsistency.

Individual response. The immediate response of individuals to natural disaster is often withdrawal, as if victims are overwhelmed and numbed by the calamity that has befallen them. The *disaster syndrome,* characterized by dazed behavior and psychic detachment, is frequently followed by shock, a sense of loss, anxiety, and in some cases, activity directed toward saving lives or restoring property to its former state. Tyhurst (1951) suggested that most victims show some stunned behavior but are not profoundly affected by the disaster, whereas 10% to 25% manifest "inappropriate" responses, including hysteria and paralyzing anxiety. Most victims appear to recover fairly quickly, though some may continue to wander about dazed and withdrawn. In a study of victims of a cyclone, Crawshaw (1963) reported that initial responses were characterized by shock, followed by denial, anger, and depression. Menninger (1952), reporting on response immediately after flooding in Topeka, Kansas, observed the inhabitants' disbelief (many did not leave their homes and subsequently required rescue), apathy, grief, and a desire to talk about the experience. The relief gained from talking about a disaster experience has been linked to affiliative tendencies (Hoyt & Raven, 1973; Strumpfer, 1970).

Fritz and Marks (1954) reviewed the effects of several disasters, including an airplane crash into a crowd of air show spectators, a series of explosions and fires, a coal mine explosion, three airplane crashes occurring within two months of one another in the same area, a tornado, and an earthquake. Based on interviews, studies of these events suggested that panic was rare and was caused primarily by an immediate threat coupled with the belief that escape was possible. However, response to the disasters was highly variable; about a third of the victims exhibited agitated but controlled behavior, less than 10 percent exhibited agitated behavior that was out of control, and a few showed signs of shock or of calm, unexcited behavior. Some victims were confused and disorganized, whereas others responded purposively. Some evidence of acute emotional and somatic responses was also reported.

Observations of responses to an earthquake in Managua suggested that early response may not be effective. Initial responses consisted of spontaneous efforts to assess effects and locate and rescue family, friends, and neighbors, but looting was widespread, and few attempts were made to limit secondary effects such as putting out fires, shutting down water mains, and so on (Kates et al., 1973). Groups that emerged were largely focused on local ties, and purposive responses aimed at regaining some semblance of normalcy were late in developing.

Several studies have shown that immediate response to disaster is not necessarily aimless or nonproductive. Bowman (1964) observed the behavior of mental patients after an earthquake near Anchorage, Alaska, on Good Friday, 1964. Contrary to Bowman's expectations, the patients' initial response was positive; wanting to help with problems that arose, the patients displayed "a stimulation of all the personnel, a feeling of unity, a desire to be helpful, and a degree of cooperation which I only wish it were possible to have at all times" (p. 314). Some felt trapped and isolated; others froze, were dazed, or ended up in a stupor, but no single response characterized the behavior among these patients after the earthquake.

Responses of organizations. Disasters can disrupt organizations and communities as well as families and individuals, and, in some cases, the functions once performed by larger groups are supported by emergent small groups of victims. For example, one of the more serious problems in disasters is coordination of various organizations and relief efforts. Despite the need for centrality of coordination in successful disaster management, organizations are often hesitant to assume responsibility for overall coordination, and there is frequently an "atomization of the community into uncoordinated organizations and isolated islands of activity" (p. 424). This atomization process and the lack of overall coordination apparently promote the emergence of cohesive local groups who must assume responsibility for those functions not being met by formal organizations. A lapse of authority also contributes to the development of these groups. Frequently, there is ambiguity regarding who has legitimate authority, and this is compounded by the tendency of leaders to avoid the assumption of responsibility early in a disaster (Loomis, 1960).

Positive social response during or immediately after a disaster event also appears to be influenced by the needs of the community. When destruction is so vast that rescue teams and official relief efforts cannot cover all needs, locally based groups may emerge to fill the void. Thus, the demands created by the disaster may require some informal group response.

When these relief efforts are adequate, those groups not involved in direct rescue efforts may exhibit more negative reactions. For example, Weil and Dunsworth (1958), reporting on reactions to an explosion and partial collapse of a coal mine in Springhill, Nova Scotia, noted that while formal rescue efforts continued, the responses of local residents ranged from initial panic, grief, and anxiety to hope and euphoria when some trapped miners made their way to safety, and later changed to stress, grief, and fatigue as the rescue attempt was finally abandoned. The development of groups in the wake of disaster may support or facilitate coping, by allowing victims to respond in a meaningful way and compare their reactions with those of other victims, while they make sense of and adjust to the event.

The notion that disasters are often met not by panic or competition for scarce resources and looting but rather by rescue attempts, prosocial behavior, and group formation, runs counter to most people's general ideas of what happens during a disaster (Goltz, 1985). Data from surveys of the public suggest that people believe that flight and incapacitating trauma are common (Wengner, Dykes, Sebock, & Neff, 1975), and that most of the information they have about disasters comes from media coverage (Turner, Nigg, Paz, & Young, 1979; Wengner et al., 1975). It is tempting to attribute the more negative view of breakdown and chaos to media accounts, although recent data suggest that this may be inaccurate (Goltz, 1985). Regardless, severe disorganization does not usually occur, although in some cases, the prosocial responses discussed by Quarantelli and Dynes (1972) do not materialize.

Effects of Natural Disasters

There is a wide range of disaster effects, varying in level of impact as well as duration, intensity, and the like. Communities, organizations, families, and individuals are affected, and each set of effects occurs in the context of these other levels: Effects on individuals, for example, are affected and influence effects on families and communities. The focus here is on individual effects—changes in health and well-being—rather than on social and organizational sequelae. Although conclusions about mental health consequences of a disaster are difficult to draw because studies have used widely varying measures of effects, it is clear that the consequences are joint products of the overall impact of the disaster and premorbid individual vulnerability. In the context of emergent disaster groups, a sense of normalcy may quickly be reestablished and psychological disturbance minimized. In such cases, effects of the disaster would be modest and short-lived. For the purposes of this review, effects discussed here are divided into acute (lasting a year or so after the event) and chronic effects.

Acute Effects

Bennet (1970) reported on consequences of flooding due to heavy rainfall in Bristol, England. On the one hand, this event was seen as mild; "compared with earthquakes, tornadoes, and other natural disasters of fiercer climates, such flooding will seem trivial" (p. 454). However, some evidence of the flood's long-term effects was noted. Flood victims and other residents whose homes were not flooded were interviewed twice, the first time within 2 weeks of the flood and the second time, one year later. Approximately 33% of the flood victims reported development of psychological or physical symptoms, compared with less than 20% of the nonvictims. Rate of physician visits increased among flood victims relative to nonvictims, and hospital referrals more than doubled among victims after the flood. Mortality also increased among victims, but not in the rest of Bristol, and, in general, the health of victims was worse one year after the flood than was that of nonvictims. The increase in mortality was seen as being the result of exacerbated health problems that were present before the flood; "death can be *hastened* by the experience of having been flooded rather than somehow being caused by it" (p. 457).

A study of victims of flooding in Brisbane, Australia, also found evidence of mental health effects up to one year after the disaster (Abrahams, Price, Whitlock, & Williams, 1976). Though relatively few lives were lost, damage was extensive and more than 6,000 households were flooded. Comparison of 695 flood victims with 507 nonvictims indicated that the former were more likely to visit a physician during the year following the disaster. The number of psychological disturbances and reports of symptoms also increased among flood victims relative to the control group, although no differences in postdisaster mortality were found. Reporting on the same flood, Price (1978) indicated that 76% of the flood victims reported one or more psychiatric symptoms during the year after the disaster, whereas only 38% of the control subjects reported any symptoms.

Melick (1976) reported a 3-year follow-up study of victims of flooding in Pennsylvania in the wake of Hurricane Agnes. Approximately 31% of subjects who had not been flooded and 46% of those who had been flooded reported that someone in their immediate family had experienced distress as a result of the disaster, men expressing more distress than women. However, this distress did not appear to last long; only about one-third of those reporting distress indicated that it lasted 9 months or more, and the mean duration of postflood distress was 6 months. No differences were found between flooded and nonflooded groups for number, type, or duration of illnesses. Nearly half of the flood victims reported that they believed that the flood had affected their health, compared with only 6% of the nonvictim group.

Logue and Hansen (1980) compared 29 women from this same flooded area who later became hypertensive with 29 women from the same area who did not develop high blood pressure. Cases were matched on age- and weight-related variables and proved comparable on a range of social and personal characteristics. Retrospective reports of experience following the flood showed that women who became hypertensive reported greater perceived property loss, financial problems, alcohol use, and distress during recovery than did respondents who had not developed hypertension. Furthermore, hypertensive individuals were more likely to continue to be bothered by thoughts of the flood 5 years later and reported greater somatic distress and anxiety than did flood victims who had not become hypertensive. The data were interpreted as evidence of "a threefold risk of hypertension" (p. 33) among flood victims who suffered substantial property loss (more than $30,000), although victims' experiences during the postflood recovery period were also associated with long-term health consequences. Other studies of the flooding in the wake of Hurricane Agnes suggest that, although victims were distressed initially, for the most part, they had adjusted to the disaster after a year or so (Logue, Hansen, & Struening, 1979; Poulshock & Cohen, 1975).

Further evidence of relatively mild mental health effects of a natural disaster is reported by Penick, Powell, and Sieck (1976). Studying 26 victims of a tornado that struck Joplin, Missouri (which killed 2, injured 87, and caused property damage for more than half of the residents), they found that the problems most likely to be reported concerned disruption of normal activities. Five months after the tornado, problems were substantially reduced; three-quarters of those interviewed reported no increase in strain and tension among adults in the household, and, although there was somewhat more reporting of psychiatric problems 5 months after the storm than there had been before it, the shift was small and involved few respondents. The authors interpreted their findings as indicating that victims of natural disasters, "do not typically experience serious emotional problems which are incapacitating" (p. 67). Another study of a destructive tornado impact also suggested that changes in mental health occurred over the 6 months following the disaster, but that the effects were relatively mild (Taylor, Ross, & Quarantelli, 1976).

A study of the consequences of evacuation during Cyclone Tracy, which devastated Darwin, Australia, on Christmas Day, 1974, provides limited evidence of lasting effects of disaster and disruption (Milne, 1977). The storm destroyed more than half of the homes in Darwin, and about 50 people were killed. Interviews of residents who did not evacuate, residents who evacuated and later returned, and residents who left and did not return were conducted 7–10 months after the storm. Those who evacuated but did not return were most affected during the disaster event, whereas those who did not evacuate reported the least stress, injury, and loss during the storm. Nearly 33% of the women who left but did not return experienced postdisaster emotional disorders, compared with about 11% of those who stayed and 12% of those who evacuated and returned. Relatively few injuries or illnesses after the storm were reported by any subjects, and differences in the use of alcohol, cigarettes, and analgesics were small. Little evidence of increases in psychosomatic complaints after the storm were found, and those complaints that were discovered may have been related to relocation rather than to the disaster itself.

These findings were consistent with those of Parker (1977), who examined psychiatric cases after the same cyclone occurred. Immediately after the disaster, more than 50% of the subjects exhibited distress, although this dropped to 22% a little more than a year later.

Research on the effects of the Mount Saint Helens volcanic eruption in 1980 has suggested that this type of natural disaster can also have negative effects on affected area residents. Adams and Adams (1984) reported posteruption increases in services to the mentally ill, emergency room visits, arrests, and domestic violence, which suggested that the eruption and subsequent ashfall were stressful. Other studies also indicate that the incident was associated with stress, although this effect may have been short-lived (e.g., Leik, Leik, Euker, & Gifford, 1982; Murphy, 1985). After a year, Shore, Tatum, and Vollmer (1986) found increased rates of anxiety, depression, and posttraumatic stress among the area residents most severely affected by the eruption and ashfall.

Chronic Effects

Chronic effects of natural disasters are not ordinarily seen; immediate reactions to most disasters are similar and short-lived, whereas long-term consequences are not as evident in most victims (e.g., Glass, 1959; Goldsteen, Schorr, & Goldsteen, 1985). In part, this is a result of a lack of studies directed toward assessing long-term effects, but the preceding review suggests that these effects are unusual. When they do occur, they have generally been attributed to the severity of disruption of individual and social functioning, to preexisting vulnerability and predisposition to psychological disturbance, and to coping and social assets (e.g., Barton, 1969; Erikson, 1976; Jacobs & Spilken, 1971; Pearlin & Schooler, 1978; Quarantelli & Dynes, 1976).

One way of examining chronic effects of disasters is to determine the ways in which recovery of daily routine is facilitated and inhibited in the postdisaster period. Drabek and Key (1976) studied the changes in individuals' relationships with friends and relatives in the wake of a destructive tornado and found that changes were common in both directions. As if the strain associated with the disaster intensified preexisting tendencies, strong social ties became stronger and weak bonds became weaker. Trainer and Bolin (1976) have argued that long-term recovery is complex, depending on the ease of regaining one's home, employment, and stable daily activity (e.g., shopping, attending school, or visiting with friends).

In order to examine this, Trainer and Bolin interviewed survivors of the 1972 earthquake in Managua, Nicaragua. The quake destroyed a major portion of the city, including the central business area and several residential areas. Thousands of victims left the city, but many returned and were able to find shelter. Up to one-third of the 376 survivors who were interviewed 8 and 17 months after the earthquake reported less social activity than before, primarily as a result of the dispersion of people throughout the area and relatively poor transportation facilities. Leisure activity was also sharply curtailed in postdisaster Managua; 45% of the respondents at the 8-month point and 32% of the respondents at the 17-month point reported that they no longer engaged in preferred leisure activities, primarily because they lacked money to spend or because entertainment facilities had been destroyed in the earthquake. Shopping was drastically altered because most markets were destroyed, and, over-all, more than half of the surviving residents were less satisfied with their life in Managua 17 months after the earthquake than before it.

Trainer and Bolin (1976) also studied survivors of a flash flood in Rapid City, South Dakota. This catastrophe left 238 dead and caused extensive damage. Some 1,200 families were homeless in the wake of the flood. Here, however, disruption of routine and recovery of daily activity were different; although a large number of the 125 survivors who were interviewed 2 years after the flood reported less social contact with neighbors, many said it was because of a lack of time. This also showed up in reported leisure activity; though a third or more reported that they no longer engaged in their preferred leisure activities, this was more often a result of a lack of time than anything else. When they had time, nearly three-quarters of the respondents indicated participation in leisure activity as they did before. Shopping and other routine activities were not affected over the long haul, and survivors of the Rapid City flood were less likely to be less satisfied with their lives than were survivors of the Managua earthquake.

In some cases, long-term social effects of disasters may be positive. Drabek, Key, Erickson, and Crowe (1975) reported that 3 years after a destructive tornado struck Topeka, Kansas, there was still evidence of heightened group cohesion and positive responses. Victims reported fewer symptoms of emotional disturbance and comparable perceptions of health than did nonvictims. In another study of the Rapid City flood Hall and Landreth (1975) found mixed evidence of positive and negative effects. No changes in suicides, juvenile arrests, drunk driving arrests, accidents, infant deaths, illness rates, or prescriptions for tranquilizers were found. However, in the 17 months after the flood, the number of divorces and annulments increased, as did arrests for public intoxication. The authors concluded that "Rapid City did not experience a major mental health crisis after the flood . . . the community in general experienced the typical post-disaster utopian mood" (p. 60).

In summary, the issue of whether the long-term impact of disasters is positive or negative has not been resolved. The data do not suggest that natural disasters are usually associated with long-term mental or physical health problems, and Quarantelli and Dynes (1972) have argued that people behave heroically during a disaster, showing a stubborn determination to "beat the storm." Stricken communities show tendencies toward increased social cohesion during and after disasters (e.g., Barton, 1970; Fritz, 1961), and Drabek et al. (1975) found long-term benefits of this increased social cohesion. However, White and Haas (1975) have argued that research has not yielded a sufficiently broad, consistent conceptualization of disaster impact to allow a determination of these long-term effects. Frederick (1980) goes a step further, noting that

> Based on a small number of research reports, for years it was thought that any mental or emotional effects of disaster were minimal. However, recent disasters have clearly indicated that this is not the case. The misperception principally has been due to inadequate, narrow research. (p. 71)

Consistent with this, Frederick argued that because the expected panic had not occurred in most disasters, "all other psychological reactions were thought to be nonexistent" (p. 72).

Effects of Humanmade Disasters

In contrast to the research just reported, the consequences of humanmade disasters appear to be more persistent. They also appear to be heavily influenced by psychological factors. For example, Adler (1943) reported on acute effects of the nightclub fire at the Cocoanut Grove in Boston and also on follow-up observations of survivors nearly a year after the fire. Accidentally set, the fire killed 491 patrons of the club and was characterized by great terror and horror. More than half of the survivors developed psychiatric complications, including general nervousness, anxiety, guilt, nightmares, and fear. Of particular interest was the finding that of those who did not develop psychiatric problems, 75% had lost consciousness during the fire, most of them remaining unconscious for more than an hour. Among those who eventually exhibited psychological difficulties, only half lost consciousness, mostly for less than an hour. Unconsciousness, and therefore less exposure to the terror and horror during the fire, was associated with more positive psychiatric prognosis.

A variety of other disasters has been studied, though in many cases the number of survivors was so small that even by studying all of them, sample sizes were perilously low. Leopold and Dillon (1963), for example, reported on a 4-year study of victims of a collision between two ships. They interviewed more than 80% of the survivors on the ship that was destroyed (34 men) and found evidence of fairly severe work-related problems and persistent psychiatric distress in more than three-quarters of the survivors. Panic did not occur, but mood disturbances increased over time, and psychosomatic disorders were reported. In addition, the majority of survivors went back to work in maritime activities, but several had to stop shortly after. Henderson and Bostock (1977) interviewed all seven male survivors of a shipwreck 1 to 2 years after it occurred and found that 71% developed some form of psychological disturbance. In a 10-year study of survivors of a coal mine cave-in, Ploeger (1972) also found substantial long-term effects among the ten men studied; nine exhibited changes in personality and experienced threatening memories, and six had developed phobic syndromes.

The Buffalo Creek Flood

One of the more carefully studied disasters was the Buffalo Creek flood in West Virginia. A slag dam gave way after extended rainfall and "unleashed thousands of tons of water and black mud on the Buffalo Creek Valley . . . [an] Appalachian tidal wave [that] destroyed everything in its path" (Titchener & Kapp, 1976, p. 295). The flood killed 125, left 4,000 people without homes, and wiped away all traces of the town of Saunders. A number of other communities were also destroyed. The dam and the company that owned it were seen as responsible for the disaster, and 654 survivors eventually filed suit against the company.

Titchener and Kapp (1976) interviewed these plaintiffs to assess the degree of psychological impairment attributable to the flood. Findings suggested substantial difficulty: Anxiety, depression, and changes in character were evident in almost all of the survivors 2 years after the disaster. The plaintiffs reported feeling sluggish shortly after the flood, had difficulty controlling their emotions, and experienced anxiety, grief, and sleep disturbances. Over time, anxieties and fears were expressed as phobia, and 80% of the group exhibited traumatic neuroses.

In long-term follow-up interviews of residents of the valley 2 and 5 years after the flood, residents reported chronic symptoms of psychopathology and more severe disturbance than was found in normative studies of the assessment instrument (Gleser et al., 1981). Furthermore, symptoms exhibited by flood victims were comparable with those of "highly distressed" psychiatric patients. Gleser et al. (1981) also reported increases in the occurrence of ulcers among flood victims since the disaster and found evidence of a rise in diagnoses of hypertension as well. Before the flood less than 5% of the men were diagnosed as hypertensive, whereas a year or more after the flood nearly 15% were so diagnosed. Women showed a similar pattern; before the disaster, 13% were hypertensive, and after it, 28% were diagnosed as having hypertension. Because predisaster rates of illness were low, Gleser and her colleagues suggest that these changes could reflect adjustment to normative standards or that the relative lack of stress in the valley before the flood may have been a factor.

Other symptoms of chronic stress were also found: Flood victims continued to experience sleeping problems 2 years after it had occurred, with 77% of the men and 87% of the women reporting some difficulty falling asleep (Gleser et al., 1981). Flood victims also reported difficulty staying asleep, which was more often related to severity of disturbance, anxiety, and depression, and more frequent nightmares than would be expected based on surveys of other populations. Alcohol consumption and cigarette smoking increased primarily among those exhibiting the greatest distress, and the extent of victimization—victims' experiences during and after the flood—were related to symptoms of distress. Bereavement and the extent of initial flood impact experienced were associated with psychopathology, as were displacement and subsequent hardship. Children were also affected, but their degree of impairment was related to that of their parents. Families tended to exhibit similar effects, as spouses were also likely to respond comparably. Families were not necessarily comparable with regard to coping, however; men who were able to begin rebuilding or restoring their homes quickly showed better mental health than did men who could not, but among women, helping or recovery activities were not related to distress. After 5 years, some decrease in symptoms of psychopathology was observed (associated with settlement of the lawsuit among the men), but there was also evidence of persistent psychological distress among almost one-third of those interviewed.

Rangell (1976) described features of the Buffalo Creek flood that help to clarify its unusually persistent or severe effects. Many are related to its technological nature; though rain swelled the creek, it was a humanmade dam that gave way and caused the great destructiveness. First, Rangell noted that the flood was not completely unexpected, as valley residents could see the dam and had expressed continuing concerns. "Another difference, which added the makings of a latent inner eruption . . . was that there were, in the minds of valley residents, people (the owners of the dam) who could and should have done something about the situation" (p. 31). Rangell observed that this may have been related to the persistence of numbness, apathy, and withdrawal in inhabitants of the valley 2 years after the flood.

The human context of the Buffalo Creek catastrophe was not the only contributing factor to chronic problems among victims. After disaster events pass and the destruction has ceased, people return to their homes and begin to rebuild. At Buffalo Creek, this was not possible; the valley had been so thoroughly transfigured by the flood that there was no home to return to for most survivors. Rangell (1976) argued that in such cases trauma does not recede with floodwaters, but rather continues and has cumulative consequences. Such a situation can result in severe blows to the social fabric holding a community together. Erikson (1976) discussed this loss of communality in the wake of the flood, suggesting that, "It is, however, a form of shock—a gradual realization that the community no longer exists as a source of nurturance and a part of the self has disappeared" (p. 302).

Erikson clearly suggests that loss of social support and destruction of social networks can cause many problems associated with disasters such as the one at Buffalo Creek. When an individual is victimized, as in the case of an automobile accident, he or she does not lose support systems as well. When a larger segment of the community is affected, however, social support may be lost. At Buffalo Creek, most survivors

> remained in the general vicinity of their old homes, working in famil-iar mines, traveling along familiar roads, trading in familiar stores, attending familiar schools and sometimes worshiping in familiar churches. However, the people were scattered more or less at ran-dom throughout the vicinity—virtually stranded in the spots to which they had been washed by the flood. (1976, p. 303)

Preflood social networks, which had depended in part on physical prox-imity, were atomized by the disaster, inhibiting recovery and posing long-term adjustment barriers.

The Three Mile Island Reactor Accident

The accident at the Three Mile Island (TMI) nuclear power station has been extensively studied as well. Until recently it was an unprecedented event, and it has attracted a great deal of attention from researchers. Unfolding over the course of one week in the spring of 1979, the accident involved releases of unknown amounts of radiation, a reported partial meltdown of the reactor core, and, at various times, reports of possible explosions or radioactive emissions. It also created an information crisis; accounts of what was happening issued by responsible officials were often incomplete, incorrect, or contradictory, and the credibility of these offi-cials suffered accordingly. Evacuation advisories were discussed and fi-nally issued, and great media attention was focused on the event.

What actually occurred (i.e., pump malfunctions leading to exposure of the core, melting of fuel rods, release of radioactive emissions, spilling of radioactive water onto the reactor building floor) seems to have been less important than what nearby residents believed to be the course of events. Dohrenwend (1983) reported that how close people lived to the reactor affected distress during acute response to the accident, and, if one had preschool children, distress was higher than if one did not. Similarly, distrust of authorities was high during acute response, but it persisted after symptoms of distress had dissipated.

The presence of stress and psychological disturbance has been the focus of several studies. Dohrenwend, Dohrenwend, Kasl, and Warheit (1979) found evidence of heightened demoralization during the month following the accident, but also reported that during the second month these effects declined rapidly. Houts, Miller, Tokuhata, and Ham (1980) conducted telephone surveys about 4 and 9 months after the accident, comparing residents living close to the plant with those living further away. Their results suggested that distress was associated with distance from the crippled reactor. Retrospective reports of levels of distress during the period immediately after the accident were higher than in either measurement period, and reported distress declined over the course of the study. After 9 months, however, a subsample of 10–20% still exhibited symptoms of stress.

Bromet (1980) and her colleagues have conducted longer-term studies of TMI area residents, comparing plant workers at TMI and women in the community with preschool children with comparable groups working at an undamaged reactor site or living nearby. Early findings indicated that mothers of young children at TMI exhibited higher levels of distress than did their counterparts living near the undamaged plant and that these problems persisted throughout the first year after the accident (Bromet, Parkinson, Schulberg, Dunn, & Gondek, 1980). Subsequent studies have indicated that these effects have persisted for more than three years (Dew, Bromet, & Schulberg, in press).

A different approach to studying the effects of the TMI accident was taken by Mileti, Hartsough, and Madson (1982), who compared rates of stress-related behaviors such as alcohol sales, death rates, suicides, arrests, psychiatric admissions, and automobile accidents during the 6 months preceding and following the accident. These archival data indicated little change in crime, psychiatric admissions, and suicides but revealed small increases in automobile accidents and in alcohol sales after the accident. From these data, the authors concluded that stress following the accident was not severe. Houts and his associates also reported that utilization of medical care following the accident did not markedly increase (Houts, Hu, Henderson, Cleary, & Tokuhata, 1984). Incidence of spontaneous abortions after the accident was comparable with baseline rates more than a year after the accident, and estimation of health effects based on the amount of radiation released during the incident suggest minimal health consequences (Goldhaber, Staub, & Tokuhata, 1983; Upton, 1981).

Response during the accident and 2-week emergency period was similar to that observed for natural disasters; panic did not occur and evacuation seems to have proceeded in a predictable fashion (Flynn, 1981). Inhabitants experienced distress but overall chaos was not the case. Within 3 weeks after the accident, the community appeared to have regained a sense of normalcy, although disagreements about what had occurred and the dangers that had been posed continued (Flynn, 1981). Thus, one might conclude that, though the accident may have caused substantial distress and disruption, response to it was not unusual and effects were largely short-lived. The data reported by Bromet and her associates (Bromet et al., 1980) provide the only suggestion that stress may have been more severe or persistent than these other accounts indicate.

Our research at TMI was initiated in 1980 to study the effects of the release of radioactive gases that had accumulated in the containment building around the reactor. Psychological, behavioral, and biochemical indexes of stress were measured in a randomly drawn sample of people living within 5 miles of the damaged reactor and were compared with responses of a control group drawn from an area more than 80 miles away. Data were collected just before, during, just after, and 6 weeks after the gases were vented into the atmosphere. Indicators in all of these stress measures were highest just before the release of the gas, as symptom reporting and levels of urinary norepinephrine and epinephrine declined as the venting proceeded (Gatchel, Schaeffer, & Baum, 1985). Elevations prior to venting may have reflected an anticipatory stress response among TMI-area residents or may have reflected chronic levels of stress that were reduced by the successful venting procedure and removal of one threat still at the plant. This is suggested by the fact that TMI-area residents exhibited greater symptom reporting, poorer task performance, and higher levels of stress hormones in their urine than did controls at all or nearly all measurement periods.

Subsequent research has also indicated that these symptoms of stress have returned to pre-venting levels or in some cases exceeded them in the 6 or more years since the accident. Symptom reporting and urinary epinephrine and norepinephrine have remained at levels greater than those observed among control subjects, even when additional control groups of people living near undamaged nuclear and fossil-fuel power plants were considered (Baum, Gatchel, & Schaeffer, 1983). Published data have shown that these symptoms of stress have persisted for at least 4 years, and preliminary data from recent measurements indicate that differences in stress levels were still significant 5 years after the accident (e.g., Davidson & Baum, 1986). Furthermore, these stress levels have been associated with health-relevant variables such as complaints to physicians, blood pressure changes, and prescriptions received (Baum et al., 1985).

These data suggest that stress has become chronic among residents of the TMI area. Vulnerability has been selective; not all area residents appear to have been affected in this manner. For example, coping and social support appear to have affected response to the TMI situation. Fleming, Baum, Gisriel, and Gatchel (1982) found that social support mediated stress symptoms that were exhibited by TMI-area residents 17 months after the accident. Those TMI subjects reporting higher levels of support reported less symptom distress than did those with less perceived social support. Control subjects did not show this relationship. However, Cleary and Houts (1984) reported that during the first 9 months after the accident, social support was not associated with stress. Number of friends was related, as were coping variables, to emotional regulation. Consistent with this, we found that direct, problem-focused coping aimed at "fixing" the situation was associated with greater distress than were coping actions that were oriented more toward making one feel better (Collins, Baum, & Singer, 1983). Self-blame—taking responsibility for one's victimization—was also associated with fewer symptoms of chronic stress than was attributing blame to others (Baum, Fleming, & Singer, 1983).

Research on situations in which toxic chemicals have leaked or contaminated nearby ground, air, or water shows similar effects. Fleming (1985) found effects of the same type and magnitude as those observed at TMI among people living near a hazardous waste dump, and data suggest that TMI- and toxic waste-area residents exhibited comparable chronic symptoms of posttraumatic stress as well (Davidson, Fleming, & Baum, 1986). Other studies have also suggested that actual or perceived exposure to toxic chemicals as a result of leaking dump sites or application of dangerous chemicals is associated with persistent distress and disturbance (e.g., Gibbs, 1986; Levine, 1982). Schottenfeld and Cullen (1985) described a different instance of chronic response to exposure to toxic substances. Following real or imagined exposure to industrial toxins, symptoms of posttraumatic stress and somatic distress were observed: "Chronic exposure which initially may not be recognized as a discrete trauma or does not gain representation in clearly defined images or words may be preferentially recalled as reexperiencing of the bodily state associated with exposure" (p. 201).

Differences Between Natural and Humanmade Disasters

Throughout this chapter, I have maintained a distinction between natural and humanmade disasters. To some extent, such a distinction is based on the disaster event more than on its impact; although natural disasters are sometimes more powerful and destructive, both are typically disruptive and differences between them are primarily those of origin and psychologically relevant variables, such as predictability and opportunity for blame. For example, a flash flood causes comparable damage whether it is caused by a torrential rainstorm or by a dam failure. Clearly, the two events are different, but not necessarily in terms of direct impact. Instead, they vary along dimensions that define the ways in which the events are experienced.

In fact, one characteristic of humanmade disasters is often a lack of visible damage; compared with coastal damage from a hurricane or destruction from a substantial earthquake, many accidents caused by technological mishaps do little physical damage. There was less likelihood of the experience of loss, terror, and horror in the Love Canal or TMI situations than there is typically among victims of fierce storms or quakes. In many cases, these impact variables are not useful for predicting the response to or the lasting consequences of humanmade disaster. Such accidents reflect unpredictable events that result from loss of control over technological systems, and there are often parties or agencies to blame. As such they are different from those caused by natural forces. When humanmade events involve toxic substances, effects may be more prolonged and recovery inhibited further.

Several writers have discussed differences between disasters of natural and human origin. Some suggest that there is value in distinguishing between them, whereas others do not. The argument is not over whether they are different, but rather whether these differences translate into meaningful impact predictors—do they really matter in the determination of response to and effects of victimization? I will briefly consider some models that discuss possible distinctions between natural and technological catastrophe and then evaluate research findings to more carefully assess effects.

Warheit (1976) has argued that natural disasters and civil disturbances differ in several important ways. Although both types of events produce many sudden demands on individual and group functioning and disrupt normal behavior, the differences in origin, warning, scope, and duration may result in different degrees of dysfunction. Natural disasters are caused by nonsocial forces outside the regulatory control of the group or community, whereas civil disturbances are usually produced by social sources within the community. In addition, natural disasters do not serve human purposes, whereas civil disturbances often do. Warheit suggests that "natural disasters occur as purposeless, asocial events; civil disturbances can be viewed as instrumentally initiated to achieve certain social goals" (p. 132). Not all humanmade emergencies share this purposive quality, but riots, demonstrations, uprisings, war, economic decline, assassination, and the like may appear to be intentional at some level.

Warheit (1976) also believes that warning is important in distinguishing between these collective stress situations. Natural disasters often provide some warning, because storms can be tracked and various levels of alerts can be issued. However, civil disturbances are viewed as inherently unpredictable and are therefore associated with less warning. Warheit also noted differences in duration, suggesting that natural phenomena usually are briefer than is disruption associated with civil unrest. When events are brief, decisions can be made more quickly; when they are more drawn out, response cannot be as decisive. As Warheit notes, "Natural disasters create a social context marked by an initial overwhelming consensus regarding priorities and the allocation of resources" (p. 133).

Rogers and Nehnevajsa (1984) discussed natural disasters and technological crises as distinct events. Natural disasters are those involving natural forces, be they geological events that give little warning, such as earthquakes, landslides, and volcanoes, or disasters of the weather system, including hurricanes, cyclones, typhoons, blizzards, and so on. A number of differences may be drawn between these general classes of natural mishaps. The weather-induced crises are typically slower-onset events and provide more warning than those involving movement of the earth, and the ability to localize where the impact of weather will be greatest is better than with earthquakes or the like.

A third group of natural hazards is more like the first in that they are hard to predict and are characterized by more rapid onset—flash floods, avalanches, and fire storms are sudden crises set off by movement of water, snow, or fire on the earth's surface. In addition, these disaster events may be caused by humans, unlike the other classes of natural hazard. Floods are also events that fit this category, though they have considerably slower onset than do flash floods and may be predicted. Finally, long-term natural disasters heavily affected by climate patterns form a fourth group—drought, famine, crop failure. These slow-onset events, in the long run, may be more resistant to intervention than are the more sudden and powerful events.

Technological crises reflect failure in technological systems. These comprise four categories as well: those derived from large system failures (e.g., nuclear power plant accidents, blackouts, dam failures), structural failures (e.g., bridge or building collapse), low-level delayed-effect crises (e.g., pollution, energy shortages), and chemical hazards (e.g., oil spills, toxic fumes, leaking toxic waste). These classes of humanmade problems vary along several dimensions. Some are sudden and unpredictable, such as system and structural failures, whereas others are slower to develop and more easily predicted (e.g., pollution). Some crises affect relatively large numbers of people, as in system failures and low-level delayed crises, whereas others are more geographically concentrated, such as chemical accidents and structural failures.

These models of types of disasters reinforce the idea that differences between natural and technological disasters are, most importantly, differences related to psychological dimensions. Sheer physical impact is less important than are factors that affect victim response and perceptions of the event. Predictability, culpability, duration, and the opportunity for exposure to toxic substances are the primary distinctions that have been proposed, and these characteristics are most important in determining how victims perceive the disaster event and cope with its demands.

Characteristics of Catastrophes and Their Psychological Effects

We have suggested elsewhere that natural disaster and technological catastrophe should not automatically be included together as one class of stressor, but rather the capacity of each one for causing stress and long-term psychophysiological change should be compared and evaluated (Baum, Fleming, & Davidson, 1983). We came to this conclusion as a result of findings from our continuing investigation of stress at TMI. Symptoms of stress, psychological disturbance, and physiological changes persisted long after we had expected them to disappear, and the reports of subjects suggested the presence of stressful conditions that had not been previously discussed. This led us to search the literature on disasters, and we found reports stating that substantial chronic effects are not often observed, but they seem more likely to occur after humanmade accidents than after natural calamities.

Earlier in this chapter, I reported evidence of chronic stress found among some TMI-area residents more than 6 years after the accident and discussed some of the sources of this lasting distress. Yet there was very little damage or property loss as a result of the accident, and, although many area residents report continued concerns about past and future harm, experts have dismissed most claims of radiation release as unsupported. Why, then, has stress persisted among these residents? It may be related to continued controversy about the accident, the reopening of the plant, and other issues that have kept the situation in the public eye.

Yet, we have also found chronic stress associated with living near a leaking toxic-waste dump that did not receive the same attention as did TMI. We came to believe that these types of disaster differ from natural disasters in ways that do not necessarily affect the intensity of distress but do support long-term problems and make cumulative effects of stress more likely. In our initial treatment of these differences, we focused primarily on the human versus natural origin distinction. Using several characteristics of disaster events, we attempted to draw psychologically relevant distinctions between natural and humanmade calamities (Baum, Fleming, & Davidson, 1983). These characteristics included suddenness, power, destruction, predictability, and the presence of a clear low point.

Natural Disasters

Natural disasters are more familiar events, occurring at seemingly greater frequency. They vary in duration from the quick but powerful impact of earthquakes and tornadoes to the long-term disruption of floods and episodes such as heat waves or drought. Such disasters do not all occur everywhere but rather each type tends to occur in only certain areas. Thus hurricanes do not affect people in the Midwest as much as they do along the Gulf of Mexico, whereas earthquakes do not traditionally occur in either locale. However, it is safe to say that there are few places where victimization by some natural force does not occur.

Natural disasters usually begin very quickly. Our ability to forecast events has made some more predictable, but onset of a natural disaster may be sudden. Hurricanes, floods, and tornadoes usually give warning of their approach, but the time gained by such warnings is often a matter of hours, and such storms may still be fairly sudden. Other types of natural disasters occur even more suddenly; earthquakes, for example, may come upon an area in a matter of seconds and are not usually preceded by a warning.

Natural disasters are also powerful. Lazarus and Cohen (1978) suggested that they are among the most universally threatening of stressors, with sufficient magnitude to cause death and great destruction. Not all people respond to these events as one would expect, but this does not appear to involve appraisal of threat so much as appraisal of appropriate coping options (Sims & Baumann, 1974).

The enormous power of natural forces engenders substantial visible damage to property that often remains after the storm has passed. In such cases, damage provides tangible reminders of the event, causes disruption, and provides a focus for recovery efforts. As rebuilding is completed, a sense of closure on the episode may be attained and recovery may be enhanced.

As I have suggested, some forms of disaster have become more predictable as our ability to forecast meteorological and geophysical conditions has improved. Floods are often predicted days before they crest, although flash floods remain unpredictable (Drabek & Stephenson, 1971; Gleser et al., 1981). Tornadoes and hurricanes are also more predictable than they used to be, but only in a general way; forecasts and warnings are issued across entire counties for hours, but the exact point and time at which a tornado touches down usually cannot be predicted. This is also true of events such as earthquakes; locations where these events are likely to occur can be specified, but there is little basis to determine when such disasters will strike. People living along a fault know that an earthquake may occur, but knowing when a specific tremor will occur is rare.

The last characteristic of natural disaster reflects something we have chosen to call a low point (Baum, Fleming, & Davidson, 1983). What we mean is a point at which the worst that is going to happen has already occurred; at the low point, "the worst is over." Although the destruction of homes and the loss of power and sanitation facilities will also create hardships, once a storm has passed or an earthquake has stopped rumbling, the worst is typically over, and people can turn their attention to rebuilding and recovery. The low point may be looked at in terms of a shift in appraisal from threat to loss, or as the point at which damage and disruption are greatest. After this point, people begin to feel better, the environment is restored, and everyday life gradually returns to normal.

Humanmade Disasters

Technological catastrophes are less familiar to most people than are natural disasters, partly because they have been less frequent. Like natural disasters, they include events that are powerful and sudden, including bridge collapses, dam failures, industrial accidents, and marine collisions. They are also precipitated by events that reflect breakdowns in technology in industries or locations where highly toxic substances are used or stored. Furthermore, these events are potentially widespread. One can argue that the proliferation of technology has made few places safe from breakdown or failure. Where technology exists, there also exists the possibility of loss of control over it.

The onset of technological catastrophes is sudden. There is little warning of a dam break or a bridge collapse, and the speed with which these events unfold often makes them difficult to avoid. As was the case at Buffalo Creek, those in the path of a flood following a dam break usually have little time to get to safety; for those on a bridge when it collapses, there is even less time to act.

Technological mishaps, like natural events, are powerful. The destruction and loss of life resulting from dam breaks are potentially as great as for natural disasters, and our present state of technological achievement has created the possibility of even greater devastation. Although the odds are small, the Nuclear Regulatory Commission has acknowledged the possibility of a nuclear accident that could claim 100,000 lives. Recent events at Chernobyl suggested, if not realized, the great potential for loss of life. Technology has allowed us to harness tremendous energy that, in the event of an accident, could cause destruction that matches or exceeds most natural disasters.

Technology is not supposed to break down. Although Perrow (1981) has argued that such accidents are inevitable, technological catastrophes are never supposed to happen. As a result, they are difficult to predict. Dams are not supposed to break, so one cannot generally predict when they will. Inspection and examination of a dam may suggest that it is weakening, but these warning signs may not be visible or may be overlooked. Parts of our technological system are expected to become obsolete, but they are not expected to fail before they are replaced. Accidents that endanger or threaten lives and property are not planned, and often there is inadequate knowledge of how to deal with an accident if one occurs. Prior to the incident at TMI, some experts believed that such an accident was nearly impossible, and most of us will not attempt to predict events that "cannot" happen.

Technological advances provide us with control over our environment; human evolution has been marked by increases in such control over the forces around us. However, when the system breaks down, control is lost. Presumably any predictive ability we have concerning technological disaster would be used to correct the situation; that is, if a prediction of a specific breakdown is possible, then something will be done to correct the problem before an accident occurs. Failures in the system reflect those problems that "slipped by" and are therefore unpredictable.

Some technological mishaps, such as factory explosions, train accidents, and mine accidents, have a well-defined low point. In these cases, coping with the disaster may follow a course similar to that of natural disaster recovery. However, it appears that some of the most powerful technological disasters may also be those without a clear low point. For example, situations in which individuals believe that they have been exposed to toxic chemicals or radiation (e.g., Love Canal and TMI) involve long-term consequences connected with the development of disease many years after the initial exposure. Thus there may be considerable uncertainty as to the degree of damage that such technological catastrophes may have inflicted. For some technological disasters, there is no clear low point from which "things will gradually get better"; the worst may be over and done with, or it may yet surface. Thus it could be difficult for some persons to return to normal lives after the actual accident or catastrophe has ended.

Currently, we are studying other variables that affect response to victimization that are associated with natural and technological catastrophe in different ways. Duration of victimization, implicitly affected by the timing of the low point, may also be affected by variables such as the possibility of exposure to toxic substances. In addition, blame or attribution of responsibility for victimization appears more likely in the case of a humanmade catastrophe than in a natural disaster. Because duration of victimization appears to be an important factor in distress resulting from disaster, and because blame has been shown to affect response to victimization in other settings, these characteristics warrant closer examination.

Effects of Toxic Exposure

The presence of toxic substances in a disaster appears to generate more persistent distress, at least in some cases. Depending on what substance is involved, different degrees of chronic disruption may be expected; radiation, for example, is odorless, invisible, and feared. Experts argue about what levels of exposure are dangerous, and, partly because of the history of nuclear energy, possible exposure to radiation evokes strong emotional responses in many. Similarly, some toxic chemicals are feared and have effects that extend beyond acute exposure. Radiation and some toxic chemicals have effects that require a long time to develop. Thus, radiation may cause cancer and birth defects, but these effects may not be detectable for years or generations. In a sense, this pattern of influence extends the duration of victimization. Long after the TMI accident or the discovery of toxic chemical leaks at waste dump sites, concerns about possible future exposure to toxic substances are compounded by worry and concern about effects that have already been set in motion. The belief that one has been exposed to toxic substances may cause long-term uncertainty and stress, as well as pose a threat to one's health. The degree to which this stress will occur depends on the perceived consequences and time course of particular toxins; when effects are severe and delayed, stress may be more persistent.

Blame as a Reaction to Disaster

The notion of blame or attribution of responsibility is an important theme in the victimization literature and is reflected in studies of disaster as well. At one extreme, some have held that assignment of blame for a disaster is rare, and victimization is explained in other ways. Others have observed that disaster victims do attribute responsibility for disasters or victimization, ranging from scapegoating and attempts to assign blame to others to the tendency to assume personal responsibility for what has happened to them. Studies also vary in the degree to which they find consequences or correlates of different responses to victimization.

Scapegoating and blaming others for victimization by disaster appears to occur most often in the case of humanmade calamities, for obvious reasons. Studies have found evidence of attribution of blame for air pollution, fires, nuclear accidents, explosions, dam breaks and resulting floods, airplane crashes, and toxic waste sites as well as after severe winter storms (e.g., Baum, Fleming, & Singer, 1983; Bucher, 1957; Drabek, 1968; Erikson, 1976; Levine, 1982; Neal, 1984; Neal & Perry, 1980; Veltfort & Lee, 1943). Blaming is more likely when someone has acted in ways that are perceived to isolate norms or community standards for his or her own benefit, most likely in the case of humanmade events (e.g., Neal & Perry, 1980). Some have argued that blaming can occur only in the case of technological accidents if one considers the cause of the event, for obvious reasons (Turner & Killian, 1972). However, under some conditions, particularly if responsibility for more than cause alone is considered, natural disasters may also be followed by scapegoating (Neal, 1984).

In a study of the Cocoanut Grove fire, victims were found to blame others for the catastrophe (Veltfort & Lee, 1943). Assignment of blame for what had happened was directed at public officials who were seen as having failed to pass laws and codes that would have resulted in fewer fatalities. Veltfort and Lee interpreted this external focus as unconscious, directed toward relieving emotionality and reducing fear, anger, guilt, and frustration. This focus was also viewed as an example of scapegoating, because victims disregarded more productive avenues of response, such as demands for better fire laws, in favor of blaming officials and clamoring for their punishment.

The pattern of assignment of blame following the fire is also of interest. The individual actually responsible for setting the club on fire (who struck a match while trying to change a light bulb) was not blamed by victims. Veltfort and Lee argued that this was a result of both his admission that he had been responsible and his own victimization. Instead, "more satisfying" scapegoats were chosen; victims would feel less guilt at seeing public officials punished, reflecting both a sensitivity to the vulnerability of the young man responsible for the fire and negative feelings for public officials in general.

Bucher (1957) recognized that few if any people attribute blame to themselves or others for natural disasters. In these cases, natural forces are seen as responsible for death, destruction, and disruption. According to Bucher, blaming other people for one's own victimization occurs only when conventional explanations are not sufficient to account for what has happened. In the case of attributing responsibility to others, two other conditions must be met: Those who are blamed must be seen as having violated moral or community standards and as not being ready to take steps to rectify the situation to prevent similar ones. This latter variable, reflecting a concern with future safety, explains why people who are directly involved in a disaster (e.g., pilots of planes that have crashed) are rarely blamed. Idiosyncratic events or individuals who are seen as unique are poor targets for blame, as they provide little predictive power in explaining a theory of how or why an event occurred. In deciding who to blame, individuals create naive theories that are directed toward identifying more stable or global factors that might also predict future catastrophes. As a result, groups of people (e.g., authorities, public officials) who are seen as having the capability to prevent such disasters in the future are more likely to be held responsible.

Drabek and Quarantelli (1969) studied attribution of responsibility in a disaster at the Indiana State Fairgrounds in 1963. An explosion during a show in the coliseum killed 81 people, most of them immediately, and injured about 400 more. Here, conventional explanations for the disaster were inadequate, and the media coverage reflected a general search for the cause and responsibility for the explosion. Gas tanks that had been illegally stored in the coliseum were eventually identified as the cause, and officials of the company supplying the tanks, managers of the coliseum, and fire department officials were blamed for the catastrophe. Such response is consistent with Bucher's (1957) conditions (moral violation, impelling action to prevent similar occurrences). Drabek and Quarantelli go on to suggest that personal blame for disasters derives directly from institutional mandates. In legal systems such as the one in the United States, responsible individuals must be identified, and societal norms seem to place greater emphasis on identifying and punishing those who are responsible than on analyzing and preventing similar events. The public "trial" and punishment of people who were involved in a catastrophe like the Indiana Fairgrounds explosion provide a greater sense of rectification—that something is being done—than does more subtle legislative action or other activity directed precisely at rectification and prevention.

These data suggest that, following disasters, the public may feel a need to assign blame. When conventional explanations are not available, when moral conduct can be questioned, when feelings of fear or guilt require expression, and when there is a perceived need to force responsible officials to act to prevent future catastrophes, blaming other people is more likely. Furthermore, it can be argued that attributing blame to others may affect the likelihood of meaningful social change and effective prevention. However, these studies have not considered how attribution of responsibility affects coping with disaster, or how personal costs may be related to how one allocates blame for victimization.

In general, attribution processes are directed toward explanation of events in ways that maintain a sense of order and provide some predictive power (Wortman, 1976). The nature of attributions that people make are related to their perception of the environment, mediating the development of learned helplessness, emotion, and social interaction (e.g., Abramson, Seligman, & Teasdale, 1978; Baum & Gatchel, 1981; Schachter & Singer, 1962; Wortman & Brehm, 1975). How people compartmentalize responsibility for failure, how they view the role of other people in contributing to stressful social situations, and how they explain internal sensations, thoughts, and symptoms affects their response to events. This may be related to the need to believe in a just world or to the defensive use of external attributions, but the need to attribute responsibility for victimization also appears to be associated with perceived control. By blaming others for one's plight, victims may also yield a sense of control over the event and the likelihood of occurrence of similar ones. Assumption of responsibility for victimization, on the other hand, may allow victims to maintain perceived control over the events in question, and such assumption may reflect a purposeful attempt to maintain or create a sense of control over the environment.

Blame may reflect the outcome of several different processes that characterize victimization, as was suggested earlier. However, there is evidence of the control-enhancing or adjustment-facilitating effects of self-blame that are inconsistent with the common wisdom on the subject (Miller & Porter, 1983). Internal attributions have been found to be both positively and negatively associated with helplessness and depressive symptoms (Abramson et al., 1978; Baum, Fleming, & Singer, 1983; Baum & Gatchel, 1981), but self-blame for victimization has been associated with better postaccident coping (Bulman & Wortman, 1977; Janoff-Bulman & Frieze, 1983). The distinction between characterological and behavioral self-blame appears to be important, because the former may not bolster perceptions of control and enhance adaptive response (Janoff-Bulman, 1979).

Attribution of responsibility for victimization in humanmade disasters may be related to the victims' desire to maintain control of their situation when it appears such control has been lost. Distinctions between technological and natural disasters are partly based on uncertainty and unpredictability. The predictability of technological disasters appears to be low, and they appear to generate greater uncertainty than do natural disasters. The nightmarish quality of some may be largely a result of uncertainty about the nature and extent of their effects. Because many effects take years to appear, technological disasters may pose long-term threats to victims' sense of control as well.

The situation at TMI is consistent with this reasoning. Research has shown that TMI-area residents report greater feelings of helplessness and less perceived control over their environment than do control subjects (Davidson, Baum, & Collins, 1982). Data also suggest that many TMI-area residents are concerned and uncertain about what effects the accident had on them (Baum, Gatchel, Fleming, & Lake, 1981). Data suggest that some TMI-area residents seek to bolster their feelings of control by assigning blame for their problems to themselves (Baum, Fleming, & Singer, 1983). Self-blame for the accident was rare but was more common when subjects were asked about the problems they experienced after the accident. Those area residents who reported that they assumed some responsibility for their situation exhibited stress levels that were comparable with control subjects' and substantially lower than TMI subjects who did not assume any responsibility for their problems. Assumption of responsibility was also positively related to perceived control.

Determinants of Chronic Consequences of Disasters

Although research has not systematically assessed the long-term effects of victimization by disaster nor resolved definitional problems regarding what distinguishes acute and chronic consequences and what constitutes an "effect," it is possible to draw some conclusions regarding natural and technological calamities and their long-term impact on mood and behavior. For example, Chamberlain (1980) reviewed a number of studies (many of humanmade disasters such as the Cocoanut Grove fire, the devastation at Hiroshima, and the Buffalo Creek flood) and concluded that physical and psychological trauma persists beyond the immediate disaster and postdisaster period. Chamberlain noted that there is evidence of long-term deterioration in health. Hargreaves (1980) suggested that when victims see a crisis or emergency as being caused by human action, the effects last longer. Similarly, Gleser et al. (1981) proposed that the cause of a disaster, whether it was natural or humanmade, contributes to the scope and duration of disaster effects. Their observations of the humanmade flood at Buffalo Creek were similar to other studies, primarily those of other technological accidents.

All of this suggests that humanmade disasters, regardless of whether or not they generate effects of the same intensity as do natural ones, are more likely to engender chronic effects such as emotional disturbances or poor physical health. Response to the event and acute effects of disaster do not appear to differ greatly as a function of origin, but long-term effects do seem to vary along this dimension. In the case of Buffalo Creek, it was difficult to determine which of several factors were associated with distress; Gleser et al. (1981) suggested that degree of threat, bereavement, prolongation of an intractable situation, loss of a sense of community, and displacement may also have been important. However, the conduct of a large lawsuit alone suggests extensive blaming of human "disaster agents," which may well have contributed to negative mental health effects.

Gleser and her colleagues (1981) also suggested that the proportion of victims who suffer psychological effects is often higher following human-made disasters than it is following natural disasters. Of those interviewed 8 days after the Cocoanut Grove fire by Cobb and Lindemann (1943), 44% exhibited evidence of emotional problems. Similarly, Adler (1943) found that more than half of the fire's victims suffered from psychiatric complications almost a year later. Leopold and Dillon (1963) reported that nearly all of the victims of a marine collision and explosion exhibited symptoms of posttraumatic stress several years after the accident, and Lidz (1946) found that all survivors of the Guadalcanal evacuation displayed long-term psychological symptoms related to the incident. These data are similar to those describing the long-term health of concentration camp survivors, nearly all of whom showed psychological problems, and the data are different from results from many studies of natural disasters.

Rates of disturbance from studies of floods, storms, and other natural disasters report lower impairment rates (e.g., Logue et al., 1979; Milne, 1977; Parker, 1977; Poulshock & Cohen, 1975). These differences may have been a result of the sampling procedures used in these studies or the method of assessing distress and may not reflect a greater extent or degree of disturbance among victims of humanmade disasters. However, a recent study that used comparable sampling and assessment procedures to compare victims of a flood with people living near a hazardous toxic waste dump as well as with a control group found differences in chronic effects of these disasters (e.g., Fleming & Baum, 1986). Those living near the toxic waste site reported greater symptom distress and exhibited higher levels of sympathetic arousal than did either of the other groups almost a year after the announcement or discovery of toxic hazard.

Data suggest that technological catastrophes have more clear-cut effects than do natural disasters. In fact, in discussing their results, Gleser et al. (1981) noted that Buffalo Creek appeared to have unprecedented effects, ones clearly different from those found for other floods. They point out that the closest approximations of the long-term effects measured at Buffalo Creek are found in the studies of nightclub fires and marine disasters. Thus, technological catastrophes appear to have effects that are similar to one another but different from those of natural disasters.

Relatively little research has been conducted on disasters involving toxic waste or radiation, but this will not be the case for long. Residents' experiences at Love Canal appear to have been stressful and should be expected to have chronic consequences for some victims, but available evidence is not conclusive about this (Levine, 1982). Research at TMI that assessed several control groups and supplemented self-report data with behavioral and biochemical measures has indicated that many residents continued to feel threatened by the plant for more than a year after the accident, and that a variety of stress symptoms has persisted for some residents as long as 17 months after the accident (Baum, Gatchel, & Schaeffer, 1983). The persistence of difficulties here is more easily explained than at Buffalo Creek, because some of the sources of danger remain at TMI. The dam that caused the flood at Buffalo Creek was not rebuilt, and the sources of threat there are no longer present. Still, the parallels between the findings for these kinds of catastrophes are striking.

Possible differences between natural and technological disasters are summarized in Table 1. Although the two share some characteristics, they appear to be different in other ways. Both are relatively sudden and powerful, and although neither is very predictable, technological mishaps may be less so than natural disasters. Both may cause visible destruction and disfigurement of the environment, but technological catastrophes can leave an area intact, producing less visible threat. Furthermore, though it is not definitive, research suggests that humanmade catastrophes can have more chronic effects than do natural disasters.

Although one can argue that technological catastrophes are less predictable than are natural ones, it is fairly clear that both are relatively hard to predict and more or less uncontrollable. Despite the fact that

Table 1
Summary of Characteristics of Natural and
Humanmade Disasters

	Disasters	
Characteristics	Natural	Humanmade
Suddenness	Often sudden, some warning	May be sudden or drawn out
Powerful impact	Usually powerful	Usually powerful
Visible damage	Usually causes damage, loss	May not cause damage, loss
Predictability	Some predictability	Low predictability
Low point	Clear low point	Unclear low point
Perceptions of control	Uncontrollable, lack of control	Uncontrollable but potentially controllable; result of loss of control
Extent of effects	Usually limited to victims	Victims' and public's loss of confidence and credibility in perceived human agents
Persistence of effects	Up to a year, mostly acute	May be chronic, long-term uncertainty

neither type of event can be controlled, however, it is likely that perception of uncontrollability will be different for each. Natural forces are, by definition, uncontrollable. We can minimize damage and loss, but the occurrence of a storm, drought, or other natural event is uncontrollable. These events have never been controllable, and the fact that nothing could be done to prevent a particular instance merely serves to highlight or reinforce one's lack of control over it.

This is not always the case, however, as technological catastrophes reflect failure by systems that once were under control. Dams, nuclear reactors, and waste dumps are normally well-regulated parts of a technological network designed to be controlled by its human masters. When a breakdown occurs, there is a temporary loss of control over the system. In one sense, these mishaps may be more controllable than are natural disasters because there are often preventive actions that can be taken to avoid an accident or to minimize an impending catastrophe. In another sense, they are uncontrollable once they begin, and a loss of control, related to the failure to foresee and prevent the accident, may be salient. Not having control when one expects to have it appears to have different psychophysiological consequences than does not having control when one does not expect it (Baum & Gatchel, 1981; Wortman & Brehm, 1975).

The public's confidence in future controllability of technology is closely related to this. One dramatic instance—the TMI accident—of loss of control over nuclear technology greatly reduced many people's confidence in the safety and viability of nuclear power, despite the fact that control over the TMI reactor was regained before the core melted down. The effects of the Chernobyl accident are not yet known. It is possible that repeated technological breakdowns can erode confidence in our ability to manage and regulate other forms of technology.

Humanmade disasters may create dangers that pass quickly but that may also pose continuing threats. This is particularly true for catastrophes involving toxic substances. The possibility of illness resulting from exposure to toxic waste or radiation continues for many years, and toxic spills, leaks, or nuclear accidents require complex decontamination and clean-up procedures that may take years to accomplish. At TMI, radioactive gas remained trapped in the plant for more than a year before it was vented into the atmosphere, and large amounts of radioactive water remained on the site for more than 6 years after the accident. Delays in decontamination, the clean-up procedures themselves, and the presence of radioactive material remaining in the plant are all sources of continuing threats that may be responsible for chronic stress among area residents.

Summary and Implications

Disasters are events or impacts that cause substantial disruption of psychological, social, or physical functioning. They may be thought of as stressors, tending to be more intense, powerful, and universal than most threatening or demanding events. They affect relatively large numbers of people and pose heavy demands on coping. And they threaten property and life, whether directly, as in victimization by a natural disaster, explosion, or fire, or by virtue of long-term threat, as is generated by exposure to toxic substances. Particularly in the latter case, perceptions of the event and associated threats may be more important in determining chronic stress and mental health effects than is the actual threat or danger posed.

Response to disasters appears to be more orderly than many people expect. Evidence of panic in the face of a disaster is rare, and many studies suggest that initial response is purposive and prosocial. I have noted the emergence of cohesive social groups that last beyond the disaster period, and have argued that the long-term effects of disasters are typically positive. Some studies have observed shock, dazed behavior, and withdrawal, and a number have reported emotional distress and dysfunction following a disaster event. However, in most cases, these effects appear to be short-lived.

Some disasters appear to be associated with psychological effects that do not dissipate quickly but rather last for long periods of time. To some extent this is associated with the duration of sources of stress, but it also appears that chronic distress is most likely to be found following human-made disasters. One explanation for this is that technological calamities are more likely to pose continuing threats, but this does not explain the persistence of problems following the Buffalo Creek flood. Rather, a combination of facts, including threats to perceived control, possible consequences, social disruption, and predictability and persistence of threats explain the differences between natural and technological disasters.

Interpretation of the disaster literature is made more difficult by the great variety of events studied and methods used. Data suggest that there is some generality of response across events, but differences in sampling procedures, design, measures, time frames, and focus have hindered meaningful conclusions about coping and consequences of disasters. From among the many levels of analysis of environmental impact, my colleagues and I have focused on psychological and psychophysiological aspects of victimization by disaster. Conclusions that we have drawn are tentative ones, awaiting systematic validation and analysis. Regardless of what is eventually learned, there are a number of implications for the psychological study of disaster.

Examination of differences between natural and technological cataclysms reveals some important modern realities. The built environment is continually expanding, and threats posed by modern technology to the natural ecosystem are well recognized. However, expansion of technology often outruns our society's ability to control it, and we have often failed to foresee the problems that the technology will create. Our current dilemmas regarding storage of toxic and radioactive wastes are cases in point. Examination of the unique effects of technology-based threats and hazards may be increasingly called for as more and more people are victimized.

By viewing humanmade disaster as different from others, psychologists may be better able to predict and treat the kinds of psychological and health consequences such events can have. Responding to a court order to consider psychological effects in its deliberations about restarting the undamaged reactor at TMI, the Nuclear Regulatory Commission in 1982 sponsored a gathering of experts on stress, disaster, and perception of hazard who were asked to make predictions about psychological health near TMI based on the "disaster literature." It soon became apparent that the predictions stemming from this research did not match the reality of the situation at TMI. Regardless of whether these discrepancies between theory and reality persist, it was clear at that time that policy decisions could not be based on the most extensive literature available. Earlier studies of natural disasters did not provide a good foundation for making decisions about TMI and will probably prove insufficient for understanding future technological mishaps.

At the outset of this chapter, I discussed the nature of disaster, focusing on questions about what constitutes a disaster. Was TMI a disaster? Was Love Canal a disaster? What is the key, the crucial factor that is required? The short-term effects of these calamities are consistent with those of events that are universally accepted as disasters; response to the TMI situation was not unlike response to storms or other natural hazards. Stress, fear, sleep disturbances, posttraumatic stress symptoms, anxiety, and depression on the negative side and social activism and more positive response in the other side have been observed. What was missing at TMI and Love Canal was the powerful surge, the destruction of property and immediate injury or loss of life, the terror and gruesome trauma, and bereavement (Hartsough & Savitsky, 1984). The primary threat at TMI never materialized, but if it had—as it apparently did at Chernobyl—it would have produced casualties and attendant experiences for area residents. Instead, the terror and threat to life unfolded over several years, and many area residents are still waiting to see how they were affected.

This suggests that the TMI situation and other humanmade accidents involving toxic substances are disasters, whether or not the amount of toxic exposure involved can be proven to be dangerous to health. Individual perceptions, coping predilections, and other personal factors determine how events are appraised and experienced, and it is this subjective evaluation that appears most closely tied to the development of physical and mental health problems. There is argument about whether stress or "emotional injury" resulting from accidents like TMI are covered under current law or whether they should be considered in decisions regarding siting of potential hazards (Hartsough & Savitsky, 1984). In the case of TMI, the Supreme Court decided it unwise or not mandated by law to consider psychological health in such planning. The chronicity of response to humanmade disasters and the role of stress in the etiology of illness suggests that the Justices were wrong. Future policy decisions and legal resolution of claims will require more systematic documentation of the issues that indicate that toxic events are disasters and that their effects may be substantial.

References

Abrahams, M. J., Price, J., Whitlock, F. A., & Williams, G. (1976). The Brisbane floods, January 1974: Their impact on health. *Medical Journal of Australia, 2,* 936–939.

Abramson, L. Y., Seligman, M. E. P., & Teasdale, J. (1978). Learned helplessness in humans: Critique and reformulation. *Journal of Abnormal Psychology, 87,* 49–74.

Adams, P. R., & Adams, G. R. (1984). Mount St. Helens's ashfall: Evidence for a disaster stress reaction. *American Psychologist, 39*(3), 252–260.

Adler, A. (1943). Neuropsychiatric complications in victims of Boston's Cocoanut Grove disaster. *Journal of the American Medical Association, 17,* 1098–1101.

Baker, E. (1979). Predicting responses to hurricane warnings: A reanalysis of data from four studies. *Mass Emergencies, 4,* 9–24.

Barkun, M. (1974). *Disaster and the millennium.* New Haven, CT: Yale University Press.

Barton, A. H. (1969). *Communities in disaster.* Garden City, NY: Doubleday.

Barton, A. H. (1970). *Communities in disaster: A sociological analysis of collective stress situations.* Garden City, NY: Anchor-Doubleday.

Baum, A., & Davidson, L. M. (1985). A suggested framework for studying factors that contribute to trauma in disaster. In B. J. Sowder (Ed.), *Disasters and mental health: Selected contemporary perspectives* (pp. 29–40). Rockville, MD: U.S. Department of Health and Human Services.

Baum, A., Fleming, R., & Davidson, L. (1983). Natural disaster and technological catastrophe. *Environment and Behavior, 15,* 333–354.

Baum, A., Fleming, R., & Singer, J. E. (1983). Coping with victimization by technological disaster. *Journal of Social Issues, 39,* 117–138.

Baum, A., & Gatchel, R. J. (1981). Cognitive determinants of reaction to uncontrollable events: Development of reactance and learned helplessness. *Journal of Personality and Social Psychology, 40,* 1078–1089.

Baum, A., Gatchel, R. J., Fleming, R., & Lake, C. R. (1981). *Chronic and acute stress associated with the Three Mile Island accident and decontamination: Preliminary findings of a longitudinal study.* Washington, DC: U.S. Nuclear Regulatory Commission.

Baum, A., Gatchel, R. J., & Schaeffer, M. A. (1983). Emotional, behavioral, and physiological effects of chronic stress at Three Mile Island. *Journal of Consulting and Clinical Psychology, 51,* 565–572.

Baum, A., Schaeffer, M. A., Lake, C. R., Fleming, R., & Collins, D. L. (1986). Psychological and endocrinological correlates of chronic stress at Three Mile Island. In R. William (Ed.), *Perspectives on behavioral medicine* (pp. 201–217). New York: Academic Press.

Bennet, G. (1970). Bristol floods 1968. Controlled survey of effects on health of local community disaster. *British Medical Journal, 3,* 454–458.

Bolin, R. (1985). Disaster characteristics and psychosocial impacts. In B. J. Sowder

(Ed.), *Disasters and mental health: Selected contemporary perspectives* (pp. 3–28). Rockville, MD: U.S. Department of Health and Human Services.

Bowman, U. (1964). Alaska earthquake. *American Journal of Psychology, 121,* 313–317.

Bromet, E. (1980). *Three Mile Island: Mental health findings.* Pittsburgh, PA: Western Psychiatric Institute and Clinic and the University of Pittsburgh.

Bromet, E., Parkinson, D., Schulberg, A., Dunn, L., & Gondek, P. C. (1980). *Three Mile Island: Mental health findings.* Pittsburgh, PA: Western Psychiatric Institute and Clinic.

Bucher, R. (1957). Blame and hostility in disaster. *American Journal of Sociology, 62,* 467–475.

Bulman, R., & Wortman, C. (1977). Attributions of blame and coping in the "real world": Severe accident victims react to their lot. *Journal of Personality and Social Psychology, 35,* 351–363.

Chamberlain, B. C. (1980). Mayo seminars in psychiatry: The psychological aftermath of disaster. *Journal of Clinical Psychiatry, 4,* 238–244.

Cleary, P. D., & Houts, P. S. (1984, Spring). The psychological impact of the Three Mile Island incident. *Journal of Human Stress,* 28–34.

Collins, D. L., Baum, A., & Singer, J. E. (1983). Coping with chronic stress at Three Mile Island: Psychological and biochemical evidence. *Health Psychology, 2,* 149–166.

Crawshaw, R. (1963). Reactions to a disaster. *Archives of General Psychology, 9,* 157–162.

Danzig, E. R., Thayer, P. W., & Galanter, L. R. (1958). *The effects of a threatening rumor on a disaster-stricken community.* Washington, DC: National Academy of Sciences, National Research Council.

Davidson, L. M., & Baum, A. (1986). Chronic stress and posttraumatic stress disorders. *Journal of Consulting and Clinical Psychology, 54,* 303–308.

Davidson, L. M., Baum, A., & Collins, D. L. (1982). Stress and control-related problems at Three Mile Island. *Journal of Applied Social Psychology, 12,* 349–359.

Davidson, L. M., Fleming, I., & Baum, A. (1986). Post-traumatic stress as a function of chronic stress and toxic exposures. In C. Figley (Ed.), *Trauma and its wake* (pp. 55–77). New York: Brunner Mazel.

Dew, M. A., Bromet, E. J., & Schulberg, H. C. (in press). A comparative analysis of two community stressors: Long-term mental health effects. *Journal of Applied Social Psychology.*

Dohrenwend, B. P. (1983). Psychological implications of nuclear accidents: The case of Three Mile Island. *Bulletin of the New York Academy of Medicine, 59,* 1060–1076.

Dohrenwend, B. P., Dohrenwend, B. S., Kasl, S. V., & Warheit, G. J. (1979). *Report of the Task Group on Behavioral Effects to the President's Commission on the accident at Three Mile Island.* Washington, DC.

Drabek, T. E. (1968). *Disaster in aisle 13: A case study of the coliseum explosion at the Indiana State fairgrounds, October 31, 1963.* Columbus: Disaster Research Center, Ohio State University.

Drabek, T. E. (1970). Methodology of studying disasters: Past patterns and future possibilities. *American Behavioral Scientist, 13,* 331–343.

Drabek, T. E., & Haas, J. E. (1970). Community disaster and system stress: A sociological perspective. In J. McGrath (Ed.), *Social and psychological factors in stress* (pp. 264–286). New York: Holt, Rinehart, & Winston.

Drabek, T. E., & Key, W. H. (1976). Impact of disaster on primary group linkages. *Mass Emergencies, 1,* 89–105.

Drabek, T. E., Key, W. H., Erickson, P. E., & Crowe, J. L. (1975). The impact of disaster on kin relationships. *Journal of Marriage and the Family, 37*(3), 481–494.

Drabek, T. E., & Quarantelli, E. L. (1969). Blame in disaster: Another look, another viewpoint. In D. Dean (Ed.), *Dynamic social psychology* (pp. 604–615). New York: Random House.

Drabek, T. E., & Stephenson, J. J. (1971). When disaster strikes. *Journal of Applied Social Psychology, 1,* 187–203.

Dynes, R. R. (1970). *Organized behavior in disaster.* Lexington, MA: Heath Lexington.

Erikson, K. (1976). Loss of communality at Buffalo Creek. *American Journal of Psychiatry, 133,* 302–305.

Federal Emergency Management Agency. (1984). *Program guide, disaster assistance programs.* Washington, DC: U.S. Government Printing Office.

Fleming, I. C. (1985). *The stress reducing functions of specific types of social support for victims of a technological catastrophe.* Unpublished doctoral dissertation, University of Maryland, College Park.

Fleming, I., & Baum, A. (1986). *Comparisons of stress persistence between victims of a toxic waste site and victims of a flood.* Unpublished manuscript.

Fleming, R., Baum, A., Gisriel, M. M., & Gatchel, R. J. (1982). Mediating influences of social support on stress at Three Mile Island. *Journal of Human Stress, 8*(3), 14–22.

Flynn, C. B. (1981). Local public opinion. *Annals of the New York Academy of Sciences,* 146–158.

Frederick, C. J. (1980). Effects of natural vs. human-induced violence upon victims. In L. Kivens (Ed.), *Evaluation and change: Services for survivors* (pp. 71–75). Minneapolis, MN: Minneapolis Medical Research Foundation.

Fritz, C. E. (1961). Disaster. In R. K. Merton & R. A. Nisbet (Eds.), *Contemporary social problems.* New York: Harcourt, Brace, & World.

Fritz, C. E., & Marks, E. S. (1954). The NORC studies of human behavior in disaster. *Journal of Social Issues, 10,* 26–41.

Gatchel, R. J., Schaeffer, M. A., & Baum, A. (1985). A psychological field study of stress at Three Mile Island. *Psychophysiology, 22,* 175–181.

Gibbs, M. S. (1986). Psychopathological consequences of exposure to toxins in the water supply. In A. H. Lebovits, A. Baum, & J. Singer (Eds.), *Advances in environmental psychology* (pp. 47–70). Hillsdale, NJ: Erlbaum.

Glass, A. (1959). Psychological considerations in atomic warfare. *U.S. Armed Forces Medical Journal, 7,* 625–638.

Gleser, G. C., Green, B. L., & Winget, C. (1981). *Prolonged effects of disaster.* New York: Academic Press.

Goldhaber, M. U., Staub, S. L., & Tokuhata, G. K. (1983). Spontaneous abortions after the Three Mile Island nuclear accident: A life table analysis. *American Journal of Public Health, 73,* 752–759.

Goldsteen, R. L., Schorr, J., & Goldsteen, K. S. (1985). What's the matter with these people: Rethinking TMI. *Mass Emergencies, 2,* 369–388.

Golec, J. (1980). *Aftermath of disaster: The Teton Dam break.* Unpublished doctoral dissertation, Ohio State University, Columbus.

Goltz, J. D. (1985). Are the news media responsible for the disaster myths? A constant analysis of emergency response imagery. *Mass Emergencies, 2,* 345–368.

Green, B. L. (1982). Assessing levels of psychosocial impairment following disaster: Consideration of actual and methodological dimensions. *Journal of Nervous and Mental Disease, 17*(9), 544–552.

Hall, P. S., & Landreth, P. W. (1975). Assessing some long term consequences of a natural disaster. *Mass Emergencies, 1*, 55–61.

Hargreaves, A. G. (1980, April). Coping with disaster. *American Journal of Nursing*, 683.

Hartsough, D. M., & Savitsky, J. C. (1984). Three Mile Island: Psychology and environmental policy at a crossroads. *American Psychologist, 39*(10), 1113–1122.

Henderson, S., & Bostock, T. (1977). Coping behavior after shipwreck. *British Journal of Psychiatry, 131*, 15–20.

Houts, P. S., Hu, T. W., Henderson, R. A., Cleary, P. D., & Tokuhata, G. (1984). Utilization of medical care following the Three Mile Island crisis. *American Journal of Public Health, 74*, 140–142.

Houts, P. S., Miller, R. W., Tokuhata, G. K., & Ham, K. S. (1980). *Health related behavioral impact of the Three Mile Island nuclear incident.* Unpublished manuscript submitted to the TMI Advisory Panel on Health Research Studies of the Pennsylvania Department of Health.

Hoyt, M. F., & Raven, B. H. (1973). Birth order and the 1971 Los Angeles earthquake. *Journal of Personality and Social Psychology, 28*, 123–128.

Jacobs, M. A., & Spilken, A. Z. (1971). Personality patterns associated with heavy cigarette smoking in male college students. *Journal of Consulting and Clinical Psychology, 37*, 428.

Janoff–Bulman, R. (1979). Characterological versus behavioral self-blame: Inquiries into depression and rape. *Journal of Personality and Social Psychology, 37*, 1798–1809.

Janoff–Bulman, R., & Frieze, I. H. (1983). A theoretical perspective for understanding reactions to victimization. *Journal of Social Issues, 39*, 1–17.

Kardiner, A., Linton, R., DuBois, L., & West, J. (1945). *The psychological frontiers of society.* New York: Columbia University Press.

Kates, R. W., Haas, J. E., Amaral, D. J., Olson, R. A., Ramos, R., & Olson, R. (1973). Human impact of the Managua earthquake: Transitional societies are peculiarly vulnerable to natural disasters. *Science, 182*, 981–989.

Lazarus, R. S., & Cohen, J. B. (1978). Environmental stress. In I. Altman & J. F. Wohlwill (Eds.), *Human behavior and the environment: Current theory and research* (Vol. 2, pp. 89–127). New York: Plenum.

Leik, R. K., Leik, S. A., Euker, K., & Gifford, G. A. (1982). *Under the threat of Mount St. Helens: A study of chronic family stress.* Minneapolis: University of Minnesota, Family Study Center.

Leopold, R. L., & Dillon, H. (1963). Psychoanatomy of a disaster: A long term study of post-traumatic neurosis in survivors of a marine explosion. *American Journal of Psychiatry, 119*, 913–921.

Levine, A. (1982). *Love Canal: Science, politics, and people.* New York: Lexington Books.

Lidz, T. (1946). Nightmares and the combat neuroses. *Psychiatry, 9*, 37–49.

Logue, J. N., & Hansen, H. (1980). A case-control study of hypertensive women in a post-disaster community: Wyoming Valley, Pennsylvania. *Journal of Human Stress, 6*, 28–34.

Logue, J. N., Hansen, F., & Struening, E. (1979). Emotional and physical distress following Hurricane Agnes in the Wyoming Valley of Pennsylvania. *Public Health Reports, 9,* 495–502.

Loomis, C. P. (1960). *Social systems: Essays and their persistence and change.* New York: Van Nostrand.

McLuckie, B. F. (1975). Centralization and natural disaster response: A preliminary hypothesis and interpretations. *Mass Emergencies, 1,* 1–9.

Melick, M. E. (1976). *Social psychological and medical aspects of stress-related illness in the recovery period of a natural disaster.* Unpublished doctoral dissertation, State University of New York at Albany.

Menninger, W. C. (1952). Psychological reactions in an emergency. *American Journal of Psychiatry, 109,* 128–130.

Mileti, D. S., Hartsough, D. M., & Madson, P. (1982). *The Three Mile Island incident: A study of behavioral indicators of human stress.* Report prepared for Shaw, Pittman, Potts, & Trowbridge, Washington, DC.

Miller, D. T., & Porter, C. A. (1983). Self-blame in victims of violence. *Journal of Social Issues, 39,* 139–152.

Milne, G. (1977). Cyclone Tracy: Some consequences of the evacuation for adult victims. *Australian Psychologist, 12,* 39–54.

Murphy, S. (1985). Conceptual bases for disaster research and intervention. In J. Laube & S. A. Murphy (Eds.), *Perspectives on disaster recovery.* New York: Appleton-Century-Crofts.

Neal, D. (1984). Blame assignment in a diffuse disaster situation: A case example of the role of an emergent citizen group. *Mass Emergencies, 2,* 251–266.

Neal, D. M., & Perry, J. B. (1980). *A note on blame and disasters: A case of the winter of 1976–1977.* Paper presented at the North Central Association Meeting in Dayton, OH.

Parker, G. (1977). Cyclone Tracy and Darwin evacuees. On the restoration of the species. *British Journal of Psychiatry, 130,* 548–555.

Pearlin, L. I., & Schooler, C. (1978). The structure of coping. *Journal of Health and Social Behavior, 19,* 2–21.

Penick, E. C., Powell, B. J., & Sieck, W. A. (1976). Mental health problems and natural disaster: Tornado victims. *Journal of Community Psychology, 4,* 64–67.

Perrow, C. (1981). Normal accident at Three Mile Island. *Society, 18*(5), 17–26.

Ploeger, A. (1972). A 10-year follow-up of miners trapped for 2 weeks under threatening circumstances. In C. D. Spielberger & I. G. Sarason (Eds.), *Stress and anxiety* (Vol. 4). Washington, DC: Hemisphere.

Poulshock, S. W., & Cohen, E. S. (1975). The elderly in the aftermath of a disaster. *The Gerontologist, 15,* 357–361.

Price, J. (1978). Some age-related effects of the 1974 Brisbane floods. *Australian and New Zealand Journal of Psychiatry, 12,* 55–58.

Quarantelli, E. L. (1985). What is disaster? The need for clarification in definition and conceptualization in research. In B. J. Sowder (Ed.), *Disasters and mental health: Selected contemporary perspectives* (pp. 41–73). Rockville, MD: U.S. Department of Health and Human Services.

Quarantelli, E. L., & Dynes, R. R. (1972, September). When disaster strikes. *Psychology Today,* pp. 66–70.

Quarantelli, E. L., & Dynes, R. R. (1976). Community conflict: Its absence and its presence in natural disasters. *Mass Emergencies, 1,* 134–152.

Rangell, L. (1976). Discussion of the Buffalo Creek disaster: The course of psychic trauma. *American Journal of Psychiatry, 133,* 313–316.

Robins, L. N., Fischbach, R. L., Smith, E. M., Cotler, L. B., & Solomon, S. D. (1986). Impact of disaster on previously assessed mental health. In J. Shore (Ed.), *Disaster stress studies: New methods and findings.* Washington, DC: American Psychiatric Press.

Rogers, G. O., & Nehnevajsa, J. (1984). *Behavior and attitudes under crisis conditions: Selected issues and findings.* Washington, DC: Federal Emergency Management Agency.

Schachter, S., & Singer, J. E. (1962). Cognitive, social, and physiological determinants of emotional state. *Psychological Review, 69,* 379–399.

Schottenfeld, R. S., & Cullen, M. R. (1985). Occupation-induced posttraumatic stress disorders. *American Journal of Psychiatry, 142,* 198–202.

Shore, J. H., Tatum, E., & Vollmer, W. M. (1986). Evaluation of mental health effects of disaster. *American Journal of Public Health, 76,* 76–83.

Sims, J. H., & Bauman, D. D. (1974). The tornado threat: Coping styles of the north and the south. In J. H. Sims & D. D. Baumann (Eds.), *Human behavior and the environment: Interactions between man and his physical world.* Chicago: Maarovifa Press.

Strumpfer, D. J. W. (1970). Fear and affiliation during a disaster. *Journal of Social Psychology, 82,* 263–268.

Taylor, V., Ross, G. A., & Quarantelli, E. L. (1976). *Delivery of mental health services in disasters: The Xenia toronado and some implications.* Columbus: Ohio State University, Disaster Research Center (Book and Monograph Series No. 11).

Titchener, J. L., & Kapp, F. T. (1976). Family and character change at Buffalo Creek. *American Journal of Psychiatry, 133,* 295–299.

Trainer, P., & Bolin, R. (1976). Persistant effects of disasters on daily activities: A cross-cultural comparison. *Mass Emergencies, 2,* 279–290.

Turner, R., & Killian, L. M. (1972). *Collective behavior* (2nd ed.). Englewood Cliffs, NJ: Prentice-Hall.

Turner, R. H., Nigg, J. M., Paz, D. H., & Young, B. S. (1979). *Earthquake threat: The human response in southern California.* Los Angeles: University of California at Los Angeles, Institute for Social Service Research.

Tyhurst, J. S. (1951). Individual reactions to community disaster. *American Journal of Psychiatry, 107,* 764–769.

Upton, A. L. (1981). Health impact on the Three Mile Island accident. *Annals of the New York Academy of Sciences,* 63–75.

Veltfort, H. R., & Lee, G. F. (1943). The Cocoanut Grove fire: A study in scapegoating. *Journal of Abnormal and Social Psychology, 38* (Clinical Suppl.), 138–154.

Warheit, G. J. (1976). A note on natural disasters and civil disturbances: Similarities and differences. *Mass Emergencies, 1,* 131–137.

Warheit, G. J. (1985). A propositional paradigm for estimating the impact of disasters on mental health. In B. J. Sowder (Ed.), *Disasters and mental health: Selected contemporary perspectives* (pp. 196–214). Rockville, MD: U.S. Department of Health and Human Services.

Weil, R. J., & Dunsworth, F. A. (1958). Psychiatric aspects of disaster—a case history. Some experiences during the Springhill, Nova Scotia mining disaster. *Canadian Psychiatric Association Journal, 3,* 11–17.

Wengner, D. E., Dykes, J. D., Sebock, T. D., & Neff, J. L. (1975). It's a matter of myths—empirical examination of individual insight into disaster response. *Mass Emergencies, 1,* 33–46.

White, G. F., & Haas, J. E. (1975). *Assessment of research on natural hazards.* Cambridge, MA: MIT Press.

Wortman, C. B. (1976). Causal attributions and personal control. In J. H. Harvey, W. J. Ickes, & R. F. Kidd (Eds.), *New directions in attribution research* (Vol. 1). Hillsdale, NJ: Erlbaum.

Wortman, C. B., & Brehm, J. W. (1975). Responses to uncontrollable outcomes: An integration of reactance theory and the learned helplessness model. In L. Berkowitz (Ed.), *Advances in experimental social psychology* (Vol. 8). New York: Academic Press.

CALVIN JEFF FREDERICK

PSYCHIC TRAUMA IN VICTIMS OF CRIME AND TERRORISM

C alvin Jeff Frederick is a professor in the Department of Psychiatry and Biobehavioral Sciences at UCLA and Chief of the Psychology Service at the Veterans Administration Medical Center in West Los Angeles. He was formerly on the faculties of the Departments of Psychiatry and Behavioral Sciences at the Johns Hopkins University and the George Washington University School of Medicine. As Chief of Emergency Mental Health and Disaster Assistance at the National Institute of Mental Health, he served as United States representative to the World Health Organization conference at the Hague on the Psychosocial Consequences of Violence. In addition, he has served as Advisor to the Pan American Health Organization on violent deaths in Central and South America, as a member of the Governor's Advisory Panel on Health Studies at Three Mile Island, and on the National Institutes of Health's Subcommittee on the Biological Effects of Ionizing Radiation. He has been on the Board of Directors of the Society for Traumatic Stress Studies, and on the Board of Directors of the Institute for Victims of Terrorism, President of the American Association of Suicidology, and a member of the American Psychological Association Task Force on Suicide Among Youth.

Dr. Frederick's work has focused on emergency mental treatment and research in psychic trauma, suicide and self-destructive behavior, and cross-cultural stressors. From such work, he has developed diagnostic Reaction Indices as posttraumatic stress disorder scales for children and adults, a Suicide Potential Rating Scale, and a treatment protocol for victims of posttraumatic stress. This chapter is based, in part, on experiences with trauma victims of crime and terrorism, including the Hanafi Muslim hostage crisis, the Iranian hostage crisis, the Beirut hostage crisis, and the Jonestown massacre.

CALVIN JEFF FREDERICK

PSYCHIC TRAUMA IN VICTIMS OF CRIME AND TERRORISM

Violent stressors have been acknowledged as precipitating factors in evoking psychic disturbances in one way or another since the time of primitive peoples. Howells graphically verified the power of positive and negative psychological responses to stressors, even among primitive cultures, in his classic work, *The Heathens* (1948). The psychological and spiritual effects of catastrophic phenomena are closely entwined. This is epitomized by the book of Revelations 6: 2–8, in the description of the Four Horsemen of the Apocalypse (War, Strife, Famine, and Pestilence or Death). The pervasive nature of violence in the United States is underscored by data from the Federal Bureau of Investigation (1985) that one violent crime occurs every 25 seconds, one murder every 29 minutes, one forcible rape every 8 minutes, one robbery every 65 seconds, and one aggravated assault every 48 seconds.

It is appropriate at the outset of this chapter to note the impossibility

Although numerous colleagues and friends have offered helpful suggestions and observations, the author wishes to thank the following persons in particular for their supportive personal comments and thoughtful discussions: Leila Dane, Consultant, U.S. Foreign Service Community; David Collett, son of Alec Collett, United Nations Works Relief Agency writer and missing Beirut hostage; Leo Eitinger, Professor Emeritus, University of Oslo; Jean German, Coordinator, Overseas Briefing Center, Foreign Service Institute, U.S. Department of State; David Jacobsen, former Beirut hostage and Administrator, American University Hospital, Beirut; Martin Jenco, former Beirut hostage and Priest, Order of Servants of Mary;

of covering all aspects and references related to the topic at hand. Therefore, I must be selective in treatment of the topic while attempting to address salient dimensions of psychic trauma relating to crime and terrorism in a reasonably organized, representative, and thought-provoking manner. Undoubtedly, the preferences of some readers may place greater emphasis on areas other than those delineated here. The information advanced in this chapter is based on (a) my personal experiences while at the National Institute of Mental Health (NIMH) during such events as the Iranian hostage crisis, the Hanafi Muslim hostage crisis, the New Mexico prison riots, the Atlanta murders of young blacks, and the Jonestown massacre; (b) treatment and research with victims and witnesses of murders, assassinations, prisoners of war (POWs), major disasters, sexual and physical assaults; and (c) an extensive survey of the literature. Especially cogent and up-to-date information is included based, in part, on my personal interactions with selected family members and hostages from the crises in Iran and Lebanon (Frederick, 1987).

In focusing principally on careful, systematic studies, it can be said that psychological and physiological impairment from some stressors has been widely reported (e.g., spousal and child abuse, rape victims, holocaust victims, and Vietnam combat veterans). Yet, to date, others have been studied far less (e.g., hostages, molested children, and victims of violent personal crime). Nevertheless, more systematically measurable data are needed, particularly concerning the effects of violent crime and terrorism. Generic similarities often appear across stressors, but the effects of some stressors may warrant sub-classification as formal diagnostic entities to permit fuller understanding and treatment. Reactions of victims to traumatic incidents can become emotionally imprinted and are quickly learned as treatment refractory responses. Such responses are frequently disguised, and thereby misdiagnosed, resulting in needless long-term sequelae. The importance of accurate diagnosis and skilled, incident-specific treatment become sine qua nons for trauma mastery. These phenomena constitute a specialized area wherein mental health professionals

Moorhead Kennedy, Executive Director, Council for International Understanding, former Iranian hostage and first Director, Office of Investment Affairs, U.S. Department of State; Penne Laingen, wife of former Iranian hostage and Ambassador Bruce Laingen and founder of the foreign service Family Liaison Action Group (FLAG); Marjorie Ness, Overseas Briefing Center, Foreign Service Institute; Shiela Platt, Overseas Briefing Center, Foreign Service Institute; Theresa Saldana, actress/author and founder of Victims for Victims; Margaret (Peggy) Say, sister of Terry Anderson, journalist and current Beirut hostage; and Brenda Bryant and Gary VandenBos, Communications Office, American Psychological Association. The author also wishes to express his thanks to Denise Paz for her assistance with statistical computations.

The views and opinions expressed are those of the author and do not necessarily reflect those of any government agency with which the writer is affiliated, such as the University of California or the Veterans Administration. Because the author is a federal employee, this chapter is in the public domain.

need to acquire particular expertise and training. Experience in both research and clinical endeavors can be a cogent aspect for understanding.

Defining Victim, Crime, and Terrorism

Victim

Certain key terms in this chapter require definition, namely, *victim, crime,* and *terrorism.* Customary definitions of the term *victim* encompass three meanings: one who (a) suffers some injurious, traumatic, or destructive action; (b) is duped, swindled, cheated, or deceived; or (c) is sacrificed in a religious ritual. The act that results in victimization may or may not be illegal or criminal and may not have an identifiable victimizer. In this chapter, primary emphasis is placed on the first meaning, in which the focus is on the impact of violent, catastrophic events and their sequelae; the initial occurrence is unexpected. In situations where subsequent unconscionable events are anticipated, such as incest and child molestation, the problem is frequently compounded with additional emotional trauma.

Inherent in my discussion of victimization are at least two basic characters that have been called, in popular parlance, victim and victimizer, or perpetrator. A perpetrator or perpetrating situation is always present when one is victimized. This must be taken into account in order to understand the events fully and appropriately. Essential to the entire phenomenon of victimization is a situational stressor and a resultant narrowing of options available to the victim. The core ingredient in victimization is the creation of conditions that the victim perceives as providing recourse only to options that will prolong the situation or worsen it. There are no positive choices that the victim can make that will resolve the problem. Feelings of powerlessness and helplessness become pervasive. For this reason, victims may think of suicide at some point (Frederick, 1977a, 1981b). Similar stressor-related phenomena obtain for children as well as adults (except for children under five or six years of age, in whom some differences from adults are found).

Crime

Borrowing from legal parlance (Black, 1951) and the U.S. Department of Justice (1984), a crime is an act prohibited by law or the failure to perform a legally required act. It is the violation of a right considered in reference to the community at large, as opposed to civil injury. It may be either a positive or negative act. Older definitions of crime denote offenses of a deeper and more atrocious cast, whereas smaller faults are called misdemeanors. For this chapter, I consider crime in the broader and more general sense, covering all infractions of criminal law. Infringements against both society and the individual are encompassed in this definition. Note that a *civil* (which derives from the Greek *civilis* or *citizen*) proceeding simply involves an action to seek recovery or redress from a private wrong that is neither a felony nor a misdemeanor.

Criminal violence has increased in developed countries throughout the world. In the early 1900s, feelings about human sexuality were one of the major conflicts among peoples of developed countries. Undoubtedly, Freud can be given primary credit for drawing attention to this area. Subsequently, there was a movement toward expressing hostility openly, because it was thought to be analogous to repressed feelings of sexuality. Aggression and violence have now become key issues for humankind. In the United States, since the early settlers moved westward, violent aggression with guns has received approbation. The behavior of some early settlers in the West (e.g., the contentious quick drawing of a gun or fighting for a piece of land) has been overextended as a model of strength, accomplishment, and success. Following wars, the expression of violence has been popularized through the sale and production of toys, magazines, and movies.

Curiously, aggression and violence have not been marked with the same taboo that characterized the expression of human sexuality. Indeed, violence has been nurtured and glorified. Although channeling it into competitive sports is generally endorsed, violence remains a major problem throughout the civilized world. Countervailing efforts toward peace, tenderness, and love coexist with, or are offset by, primitive forces toward personal iconoclasm and Procrustean political zealotry. Killing and plundering during wartime has existed for centuries and probably will continue. One can philosophize that war is more justifiable and less psychopathological than individual crime and terrorism because of a presumed higher motive. The highly developed cerebral cortex of humankind is capable of becoming more productive and creative in the expression of human needs. Ironically, the more highly developed brain of Homo sapiens is a two-edged sword capable of both productive and destructive phenomena.

Terrorism

The term *terrorism* denotes explicit domination or coercion through intimidation and fear. Its perpetrator's aim is to gain control of others. Cline and Alexander (1986) defined state-sponsored terrorism as the employment of violence or the threat of it to attain strategic objectives by criminal acts intended to create overwhelming fear in the target population. Perpetrators themselves may experience pressure from a narrowing of options similar to those they create in their victims. Perpetrators rationalize their own actions, however, in terms of an avowed putative wrong they wish to set right.

Physical brutality is not always present in terrorism. Persons in some countries with ongoing political unrest may object to using the word *terrorism* and advocate substitution of the term *insurgency*, at least for many politically motivated acts. *Insurgency* simply denotes insurrection, rebellion, and revolt against an existing dominant regime. I have noted the advocacy of the use of the term *insurgency* in the Irish Republic, for example, where some professional colleagues pressed for its adoption over *terrorism*, because it is not as pejorative and is less likely to arouse negative responses.

Group versus individual victims and perpetrators. Terrorist activities may be perceived on an individual and a group basis for both perpetrators and victims. The views set forth here rely heavily on the works of Eichelman, Soskis, and Reid (1984), Jenkins (1985), Cline and Alexander (1986), Eitinger (1961, 1962, 1965, 1978, 1980), and my own work and opinions derived from personal interaction with hostages and other victims.

Individual terrorists are likely to suffer from a definable emotional or mental disturbance, such as borderline personality, paranoid personality, or antisocial personality disorder. They are often impulse-ridden and exhibit little or no thought or careful planning in their actions. In gang terrorists usually no clear cut emotional or mental disorder is present, per se. Procedures are generally organized, often with much precision and thoughtful planning. Gang terrorists may be consumed with a commitment to cause célèbre. The end justifies the means as they perceive it.

Emotional disturbances occur to some degree in the majority of victims, irrespective of the stressors. Support from significant others and from authorities can aid in ameliorating the distress. Psychic trauma is frequently pervasive and may generalize into numerous avenues of the victim's life. When there has been a prior relationship with other victims in a group, sharing and support can be salutary in its effect. In the absence of such associations, victims are likely to feel that "it's everyone for himself or herself." Widespread negative emotional and mental sequelae customarily follow.

It is historically significant that during the 1970s, concurrent with the formulation and introduction of posttraumatic stress disorder (PTSD) into the DSM-III (American Psychiatric Association, 1980), I and a small cadre of my colleagues at NIMH, including Frank Ochberg, Susan Salasin, and Julius Segal, working in a variety of program areas, recognized and stated the precursors to PTSD in our responses to program goals and procedures. In 1981, my colleagues and I gathered at an international conference, co-sponsored by the Netherlands government and the World Health Organization, to address the psychosocial consequences of violence. We adopted what we felt was a cogent working definition of violence, that violence is the inter-human infliction of significant and avoidable pain and suffering. We also noted Article V of the Universal Declaration of Human Rights that emphasizes that no person should be subjected to torture or cruel, inhuman, or degrading treatment or punishment.

These declarations have served to underscore an essential conso-nance between current formal, professional health perspectives and the beneficent, forbearant policies and procedural positions extant with re-gard to human harrow and anguish in the developed countries. In this context, at my request, the conference membership graciously acknowl-edged and recommended that PTSD should be recognized as a suitable official diagnosis for appropriate cases among victims of violence.

Infrahuman and Physiological Aspects of Psychic Trauma

The eminent physiologist Walter Cannon (1942) described the effects of profound psychic stress in primitive cultures nearly a half century ago. These early writings pointed out that the sympathetic nervous system responds to fright by supplying increased amounts of glucose and adrena-lin, causing vascular contractions. In the absence of appropriate musculo-skeletal responses for a persistent emergency, heavy sympathetic stimula-tion elicits shock (i.e., blood pressure drops, the heart deteriorates, and the arterioles contract near to the skin reducing oxygen in the blood, which permits plasma to leak into the tissues, leaving the red blood cells without vital nourishment). Inadequate food and water accentuates this vicious cycle and produces only normal amounts of adrenalin, which perpetuates the condition until the subject dies.

Although humankind is capable of experiencing more exquisite as-pects of stress, stress is by no means confined to higher organisms. In-deed, the primitive paradigm for stressful responses has been well estab-lished at the infrahuman level. In laboratory experiments, animals unable to avoid shock produced decreased noradrenaline responses. Thus the availability of escape or avoidance contingencies is extremely important. It has been observed, generally, that the pairing of a warning signal with an otherwise unsignaled aversive event can reduce the magnitude or duration of behavioral and physiological changes from response norms. Availability of aversion-stimulus delay or escape contingency exerts a major influence on hormone responses. Plasma cortisol was significantly greater in monkeys who could not escape high-intensity noise (Mason, Brady, & Tolson, 1966). Aberrant-behavior responses have also been ob-served under conditions of crowding and social isolation. These results have been reported in depth by Turkkan, Brady, and Harris (1982). Institu-tional and genetic factors, of course, can influence responses such as blood pressure and cardiovascular pathology as reported by numerous investigators (e.g., Lawler, Barker, Hubbard, & Allen, 1980).

A number of physiological aspects of stress and psychic trauma re-quire elucidation. The influence of stressors on psychic trauma is appar-ent in several dimensions. Lazarus (1966) has noted that investigators have had difficulty in defining stress in a useful fashion. He did not attempt a definition of stress, per se, but wrote of a field of stress, encompassing physiological, sociological, and psychological phenomena. He viewed stress as neither a stimulus nor a response but as a broad intervening variable. It is perhaps more useful to speak of various types of stressors and focus on their impact on behavior. A variety of stressful stimuli relate to this issue, including failure, threat of failure, noxious conditions, loss of body and intellectual functioning, frustration of goal attainment, sensory flooding, and approach–avoidance conflicts. The field of psychosomatic medicine was developed from this line of thinking. The importance of research into significant life events led to empirical studies by Rahe (1968), Holmes and Rahe (1967), and Dohrenwend, Krasnoff, Askenasy, and Dohrenwend (1978). They presented a strong relation between health changes and life crises, which they defined in terms of about 150 life change units in the course of a year. These events were weighted, so that the greater the number of heavily weighted events, the more likely a negative outcome.

Blood pressure and the heart rate are phenomena that have been demonstrated more reliably in animals below the primate level. When diastolic blood pressure was used as a baseline contingent, baboons were conditioned to raise their blood pressure level 30% to 50% above preconditioning baseline levels and to maintain that increase during a 12-hour training session (Harris, Gilliam, Findley, & Brady, 1973; Harris & Turkkan, 1981a, 1981b). This included a program combining food reward, shock avoidance, and visual biofeedback, all dependent on diastolic blood pressure. Irreversible cardiovascular pathology has shown necrotic changes in the myocardium of animals exposed to avoidance–shock conditioning for extended periods (Corley et al., 1979). When animals on a shock avoidance schedule were vagotomized or received a beta blocker (Propranolol), results indicated that the myocardial pathology developed from increased sympathetic activity. Conflict schedules in rats selectively bred for susceptibility to hypertension produced cardiovascular disorders (Lawler et al., 1980). Elevated systolic blood pressure consistently developed in genetically susceptible rats under a conflict condition when compared to various control conditions (including random shocks, food deprivation, maturation level, and normal tensive strains), which did not produce such elevations.

In an infrahuman model for captivity experience, taken from a contrasting procedure, researchers have used rats housed in pairs in soundproofed rooms. Sound-withdrawal hypertension was reported to have developed under these conditions over a 1-month period and indicated an elevation in mean systolic blood pressure, which was well above the control group housed in non-soundproofed rooms. When the sounds from the control chamber were relayed to the soundproofed rooms, pressure elevations did not develop. Placing the experimental animals in the soundproofed chamber for 3 months, however, produced pathological changes in the arterioles. In another dimension, of course, high-intensity sound alone can produce hypertension (Andriukin, 1961). Although the data are less equivocal at the nonprimate level, primate data on cardiovascular effects of noise are in evidence in monkeys exposed to high-intensity sound for 9 months (Peterson, Augenstein, Tanis, & Augenstein, 1981).

The effects of extreme environmental stress on physiological and psychopathological responses in adult humans and children as well as among infrahumans, encompassing various endocrine functions, catecholamines, plasma cortisol levels, aggression, internal locus of control, saline level, and hypertension, have been described by numerous authors (Hanson, Larson, & Snowdon, 1976; Hocking, 1970; Houston, 1986; Howard & Gordon, 1972; Marks, Viswanathan, Lipsedge, & Gardiner, 1972; Mason, 1968; Mason, Brady, & Sidman, 1957; Mason, Brady, & Tolliver, 1968; McCarty & Kopin, 1978; Melick, Logue, & Frederick, 1982).

Diagnostic Criteria for Psychic Trauma

In order to set the stage for the topic of victims I quote one victim, whose reaction is cogently characteristic of reactions to the many crimes committed daily in the United States: "I was forced to take some drastic steps to protect myself. At first I blockaded myself in my apartment and began to carry a pistol. Later, I moved to another city, got an unlisted phone number, and continued to carry a weapon. Even though I had done all of this, I still lived in fear"(President's Task Force, 1982). Comments made by such victims often poignantly express how the effects of traumatic stress become manifest in those affected.

Although this account was given by a crime victim, to date, much of the data concerning the effects of PTSD have been derived from studies of stressors other than crime. Most of the information heretofore was based on experiences of combat veterans, concentration camp inmates and their families, and refugees, and of victims of physical assault and sexual abuse, natural and human-induced disasters, and hostage-taking (Bard & Sangrey, 1979; Blank, 1982a, 1982b; Burgess, Hartman, MacCausland, & Powers, 1984; Cohen & Ahearn, 1980; Danieli, 1981, 1985; Eitinger, 1961, 1962, 1965, 1971, 1980, 1983; Fields, 1976; Frederick, 1980, 1981a, 1981b, 1983, 1985a, 1985b, 1986a, 1986b; Gil, 1970, 1985; Green, 1978a, 1978b, 1983; Green, Grace, & Gleser, 1985; Hilberman, 1977, 1980; Kennedy, 1986; Lifton, 1986; Lipkin, Blank, Parson, & Smith, 1982; Lynn & Belza, 1984; McGee, 1984; Modlin, 1986; Ochberg, 1978; Rofe & Lewin, 1980, 1982; Rosenfeld, 1979, 1981; Schoettle, 1980; Seigel, 1984; Sgroi, 1982; Stone, 1980; Symonds, 1980; Terr, 1981, 1983, 1984). The significant effects of stranger-to-stranger violence have been emphasized by Saldana (1986).

Some stressors almost invariably evoke psychic trauma; others produce it with less frequency or severity. In general, stressors that are perceived as life threatening or disabling produce the most severe reactions. Concomitant physical trauma may or may not be present. Psychic trauma may develop as a result of an individually experienced stressor or one that occurs among a group of people. An example of the former may be seen in physical battering or sexual abuse, and the latter can be exemplified by people taken hostage in a hijacking or in a natural or human-induced disaster. The type and intensity of the reaction depends on the victim's perception of the trauma. The disturbance is generally presumed to be more severe and to require more skilled and prolonged treatment when the stressor is human-induced. Suddenness of impact often intensifies the problem because the ego does not have time to prepare for or process such an assault on the psyche, as evidenced by the writings of Lindemann (1944), Titchener and Kapp (1976), Lifton and Olson (1976), and Horowitz (1982). Although children and the elderly can be especially vulnerable victims, other age groups are by no means immune to severe long-term psychic trauma.

The criteria essential for identifying PTSD are as follows:
- a traumatic event outside the range of ordinary human experience
- a persistent reexperiencing of reactions associated with the event
- an ongoing avoidance of trauma-associated stimuli or numbing of responsiveness
- persistent symptoms of increased autonomic arousal
- symptoms all present within the same 6-month period.

Symptoms that signal PTSD are symptoms that did not exist prior to the trauma (symptoms such as hyperalertness, startle reactions, lack of concentration, sleep disorders, avoidance of stimuli that represent the event, and guilt). A proposed revision of the diagnostic criteria for PTSD is shown in Table 1.

Unmasking Symptoms

The importance of diagnostic acumen cannot be overemphasized. This warrants particular attention to the inclusion of those phenomena that traumas encompass. Effective treatment and problem resolution rely on the principle that every diagnosis constitutes a prognosis. Accurate diagnosis and assessment of the implications of a sore throat will serve to illustrate this principle. A raw, inflamed throat may indicate a variety of conditions, such as a streptococcal infection, which can lead to a cardiac disorder; poliomyelitis, which can become a precursor to muscle atrophy and paralysis; or an incipient virus cold, which is usually relatively benign but may develop into pneumonia in the presence of a suitable host.

Thus not only is assessment or diagnosis of major significance, but obtaining appropriate treatment is frequently critical. Gargling with warm

Table 1
Diagnostic Criteria for Post-Traumatic Stress Disorder

A. The person has experienced an event that is outside the range of usual human experience and that would be markedly distressing to almost anyone, e.g., serious threat to one's life or physical integrity; serious threat or harm to one's children, spouse, or other close relatives and friends; sudden destruction of one's home or community; or seeing another person who has recently been, or is being, seriously injured or killed as the result of an accident or physical violence.

B. The traumatic event is persistently reexperienced in at least one of the following ways:
   (1) recurrent and intrusive distressing recollections of the event (in young children, repetitive play in which themes or aspects of the trauma are expressed)
   (2) recurrent distressing dreams of the event
   (3) sudden acting or feeling as if the traumatic event were recurring (includes a sense of reliving the experience, illusions, hallucinations, and dissociative [flashback] episodes, even those that occur upon awakening or when intoxicated)
   (4) intense psychological distress at exposure to events that symbolize or resemble an aspect of the traumatic event, including anniversaries of the trauma

C. Persistent avoidance of stimuli associated with the trauma or numbing of general responsiveness (not present before the trauma), as indicated by at least three of the following:
   (1) efforts to avoid thoughts or feelings associated with the trauma
   (2) efforts to avoid activities or situations that arouse recollections of the trauma
   (3) inability to recall an important aspect of the trauma (psychogenic amnesia)
   (4) markedly diminished interest in significant activities (in young children, loss of recently acquired developmental skills such as toilet training or language skills)
   (5) feeling of detachment or estrangement from others
   (6) restricted range of affect, e.g., unable to have loving feelings
   (7) sense of foreshortened future, e.g., does not expect to have a career, marriage, or children, or a long life

D. Persistent symptoms of increased arousal (not present before the trauma), as indicated by at least two of the following:
   (1) difficulty falling or staying asleep
   (2) irritability or outbursts of anger

Continued

Table 1, continued

(3) difficulty concentrating
(4) hypervigilance
(5) exaggerated startle response
(6) physiologic reactivity upon exposure to events that symbolize or resemble an aspect of the traumatic event (e.g., a woman who was raped in an elevator breaks out in a sweat when entering any elevator)

E.   Duration of the disturbance (symptoms in B, C, and D) of at least one month.
Specify delayed onset if the onset of symptoms was at least six months after the trauma.

Note. Reprinted from the American Psychiatric Association (1987) by permission.

salt water for a sore throat when a virus cold is present may help abate the problem until the cold runs its course with no untoward effects. However, if the underlying problem is a streptococcal infection or poliomyelitis, then grave sequelae may develop without skilled and knowledgeable intervention. It is often assumed that the criteria for psychological diagnoses are more caliginous than physiological ones. Although there may be some truth in that position, it is by no means immutable. Psychology and physiology, neurophysiology in particular, are closely entwined. Symptoms of the one interdigitate with the other to an appreciable degree. This principle obtains when a strong stressor has evoked a psychic trauma: Physical symptoms may overshadow or mask psychic impairment. Unfortunately, to the unskilled observer, symptoms may not become readily apparent but may lie fallow for prolonged periods only to surface later in conjunction with some improbable stressful event.

Psychic trauma may be camouflaged; therefore, its diagnosis and treatment must be specialized. Its complexity is evidenced by the wide spectrum of stressors that evoke it as well as the various dimensions that the condition encompasses. Researchers who do not have firsthand clinical exposure to such cases should avoid participating in direct clinical intervention until training and experience have been acquired. This does not imply that proficiency cannot be readily learned or that related activities, such as information gathering and supportive services, should not be performed by those with less experience.

Traumatic conditions are often confused with depressive reactions, organic disorders, adjustment reactions, an anxiety state, or a borderline disorder. Because depressive-like symptoms frequently appear, such as diminished interest, detachment, and sleep disturbances, inaccurate assessments and ineffective treatment protocols may follow. Individuals with PTSD who are treated with antidepressants may show some improvement from those symptoms, while the underlying condition is missed and progresses untouched. Naive and inexperienced clinicians will mistakenly conclude that the patient has been treated effectively.

The acute quality of severe distress may resemble borderline psychotic states, whereas the phobic aspects and avoidances can mimic paranoid reactions. After the acute period, anger, resentment, and impulsive urges may be suggestive of a personality disorder. In point of fact, none of these signs conveys the full meaning of the primary and secondary features inherent in a victim's psychodynamics. Differential diagnosis may be improved and established more quickly with the aid of psychological tests, wherein measures of PTSD can be obtained along with other psychodynamic aspects of the case.

Assessment Instruments

Psychodiagnosticians have needed to formulate a useful battery for diagnosing PTSD. To my knowledge the Reaction Index (Frederick, 1985b) is the only instrument that is specifically based on DSM-III criteria in the assessment of PTSD in a broad range of stressors. Some researchers have, however, used selected items of the Minnesota Multiphasic Personality Inventory, or MMPI (Hathaway & McKinley, 1967), in attempts to diagnose PTSD among combat veterans (e.g., Keane & Fairbank, 1983; Keane & Kaloupek, 1982; Keane, Malloy, & Fairbank, 1984; Malloy, Fairbank, & Keane, 1983). Needless to say, careful social, medical, and military histories are essential. Earlier efforts at assessing fear and anxiety have been described by Greer (1965); Spielberger, Gorsuch, and Lusbene (1970); and Stern and Marks (1973).

In concert with policy caveats in assessment set forth in the *VA Practitioner* ("Application of Psychological," 1986), Dalton, Garter, Lips, and Ryan (1986) and Dalton, Pederson, Blom, and Besyner (1986) have provided helpful summaries of recommended psychological tests by surveying programs in which PTSD has been treated by the Veterans Administration. They recommend that when a test battery is used for treatment as well as assessment, it should address differential diagnosis, personality description, description of mood, and cognitive functioning. Although the MMPI has shortcomings, it is still the most widely used among tests given regularly, and it should be included in a battery. The Millon Clinical Multiaxial Inventory (MCMI) requires further use in this context before its efficacy can be determined. An assessment of depressive trends using the Zung Self-Rating Depression Scale, the Beck Depression Inventory, or the NIMH Center for Epidemiological Studies-Depression Scale along with an evaluation of suicide potential (Frederick, 1977a, 1981b) is always important. Motor expressive measures, such as the Bender–Gestalt Test, along with skilled use of the Wechsler Adult Intelligence Scale (WAIS), can be invaluable in both personality and neuropsychological assessment. Moreover, the Shipley-Institute of Living Scale for Measuring Intellectual Impairment, The Hooper Visual Organization Test, and the Trail Making test can add to the efficacy of the appraisal. The Reaction Index and an incomplete sentences test can round out the assessment. A pulse meter to assess physiological responses is a necessity for both diagnosis and treatment.

The need for accurate diagnosis as early as possible can lessen or abort the effects of long-term reactions. I agree with Modlin (1986) that with appropriate and timely treatment, remission of troublesome symptoms can sometimes occur within a few sessions. More refractory cases should be referred to professionals who have specialized training and experience with psychic trauma. My appraisal of the use of tranquilizing agents with PTSD victims is consonant with Modlin's view as well: Minor tranquilizers are of little use and may be countertherapeutic, because their use implies that the patient has a physical disorder. Antidepressant medication is contraindicated for similar reasons. The pervasive and continuing worry and discouragement the victim may frequently display are not symptoms of clinical depression or a borderline state but are normal emotional expressions under the existing conditions. A drug may simply treat the symptoms of anxiety or depression rather than the condition of PTSD. If truly debilitating anxiety continues to manifest itself, an anxiolytic agent administered at night to promote sleep may be considered. It should not, however, interfere with psychotherapy.

Comparing Psychological and Physiological Effects of Psychic Trauma

Despite the growing importance of PTSD, victims of various forms of violence have not been assessed and systematically compared to date. I attempted to provide such information in the following study. In expanding upon previous work, I studied the emotional responses to trauma of groups comprising a total of 300 subjects who were victims of different violent acts as stressors (Frederick, 1985a, 1985b; see Table 2). In the study, there were 50 subjects who had been prisoners of war, 50 victims of physical assault, 100 victims of disaster, 50 subjects who had been hostages, and 50 who had been victims of sexual abuse. All were White adults of both sexes ranging in age from 20 to 67 years. Subjects were assessed by the Reaction Index, a scale measuring the presence and degrees of severity of PTSD, ranging from *doubtful* to *very severe*. Previous studies showed that in a total population affected by a traumatic event, 25% will fall into the doubtful category with 50% being mild to moderate and 25% being clearly observable (severe). The population groups in this study exceeded the expected ranges. The study addressed the question of whether or not the percentage of doubtful cases is the same for each group. Clearly it is not. A second question addressed in this study is whether or not, within each group as a separate category, the

Table 2
Groups Exceeding Statistical Significance
on the Reaction Index

Groups	Percent doubtful	95% confidence interval	Percent positive
POWs	8	19 highest 3 lowest	92
Physical assault victims	10	21 highest 4 lowest	90
Disaster victims	11	19 highest 6 lowest	89
Hostages	4	13 highest 1 lowest	96
Rape victims	6	16 highest 2 lowest	94

percentage rated doubtful significantly differs from 25%. These data also unquestionably show that the percentage of such cases is, indeed, different from 25%.

In this study, 50 cases, 10 from each of the 5 groups noted, correlated 0.87 with an MMPI scale designed to assess PTSD (Keane, Malloy, & Fairbank, 1984). A score of 25 and above was used as the cut-off for the Reaction Index and a score of 30 and above was used as the cut-off for the Keane MMPI scale. One limitation in this comparison is that data for the Keane study came from Vietnam combat veterans and psychiatric inpatients and outpatients, whereas the subjects for my study were taken from a spectrum of five groups of trauma victims, including POWs. Higher scores from each scale as cut-off points would have undoubtedly discriminated even more selectively. A score of 40 and above for the Reaction Index selects out severe cases and produces a 98% probability of PTSD. Scores of 35 reveal the probability of PTSD at 87% and a score of 40 shows a probability at 90% for the scale derived by Keane and Fairbank (1983). A regression line chart for MMPI and the Reaction Index may be seen in Figure 1. Recent preliminary data indicate further that no false negatives have been found with the Reaction Index although 5% of the cases have resulted in false positives. Although both the MMPI and the Reaction Index are of value, the use of the MMPI scale in my study has been somewhat less sensitive to PTSD than the Reaction Index.

The Reaction Index discriminated at a statistically significant level ($p = .01$) in psychic trauma symptoms shown between police officers present and those not present at the San Ysidro McDonald's drive-in massacre (Lipson & Dubner, 1985).

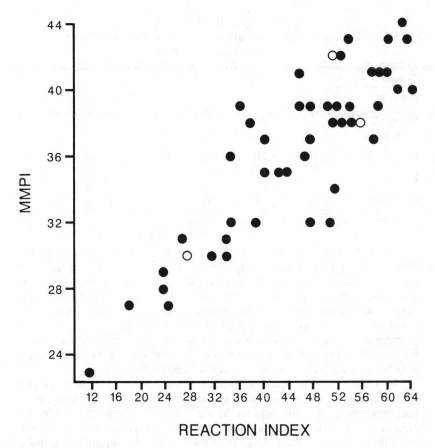

Figure 1. Regression scores comparing MMPI PTSD Scale with Reaction Index. $N=300$. Each o = 12 cases; each ● = 6 cases.

A reliability coefficient yielded an interrater reliability of 0.77 for a single rater in which 50 cases were given anonymous clinical ratings including levels of severity by three raters. An analysis of variance with sums of squares and correlation matrix of the orthogonal components was significant at the .02 level. A Greenhouse–Geisser probability of .92 and a Huyn–Feldt probability of .95 were found when Epsilon factors for degrees of freedom adjustment were applied. These data reveal the unmistakable prevalence and degrees of severity of psychic trauma occurring among victims of various traumatic events, including selected cases of a criminal nature. Table 3 indicates the various degrees of severity on the Reaction Index scale measuring psychic trauma for five populations. A Pearson Chi Square value of 28.97 was statistically significant for 16 degrees of freedom at the 0.02 significance level.

Table 3
Subjects Scoring at Different Severity Levels
on the Reaction Index

Groups	N	Doubtful	Mild	Moderate	Severe	Very Severe
POWs	50	4	7	14	17	8
Physical assault victims	50	5	9	18	14	4
Disaster victims	100	11	19	42	21	7
Hostages	50	2	5	10	19	14
Rape victims	50	3	8	12	16	11

Note. Pearson Chi Square $= 28.97$. $df = 16$. $p = .02$.

Table 4 shows a comparison of psychic trauma experienced by victims of five types of traumatic events. As can be seen, victims pass through phases on the road to reconstitution and adjustment from severe stressors, although similarities and differences obtain. Most authorities agree that phases occur, despite variations in number and composition. My own work, on more than 2,000 cases, describes various phases in keeping with those listed in Table 4. In addition, the psychological, behavioral, and psychophysiological symptoms have also been set forth roughly in order of occurrence for each of five selected stressors.

In addition to the primary trauma, secondary or gratuitous psychic traumas may occur because of frustrations with authorities and agencies, and reactions of specific persons in one's life. This indicates a negative response to perceived harsh stimuli during a vulnerable period. Victims feel that people respond to their plight with a lack of support and understanding, adding insult to injury, so to speak. Such responses may actually exceed the initial primary trauma.

These reactions are not uncommon and should be anticipated by the astute clinician when dealing with cases of marked psychic trauma. Victims may feel that friends do not want to hear about the tragedy and may tend to avoid the friends, lest they overburden their listeners with feelings of anxiety and depression. This perception may cause a forced facade of happiness and pressure to maintain it. Lack of sensitivity and acceptance of depressive moods will cause the victims even more pain.

Gratuitous traumas may be present from all stressors in addition to the primary psychic trauma. In severe cases, in my experience, suicidal ideation may appear as a distressing thought pattern when depressive trends appear. When hopelessness is added to haplessness and helplessness, the likelihood of suicide increases appreciably. Psychological, behavioral, and psychophysiological symptoms are evident with any stressor. In the interest of brevity, only significantly varying symptom patterns will be elaborated in the following sections of this chapter, which deal with victims of natural disasters, hostage-taking, POW trauma, physical assault, and sexual abuse.

Natural and Human-Induced Disasters

Disasters can serve as an established and interesting base of comparison for other stressors with five phases affecting most victims, (1) impact/ shock, (2) heroic, (3) honeymoon, (4) disappointment, and (5) reorganization and recovery. Each of these phases may vary from one victim to another. There is universal unanimity regarding the presence of some impact and shock with severe stressors. During this period, the victim finds it difficult to accept the full occurrence of traumatic stress. Following that, an heroic phase develops wherein much energy is expended in working long hours to ameliorate the victim's plight. The third, or honeymoon phase, is one in which positive trends are seen in anticipation of compensation for losses along with assistance from various government agencies. A fourth phase then comes into play, wherein disappointment develops because matters have not rectified themselves as anticipated. Resentment toward certain government agencies for delays or failures in meeting expected needs and hostility is frequently directed toward one's family or neighbors. In part, this is caused by psychological and physical burnout due to an overexpended energy for protracted periods of time. If progress toward amelioration of the trauma develops, a fifth phase occurs wherein victims become resigned to the existing facts.

Hostage-Taking

Phases through which hostage victims generally pass are as follows: (1) impact/shock, (2) interaction, (3) acceptance acquiescence, (4) ambivalent anger, and (5) trauma mastery/recovery. Feelings of disbelief and denial of the serious nature of the event are manifested from the outset. The impact/shock phase is relatively short-lived, regardless of the stressor. Although no precise time limit can be placed on the presence of this phase, it often lasts a matter of hours and occasionally no more than a few days. In contrast with victims from other psychic stressors, including more common crimes, the person taken hostage or a prisoner of war must experience an interaction with the captors or the perpetrators.

In general, people who are kidnapped or held hostage show a greater similarity to victims of rape than to victims of other stressors. It is important for the captors to make their presence known and establish contact with others, thus effecting the impact on the victim. Interaction between captor and victim is of unique importance. Hostages often feel that people

Table 4
Phases and Symptoms of Selected Stressors

	Natural Disasters	Hostage-Taking	Trauma	Physical Assault	Sexual Abuse
Phases	1. Impact/shock	1. Impact/shock	1. Impact/shock	1. Impact/shock	1. Impact/shock
	2. Heroic	2. Interaction	2. Insensibility/ resignation submission	2. Submission/ withdrawal	2. Withdrawal/ repression
	3. Honeymoon	3. Acceptance/ acquiescence	3. Unrealistic optimism	3. Ambivalent anger	3. Regression
	4. Disappointment	4. Ambivalent anger	4. Euphoria/ emotional anesthesia	4. Dependent aggression	4. Compliance/ anger
	5. Reorganization	5. Trauma mastery/ recovery	5. Trauma mastery/ reconstruction	5. Trauma mastery/ recovery	5. Trauma mastery/ recovery
Psychological/ behavioral symptoms	Anxiety	Phobias/ perpetrator	Phobias/anxiety	Phobias/ perpetrator	Phobias/ perpetrator
	Depression	Helplessness/ depression	Feelings of failure	Recurrent thoughts	Paranoid reactions
	Phobias	Anhedonia	Helplessness/ depression	Suppression	Intrusive thoughts
	Hostility	Memory deficit	Self-abnegation	Anger/fear	Isolation
	Resentment	Loss of concentration	Loss of concentration	Depression	Blunted emotions
	Intrusive thoughts	Intrusive thoughts	Paranoid reactions	Isolation	Sexual confusion
	Loss of concentration	Anxiety	Flashbacks	Guilt	Guilt
	Paranoid reaction		Irritability	Blunted emotions	Self-blame
	Substance abuse				Shame/

Marital discord	Marital discord Substance abuse Stockholm Syndrome Distortion of time & place Dissociation	Hostility/anger Intrusive thoughts Dissociation Substance abuse Marital discord		humiliation Conduct disturbances Inefficiency Distorted perceptions Irritability Anger Marital discord
Psychophysiologic symptoms	Insomnia/nightmares Anorexia Skin disorders Vomiting Sexual inhibition Trembling Hypertension Diarrhea Hyperalertness/startle Diaphoresis Tachycardia Weight loss Startle	Fatigability Diarrhea Skin disorders Insomnia/nightmares Digestive disturbances Restlessness Respiratory disorders Headaches Back trouble Vertigo Hypertension Weight loss Hyperalertness Diaphoresis	Insomnia Hyperalertness Headaches Cardialgia Hypertension Sexual inhibition	Insomnia/nightmares Stomach distress Diarrhea Hypertension Hyperalertness/startle Sexual inhibition Tachycardia Anorexia Emesis Enuresis/encopresis
	Insomnia/nightmares Enuresis/encopresis (children) Anorexia Hypertension Hyperalertness/startle Sexual inhibition			

Note. Listed in approximate rank order of occurrence

acting in a negotiating capacity have frequently been inept in understanding this complicated interplay. Symonds (1975, 1980) takes cognizance of the special relationship between kidnapper or hostage-taker and victim by noting that the former cannot remain anonymous as he or she would wish to do in most other crimes. The victim is used as a weapon to achieve a given goal. Hence, the captor must make certain that the victim remains alive or that an impression is created that the victim is alive.

In some instances, as the captivity continues over time, the so-called Stockholm Syndrome often manifests itself. This rather overworked term derived its name from an incident involving some young women who were held hostage in a Stockholm bank. After the incident was terminated, some of the victims attacked police and defended the criminals. Hostages frequently perceive of their captors as protectors and believe that the perceptions and actions of police and family are jeopardizing the victim's life. In that sense, hostility often develops toward police and family for lack of understanding and acceding to their captor's demands.

Similar to my findings, Symonds (1975, 1980) described four phases he has observed among crime victims: (1) disbelief and shock, (2) psychological infantilism, (3) characterological manifestations, and (4) resolution. Victims frequently truncate reality and view police and family as enemies. This perception is more than mere identification with the aggressor. When pervasive fear is present, it encompasses a feeling of gratitude toward the captor for allowing the victim to remain alive and unharmed, if that is the case. Loss of self-determination and power is sustained or regained by this process, even if it is distorted, indirect, and incomplete. A third stage encompassing acceptance and acquiescence is characteristic of the hostage-taking experience. The victim is in a low-key state and remains so as a form of self-protection. This may vary from what Symonds (1980) called "frozen fright" to a more benign state. The focus here is on self-preservation, the need to remain alive and unharmed. If the incarceration or captivity is extended over a period of more than a few hours, then it is wise, in particular, to help maintain oneself as a human being. While maintaining a low-key unprovocative posture, it is also of paramount importance to get the captors to recognize the victim as something more than a simple piece of property that is expendable.

Making remarks about one's own family and other interests in a nonargumentative and nonthreatening manner can help establish in the mind of the captor the recognition of the captive as a human being rather than an object. The behavior of the hostage can indeed be lifesaving as observed by Niehous (1985), Richardson (1985), and Jacobsen (1987). The fourth phase constitutes an ambivalent anger manifesting itself. The individual begins to move away from the low-key, feared, self-protective, survival response to one of assertion and anger. Due to lack of personal security, this is done tentatively and periodically. Even after release, the tendency exists for the victim to repress the episode, particularly where legal involvement obtains. The victim, however, must reach a state in which anger and resentment are expressed in order to reconstitute feelings of self-worth.

Symptoms of Trauma in Hostages

Among the symptoms most apparent in hostages are phobias specific to the perpetrator. The hostage may have thoughts, even if unrealistic, that the perpetrator or a perpetrator cohort will exact some additional maltreatment on the victim or the victim's family. Frequent psychological symptoms are helplessness and depression, anhedonia, memory deficit, loss of concentration, intrusive thoughts, generalized anxiety, and wavering feelings toward the captors. Distortion of time and place and dissociation will occur with less frequency.

Unrealistic expectations are present on the part of both the victim and family members. The victims wish to return to a normal way of life although they usually cannot accept the ordeal quickly after it is over. Following the early days after release, when much attention has been given to the former hostage, it is expected that tensions will diminish and matters will return to normal. The belief is held, by all parties concerned, that there will be a virtual reestablishment of conditions as they were prior to release. Family members may become inwardly resentful over the attention, feeling it impossible for anyone else to understand their experiences. This may cause them to become unduly defensive. Psychophysiological symptoms such as insomnia and nightmares occur in varying degrees depending on the experiences of the victim. Fatigability, skin disorders, back trouble, sexual inhibition, hypertension, diarrhea, and other cardiovascular disturbances are usually quite apparent and gastrointestinal disturbances frequently appear. However, more serious sequelae can resemble the KZ (concentration camp) syndrome, set forth by Bastiaans (1982), in which exhaustion and life endangering cardiovascular problems occur.

Diagnosis and Treatment of Hostage Victims

As noted earlier, a number of psychological disturbances may appear, including PTSD. In my experience, this three-pronged approach is most fruitful: (a) supportive therapy involving family members when possible, (b) incident-specific treatment of troublesome aspects, and (c) physiological/biofeedback procedures to correlate physiological responses with verbal ones. The psychodynamic correlates of each of these must be individually tailored to suit the person's needs. Pulse rate measures at significant points will verify troubled areas. This therapy provides direct information and assurance to the person under treatment in a collaborative therapeutic effort by substantiating gains in stress-laden spheres. Positive and negative association with other phenomena in the victim's life can prove salutory in effect. Relaxation procedures accompany (b) and (c) in the previous list. Although aspects of this effort are related to behavior therapy, the total approach is much more encompassing.

Such treatment must be undertaken as early as possible. An initial caveat must be noted: Serve the emergency needs of the patient first. Treatment may be done in vitro, in an office situation with a skilled professional therapist who is knowledgeable about such matters, as well as in vivo. Incident-specific or trauma-specific treatment is a sine qua non for trauma mastery (Frederick, 1985a). This holds regardless of the stressor. I am convinced of the efficacy of this position based on contact with more than 2,000 victims of psychic trauma. A final phase comes into play, if all goes well, constituting trauma mastery and recovery from the experiences endured. This is accomplished by nurturing the need to ventilate feelings and by supplying an appropriate, accepting attitude, which will allow and encourage such expressions to develop. A victim needs support in movement at an optimal, personal pace. The value of confirming the diagnostic impression by descriptive replay can be explained to the patient with a view to measuring improvement as treatment progresses. In some instances, the victim's perception of negative reactions by other people is essentially accurate, whereas in other cases it may reflect a sensitive state of mind and need for specific support.

The therapist must be ever mindful of the fact that gratuitous traumas can become very damaging to the victim. Irrespective of the degree of accuracy involved, it is essential to understand the feelings expressed and provide support and guidance through this period. Victims need to be reassured that any feeling is acceptable. Many victims of psychic trauma are fearful that they may be losing their minds when such a panoply of emotions and feelings encompass their thoughts. Therapists must be cautioned against prematurely moving into emotionally charged areas. Good clinical judgment will always honor the person's feelings, defenses, and prior values on performance and failure.

Case Example: The Hanafi Muslim Crisis

In the nation's capital in 1977, a group calling themselves the Hanafi Muslims took hostages in three buildings, the B'nai Brith Building, a mosque, and the District Building (City Hall). During this takeover, a Black newspaper man was shot and killed while leaving an elevator. The largest number of hostages were taken captive in the B'nai Brith Building, where more than 100 people were held for about 40 hours. The victims were taken to a large room, so that they could be made to lie flat on the floor against each other. All victims were subjected to threats from their captors, but some were abused more flagrantly than others. They were restricted from going to the toilet, except at the whim of their captors. They were permitted to move only singly. Machetes were waved about their heads while they were repeatedly threatened with decapitation. One victim, a cardiac patient, implored his captors to release him, because he feared that he might die with a heart seizure, to which one of his captors replied that he would simply decapitate him with a machete and thereby resolve the issue of a heart attack.

The captors espoused specific religious views with regard to their beliefs. One male hostage initiated a somewhat argumentative discussion regarding the value of the captors' religious beliefs. This was an unwise decision, because the Hanafi Muslims later reported that if they had carried out their plan to execute and decapitate some of their prisoners, he would have been the first to die. It is wiser to maintain a low-key posture. During the Van Cleef and Arpels hostage-taking in Beverly Hills, California in July 1986, the security guard was killed because he failed to keep his mouth shut, as the captor put it. Symonds (1980) reported a similar case in which an infantile response to danger by crying created tension that brought tragic results. For example, during a robbery, a youngster cried incessantly, despite efforts by other victims and captors to silence her. In a burst of anger, one of the robbers shot her to death.

After release, many of the B'nai Brith victims had unmistakable phobias about returning to the building. Among the victims I treated was a 30-year-old woman who was unable to return to her office and felt compelled to take a holiday and leave the area where the event occurred. I assured her that this would not resolve the problem and urged her to contact me immediately upon her return. While away, she was fearful that her captors or their cohorts would follow her, forcibly enter her room, and rape and kill her. Even though she recognized the fact that this was unlikely in reality, these images invaded her thoughts with unrelenting persistence. After returning more acutely distressed than when she left, she contacted me to undertake treatment.

At the outset, she stated that she wanted to change jobs and find a position away from the city, because the immediate area invoked unsettling thoughts. I advised her against such a move and explained that this would merely constitute an avoidance of the fear that would make the healing process more difficult in the long run. She accepted the suggestion to remain in her job during the period of treatment, realizing that she could leave upon its termination. I explained to her that such fears would mount and generalize to other areas of her life; to wit the traditional illustration of fears from falling off a horse. Unless the victim is helped to address the fear not only will the individual continue to be afraid of that proverbial horse but also other horses, large four-legged animals, and so forth. Damage from psychic trauma is insidious and may spread rapidly in its malignancy into unexpected areas of the victim's life.

I began incident-specific or trauma-specific treatment with this young woman after initial dynamic supportive psychotherapy and a careful detailing of the incident in a controlled manner in words palatable to her. Along with measures of pulse rate and blood pressure, descriptive events were recaptured in vitro, in the office, in a planned and acceptable fashion. This three pronged approach is essential to trauma mastery. In contrast to more elaborate muscle tension electrodes on the forehead and trunk, such treatment is non-invasive, and it corroborates troublesome areas and validates conflict resolution. Victims themselves should articulate and verbalize, as dramatically as possible, the various aspects of traumatic incidents. When this is difficult, the therapist may help verbalize the scenes for them. Symbolically, it is analogous to assisting an individual in the removal of a splinter that has become infected in subcutaneous tissue. The needle may be applied under direction by the patient so as to extract the splinter and debride the infected area of invasive leukocytes.

After reliving and replaying scenes in vitro, at a point agreeable to both of us, we returned in vivo to the scene of the trauma. As expected, when approaching entry into the building, heightened anxiety and mild panic engulfed her. I assured her that this would abate and that we would proceed at a pace that was tolerable. I told her to inform me when the anxiety had abated, and at that point we entered the building. Upon crossing the lobby to the elevator that would take us to the floor where the victim had been held hostage, the panic-like state welled up again, as anticipated. The previous process was repeated and we waited until the anxiety faded.

Step by step, we worked our way up to the room where she had been held hostage. When entering the room, I asked her where she had been lying on the floor during the ordeal. She could not look at the spot, but she turned her head away and pointed. Gradually, in a guided but unforced manner, we approached the spot where she had lain for 40 hours. Here we remained, while she relived the scene, describing all the events that she could recall and her feelings about them. Personal associations past and present were encouraged with a suitably psychodynamic amplification and exploration of each.

The entire process must be done in an unhurried, supportive fashion, and the therapist should emphasize the patient's need to experience any feeling associated with the trauma. In this instance, the procedure was carried out in a single day, during one block of time. Other occasions may require moving in segments. Once begun, each portion must be completed with anxiety reduction always the final result. One must never leave a situation during a period of heightened anxiety or panic. That will merely strengthen the fear and reinforce the avoidance mechanism that was used to reduce the anxiety. The avoidance response from fear can become as deleterious as the trauma itself and result in an effect inimical to the one desired. The problem will thereby increase rather than decrease in strength. The patient must be shown that anxiety is bearable. Physiologically, anxiety cannot remain in a heightened panic state. When anxiety is allowed to abate, it lends credence to the therapist's concept of trauma mastery and acts as a powerful confidence-builder by reinforcing the belief that the deleterious effects of the psychic trauma can be resolved. With this treatment, the patient was able to return to work in the feared building and become an effective employee again. At a later point, she became employed elsewhere, but under conditions whereby she was no longer avoiding her fears.

Secondary Effects on Hostages

Hostage victims may suffer from reactions similar to prisoners of war. Traumatic situations can evolve during the period of captivity and after release. People often develop gratuitous injuries or secondary traumas after they have been released. Lack of sensitivity and understanding and unreasonable expectations are not uncommon. Presumably, an exception to prevailing psychic trauma responses for hostages has been delineated by Niehous (1985), who was an employee of the Owens Illinois Company at the time of his capture and returned to work within 3 months after he was rescued. He has presented five keys to survival, which he believes helped him. In underscoring the fact that there is no single way to survive, he has shared what proved fruitful in his own case.

First, he attempted to get the captors to recognize him as a human being, rather than as an expendable item. He discussed his family and other personal topics with his captors. Second, he fostered communication by speaking on nonthreatening topics. Being able to speak Spanish, he talked about international sports, the weather, and even politics. Third, he set goals for himself, believing that he would live until his son's graduation or a family birthday. To avoid utter despondency when he was not released by those dates, he reset other times and goals. Fourth, he ate and exercised in an attempt to condition his body. Although he was chained to a tree or pole nightly, which prevented him from doing strenuous exercises, he adapted the exercises to the restrictions he was under. Fifth, he felt that maintaining hope and faith in his company, family, friends, God, and even his captors were of great value. Although the initial prognosis for Mr. Niehous, happily, appears to be positive, a delayed stress syndrome would not be unusual.

Similar stress reactions have been noted in individuals who have been traumatized due to rape, child molestation, or physical battering, or being taken as a prisoner or hostage. Insensitive reactions are forthcoming from other individuals in the victim's life. People who are battered or raped are often asked what they might have done to contribute to the problem. Molested children are not believed or they are shamed. POWs may be made to feel that they might have done something more to prevent being captured. Hostages may be criticized for making sympathetic comments toward the captors and their beliefs. Feelings of some degree of guilt are not uncommon among victims because they may believe that they have not behaved according to expectations set by themselves or others.

In the New Mexico prison riots (Hillman, 1981), employee victims were told that they should not have been working at such jobs in the first place. Victims often remain captives of their own emotions and fears and of the perceptions and attitudes of others. Victims are vulnerable to gratuitous traumas or secondary injuries resulting from the lack of recognition by others. They may be treated as if they are mentally ill on the one hand, or have factitious symptoms on the other.

Family Members as Co-Victims

The information in this section is distilled from the invaluable interactions I have had with the many hostages and their families over the past several years. Most recently, I am indebted to Penne Laingen, wife of ex-Iranian hostage and diplomat Bruce Laingen, for her perspicacious comments (personal communication, March 21, 1987). Conversations with such family members necessitate emphasis on the following issues: (a) preparation and pre-planning among family members in high risk areas, (b) recognition of family members as normal people reacting to extreme stress rather than as mental patients, (c) support, skill, and direction in dealing with the media, (d) power of unity among hostage families, (e) need for sensitive crisis managers within government and other agencies, and (f) importance of devaluing the hostages as bargaining tools.

Both family members and direct victims of terrorism experience various kinds and degrees of responses, many of which may not be predictable, especially by professionals who are neither knowledgeable nor trained in the burgeoning field of psychic trauma. By no means do all victims show manifestations of the Stockholm Syndrome, nor do they inevitably come through free of negative emotional sequelae while always displaying the spirit of rugged American individualism. Laingen (1987) observed that the family members experience similar reactions to stress, threats, and rumors as the hostages themselves along with comparable cycles of denial, bargaining, anger, and depression. Moreover, she underscored the fact that when feelings are repressed over time, especially after the primary victim's release, severe psychological sequelae can follow. Both hostages and family members must possess patience and understanding in order to bridge the changes and emotional gaps created by lengthy and anguish-laden separations. Hostages and family members alike repeatedly emphasized that they must be viewed as human beings reacting to trauma in a normal fashion rather than as patients who are emotionally or mentally disturbed. Expecting positive behavior will promote reactions of strength and subsequent reinforcement will heighten self-confidence. This is especially helpful when children can perceive such steadfastness in parental figures.

In maintaining that we can best favor our country's hostages by devaluing them, Laingen (1987) advanced the belief that government officials, the media, and hostage family members must establish mutually agreeable guidelines to accomplish this goal without making it necessary to relinquish individual freedom. Being adversaries, scapegoating in search of blame for crises, and permitting political considerations to pressure leaders into ill-advised decisions will lead to chaos and divert focus away from the real enemy. Frank and honest cooperation enhances the likelihood of reaching attainable solutions to such crises, all of which will aid in diminishing the unnecessarily gratuitous aspects of psychic trauma.

Although not immutable, the robust consistency of the phases described in Table 4 has been striking, with correlations of .85 to .90. In supporting my five stages as generally extant among hostages, P. Laingen (personal communication, March 21, 1987) reported that, as co-victims, family members often go through phases of their own: (1) impact/shock, (2) denial, (3) integration, (4) heroic, (5) anger, (6) trauma mastery, and (7) acceptance. In brief, impact/shock ordinarily lasts from 3 days to a week and includes disbelief, disavowal, and physiological unrest. Denial can be partly inherent in the first phase; yet, it often stands apart as a justifiably separate condition. Integration comprises meeting other families, meeting and knowing officials, and moving beyond the bounds of the customary life of the family. A heroic period is likely to occur around the fifth month. It involves a realization that the government is not able to solve the problem quickly and is accompanied by personal organization efforts to address issues with officials, the media, and other affected families who are active.

Acknowledgment of ambivalent anger is especially important because of its presumed negative aspects. It may be felt almost immediately and may wax and wane but will continue even after the hostages return. It may be diffuse, unfocused, and disruptive rather than toward a single person. This comes as a surprise because expectations for positive resolution may not develop. Trauma mastery is nurtured by helping others, involvement with constructive causes, and dealing with the media effectively. Complete acceptance may never be reached. The entire phenomenon remains unclosed. Family members learn not to be overly hopeful. They become skeptical about reports until verified and become distrustful of the frequently aggressive and intrusive actions of the media. Many of these responses remain after hostage return.

In his thoughtful work on hostage experiences, Kennedy (1986) underscored the impact of feelings of powerlessness and the inevitable depressive-like symptoms that can be emotionally debilitating. Dane (1986) has made a seminal contribution to this sphere of work in a systematic dissertation study of 14 wives of Iranian hostages. In employing a structured interview and the Bugen-Hawkins Coping Assessment Questionnaire, she found that although most wives felt they coped well in general, at times the intensity of the experience was such that they believed no amount of support could suffice. The intensity of a prior crisis was seen as a useful buffering agent and people regarded as most supportive were those able to communicate within the context of that intensity. She also highlighted the subject's need to affiliate with symbols of strength. Curiously, there were rather widespread negative reactions to pre-release stress inoculation sessions, which underscores the problem of treating individuals as patients with mental disturbances rather than as persons who are involved in a social crisis. A procedure that focused on symptoms was not seen as particularly adaptive, whereas assistance with the development of coping strategies appeared to elicit constructive activity.

Ex-Beirut hostage David Jacobsen (1987) takes pride in not developing the Stockholm Syndrome and in not having been "brainwashed" or exercising any form of apostasy. For some, acts that might be viewed as pusillanimous are inimical to ego strength and positive self-concept. Undoubtedly, activities that stood Jacobsen in good stead were his arguments with fellow hostage Terry Anderson, games of goal-setting surrounding release with hostage Father Martin Jenco, and fantasies about carrying out the duties of his job and family life and maintaining faith. Immurement cannot help but be dehumanizing, especially if it is accompanied by any psychological or physical maltreatment and punishment. One type of responder to traumatic stress calls on personal strong-willed resources, whereas another may use a soft-sell approach to weather the ordeal. No reaction pattern should be execrated or denigrated but should be accepted as a meaningful and valuable response in its own right. Such gratuitous reactions from others can appreciably worsen an already difficult situation. The importance of partner reaction to trauma has been described by Burgess and Holmstrom (1978).

Prisoners of War

Most studies of POWs are from World War II and the Korean conflict. Although there has been a sizable body of work focusing on Vietnam era veterans, apart from such thoughtful writings as those of Segal, Hunter, and Segal (1980), it has dealt principally with combat versus noncombat subjects rather than POWs as such. Because my work cited herein deals with POWs, it will suffice to refer the reader to other references pertaining to combat in Vietnam (Blank, 1982b; Egendorf, Kadushin, Laufer, Rothbart, & Sloan, 1981; Figley, 1978, 1985; Foy, Sipprelle, Rueger, & Carroll, 1984; Keane, Malloy, & Fairbank, 1984; Stretch, Vail, & Maloney, 1985). Discussions of traumatic war neuroses, of course, date back to Grinker and Spiegel (1945) and Futterman and Pumpian-Mindlin (1951).

Studies of military personnel stationed in the United States and Europe have provided much useful information. Professor Eitinger in Norway has probably examined POW and concentration camp phenomena more extensively than any other investigator in the world (1965; 1971; 1980; 1981; 1983). Eitinger, himself an ex-prisoner at Auschwitz, has devoted much of his life to gathering objective data concerning the physical and psychological effects of such confinement. My own studies of POWs from World War II, Korea, and Vietnam are consonant with Professor Eitinger's findings (see Table 1).

Apparent phases of POW trauma are as follows. The first stage entails impact/shock reactions with loss of power over one's own fate. The second stage is resignation, submission, and insensibility. Significant aspects of captivity include well-known accounts of sensory deprivation (Dubek, 1969). Torture or restraint and inadequate food and living quarters are often experienced by POWs. The impact of being held in captivity like a caged animal elicits the onset of feelings of insensibility. Due to physical maltreatment, numerous prisoners have noted that their bodies can become numb to pain, as a means of survival. Eitinger (1978) observed that POWs who survived best with less psychopathology never actually experienced any identification with the aggressor. This is somewhat antithetical to the belief that some people do so in order to protect themselves psychologically. In the third phase prisoners engage in unrealistic optimism; they imagine that the world outside to which they will return has been positively reconstituted, which results in later disillusionment.

The fourth phase develops upon release with a dichotomous expression of euphoria and emotional anesthesia with fluctuation between these two extremes. Feelings of elation and euphoria attending release are temporarily followed by recollections of captivity, which elicit an emotional anesthesia or psychic numbing. Although investigators emphasize the fact that premorbid psychopathology is of no great significance, many believe that some degree of vulnerability may heighten trauma responses. However, premorbid conditions are by no means a necessary or even a sufficient condition for development of PTSD. There is strong evidence to indicate that support from families and friends is of particular significance with regard to the severity of the psychic trauma experience (Eitinger, 1980). Eitinger noted that Norwegian prisoners of war who returned to families that accepted their low level of functioning fared better than Jewish POWs who had no families giving similar psychological support. The fifth phase of trauma mastery and reconstruction or recovery is materially enhanced by such support.

Symptoms of POW Trauma

Among the psychological and behavioral symptoms experienced are phobias and anxiety. Phobias are specific to experiences during the captivity, whereas anxiety is of a generalized nature. Feelings of failure often set in because individuals are no longer able to function in keeping with previous expectations. Feelings of depression, helplessness, self-abnegation, loss of concentration, flashbacks, irritability, hostility, anger, intrusive thoughts, and dissociative phenomena are prominent along with marital or familial discord. Among the physical and psychophysiological symptoms present, fatigability is especially prominent. Chronic fatigue is a consistent symptom of post-POW trauma. Diarrhea, skin disorders, insomnia, nightmares, digestive disturbances, restlessness, respiratory disorders, headaches, back trouble, vertigo, and hypertension are also prevalent. These are confirmed across populations in the United States and in Europe. Where neurological disturbances exist, a physical trauma, such as head injury, is likely. Malnutrition has also evoked physical and psychic problems. The principles surrounding diagnosis and treatment do not vary from the other stressors listed.

Physical Assault

The definition of *physical assault* used in this chapter is spousal abuse, domestic violence, and other assaults against a person. The tabularized data on physical abuse reported in this chapter relates to adults, but it is fitting to cite some representative work with children and the elderly as well. Straus, Gelles, and Steinmetz (1980) have estimated that up to 4 million children are kicked, bitten, or hit by a family member at some time during their lives. Their figures indicated such occurrences about nine times the previous year, whereas actual beatings took place an average of six times during that period. Moreover, at least one act of violence by a spouse occurred during the previous year in 16% of the cases and among nearly 30% of the couples at some point in the marriage. Gelles (1974) selected neighbors of violent people as a control group and found that violence had occurred in 37% of the control sample. Widespread abuse and neglect of the elderly reaching nearly 2.5 million cases yearly have been cited by the U.S. Congress (1980) and Rathbone-McCuan and Voyles (1982).

The fact that violence begets violence is shown by George and Main (1979), who discovered that even abused toddlers assaulted and harassed their peers more frequently than did matched controls. Differences have appeared between abused children and matched peers in social, emotional, and cognitive development. Kempe and Helfer (1972) noted that abusive parents were themselves abused and more children are killed by parents than die from disease. Some researchers (e.g., Gil, 1985) asserted that violence in this country will never be controlled because of society's acceptance of corporal punishment. Gil's work indicated that physical child abuse is committed by basically normal people who become angry and frustrated and experience loss of control, often because the child would not stop crying. Common parental responses include remarks such as "he has to learn" or "she needed to be taught a lesson" and "I was at my wit's end." Gil stated further that both sexes compose the abusive population, with fathers and stepfathers guilty in two thirds of the cases, and mothers and stepmothers blameworthy in one third of the cases. Although parents of all ages are abusers, severe abuse comes largely from those under 25 years of age. Garbarino and Sherman (1980), Pelton (1982), and Newberger and Cook (1983) highlighted socioeconomic issues and personal needs of parents as important factors contributing to child abuse.

People who are subjected to physical assault experience the following five phases: (1) impact/shock, (2) submission/withdrawal, (3) ambivalent anger, (4) dependent aggression, and (5) trauma mastery and recovery. During the impact/shock phase, in which the individual experiences disbelief, a second phase of submission and withdrawal evolves. Apprehension and fear are particularly prominent in cases in which a continuing relationship exists (e.g., in the case of spousal or lover abuse). Assault is often not reported at the outset. Victims frequently return to the abusing perpetrator. Financial constraints may be present in some instances. This is by no means a logical or persuasive reason for the victim's actions in returning to the source of the abuse. These individuals require support to separate themselves from the source of the assault. Men are the most frequent perpetrators of violent acts, but they by no means have a lock on them.

Giles-Sims (1983) computed a violence index and an abuse index for both sexes. She concluded, "Over time violence may become a patterned way of relating in the system rather than a behavioral response to stress and frustration" (p. 58). Using the violence index, Giles-Sims (1983) compared the percentage of the women who reportedly used violent acts at least once on the second occasion. They found that 5% of the men and 42% of the women reported engaging in such acts. It should be noted, however, that the number of women never engaging in violence was considerably lower than the number of men who were never violent. Moreover, women suffered more severe violence than their partners, experiencing serious injury or life-threatening acts.

Symptoms of Physical Assault Trauma

Psychological and behavioral symptoms may include fears of the perpetrator reenacting the initial assault. Recurrent thoughts and an attempt to suppress what occurred are common psychological manifestations. Marked ambivalent anger or fear is demonstrable and many women in particular felt that they were in a situation that was inescapable. Feelings of isolation and blunted emotions followed. Giles-Sims (1983) found that women particularly felt guilty about leaving, especially when children might be deprived of interacting with their fathers. Her work as well as my own, covering a 2-year follow-up period, indicated that insomnia is the most prevalent. It was clearly apparent that victims of physical assault experienced hyperalertness or hypervigilance. A state of hyperarousal became conditioned with thoughts of further assaults. Headaches were common, as were cardialgia, hypertension, and sexual inhibition. Upon returning to the partners who have abused them, rewarding sexual intimacy was not readily forthcoming.

Although assault or battery can be perpetrated or experienced by either sex, it is most common for the man to be the perpetrator and the woman to be the victim. From research in this area it seems clear that violence within the family is more widespread than is commonly believed (Gelles, 1974). Straus (1977) has remarked that a marriage license becomes a "hitting license." Like other forms of violent behavior, much of this activity is underreported due to fear and shame. Moreover, dangerousness continues to be a source of disagreement among authorities and is a poorly defined concept, even in the courts (Frederick, 1978).

Retrospective studies on the psychosocial consequences of violence among battered women support the presence of some unsettling psychological sequelae (Carmen, Rieker, & Mills, 1984; Hilberman, 1977, 1980). Van Rappard (1983) observed feelings of fear, sadness, doubt, guilt, and conflicts over seeking independent status after having been assaulted or battered. She described these women as fearful of being alone, jumpy and nervous, and poor sleepers. In addition, suicidal attempts often follow when these victims become isolated and alone after leaving the home setting.

Carmen et al. (1984) reported on victims of violence and psychiatric illness in 188 male and female psychiatric patients. They reconstructed the events studied through an in-depth examination of psychiatric inpatient records. Almost half of the patients had histories of physical or sexual abuse, and 90% of the patients had been victimized by family members. Chronic abuse left victims with ongoing problems such as inability to cope with aggression and anger, impaired self-worth and self-esteem, and the inability to trust others. It became readily apparent that the women were much more likely than men to have histories of abuse. From among 80 abused patients, 53% had been physically abused, 19% had been sexually abused, and 23% had been abused both physically and sexually. Of the 38 patients who experienced sexual abuse, only 4 were men. Blacks were slightly more apt to have suffered abuse than Whites; 50% for the former compared to 41% for the latter. Although these patients were not specifically classified as having PTSD, the symptoms described appear to fit that category.

A sample of 59 battered children were studied by Green (1978a, 1978b). Cases consisted of those who were openly abused, those neglected, and those who were neither abused nor neglected. Assaultive or openly self-destructive behaviors were apparent in 41% of the abused sample, 17% of the neglected subjects, and 7% of the controls. A report of psychic effects on battered youngsters was further developed by Stone (1980). Similar symptoms appear in PTSD in children.

Sexual Abuse

Victims of sexual abuse pass through the initial impact/shock stage followed by withdrawal and repression. Both victims of rape and child molestation frequently avoid disclosing the incident. Fear of disclosure is accompanied by fears of rejection, feelings of unworthiness, and by disbelief, self-blame, and guilt. Although there are no reliable figures, there appears to be little doubt that withdrawal and repression are the defense mechanisms manifesting themselves in a large percentage of cases. This attempt to control anxiety carries the hope that any continuous sexual abuse will cease. Although far less frequently, women can also be perpetrators of sexual abuse. Among my cases I have observed that when boys are the victims, the perpetrator is likely to be a stepmother or aunt rather than the natural mother. This kind of sexual abuse may constitute statutory rape or incest.

The gratuitous traumas or injuries secondary to the primary trauma of rape victims are reported in a detailed NIMH-supported study by Bart and O'Brien (1985). They found no differences in the frequency of depressive reactions between women who successfully avoided rape and those who did not. However, a small number in the sample avoiding rape felt strengthened by the experience, apparently gaining self-confidence.

Symptoms of Trauma in Victims of Sexual Abuse

Intrusive thoughts, paranoid reactions, perpetrator phobias, isolation, blunted emotions, self-blame and shame, along with distorting perceptions and irritability are especially prominent in victims of sexual abuse. Victims use mechanisms of denial and conscious suppression and repression to control the frustrations and anxiety surrounding the trauma. Conduct disturbances, a drop in efficiency, sexual confusion, and an overriding fear of discovery by peers constitute reactions occurring largely in age groups under 21 years.

Psychophysiological reactions that are in clear evidence are sleep disturbances, stomach distress, diarrhea, hypertension, hyperalertness, startle reactions, sexual inhibition, tachycardia, anorexia, and emesis, and in young children, enuresis and encopresis. When boys are molested, they almost invariably have not only thoughts of suicide but fears of homosexuality and their own identity as effective future husbands and fathers.

Victims should be reassured that such responses are normal reactions to traumatic situations and be supported in a collaborative effort with the therapist. Great sensitivity is needed to accomplish this in the most optimal fashion. Goals to manage effects of the trauma are fully explained to victims at the outset. It is imperative to enlist their cooperation and to avoid any misunderstanding about the value and importance of such treatment. Of course, it is wise to always obtain informed consent in a nonthreatening manner before proceeding.

Terrorism

The Role of the Media: Gratuitous Trauma

The contribution of the media to terrorist activities continues to be weighed against the principle of freedom of the press. Gaining media attention is an avowed terrorist goal that can evoke an ambivalent response by the media. The sheer drama of terrorism heightens its appeal and reinforces the desire to publicize it, as exemplified by the 1985 TWA hijacking, in which media coverage was widespread. As a policy, the primary use of dramatic tactical assault or surgical strike has not yielded a superior record of success and is not endorsed by most governments. Journalists have pointed out that although the Israeli government has shown a pronounced tendency to use the assault option, even that country has been unable to resolve all incidents by force; nor has the use of force option in hostage incidents eliminated the problem for Israeli citizens.

In July 1985, David Martin, a CBS News Pentagon correspondent, reported, "twenty-two Americans were killed by terrorism during this past year. Compared with other ways Americans lose their lives it is really not so many. That may simply be a price we have to pay for doing business in the world." This may be a rather oversimplified, capitulatory view of a troublesome situation affecting the entire world. Nevertheless, the fact must be faced that the so-called terrorist strike force unit from the United States can be ineffective due to proscriptions from other countries. The element of a surprise attack is thereby neutralized and rendered ineffectual.

The controversy over the right of the public to gain information (i.e., freedom of the press versus the citizen's right to privacy) continues to manifest itself as a form of gratuitous trauma. Most victims agree that the media has a responsibility to gather news, to inform, and to report to the public ethically and professionally. But some journalists or editors circumvent good taste, privacy, and ethics in their editorial judgment and conduct.

On the positive side, the media can supply comforting direct information to victims' families, disseminate valuable propaganda, and provide educational avenues for professionals and relatives of victims themselves. Most professionals and families of victims are mindful of the fact that most journalists act responsibly and are frequently placed between Scylla and Charybdis in executing sensitive but dramatically newsworthy assignments. Most assuredly, experiences with the media are predominantly positive and useful; yet, victims of each stressor covered in this article have expressed negative media experiences, which they have regarded as unnecessary. It would be well for victims and families to remember that despite pressures to the contrary, they can always simply refuse to speak with media personnel until they wish to do so.

Laingen (1987a) suggested that because those interviewed are unable to edit a live audio or video program, it may be wise to request taping before airing. This maneuver can prevent the interviewee from being blindsided by queries that are disquieting and ad hominem. This can, perforce, allow the media personnel to disavow any implied coercion and mitigate potential ill will. On the negative side, numerous victims and relatives have reported stakeouts involving their children as well as themselves; aggressive invasions of privacy of person and property; interrogation about personal medications, alcohol use, emotional states, and sexual liaisons. They often feel that media reporters assume an importunate posture that evokes impuissance on the part of the victims and their families.

Professional Participation in Terrorism

Psychologists may become propaganda participants in insurgency or terrorism, and physicians can and do become terrorist technicians. The latter has been discussed by Goldstein and Breslin (1986). Numerous instances of abuse by treating professionals have been reported from ancient times, principally by physicians, because of their practice, expertise, and knowledge relating to bodily functions. Negative treatment or the absence of positive treatment by medical personnel under a previous regime in Uruguay illustrates this point. In March 1984, Lucia Ursuaga Gilboa reported that during initial interrogation as a political prisoner she had been stripped nude, kicked, beaten, and then suspended by a rope tied to her bound wrists. In this position, electric shock sticks were applied repeatedly. After losing consciousness during one such period, she was told upon awakening that she had experienced convulsions. Following examination, the attending physician informed her interrogators that they could continue but recommended that she be allowed to sit to avoid permanent trauma.

Uruguayan military physicians diagnosed a woman with unmistakable carcinoma of the breast as merely a case of "nervousness," and after several months of neglect and a marked weight loss, a radical mastectomy was performed. Another severely depressed woman who had attempted suicide was placed in periodic isolation until she ultimately did kill herself. Any psychologist or physician with a modicum of knowledge about depression and suicide knows that isolation in such cases is contraindicated.

At Auschwitz, SS Colonel Hess, who had previously served at Dachau, described the activities of medical officers who classified those fit for work and sent the others (about 75%) to the extermination chambers, which were designed to resemble delousing baths, with showers, pipes, and drains. Prussic acid (HCN hydrogen cyanide), which mixes with oxygen instantly to become lethally toxic, was introduced through a specially constructed opening in the ceiling. Its victims became stunned with the first breath and died within three to fifteen minutes, depending on atmospheric conditions and the number of people confined. Prisoner dentists removed any rings and gold teeth from the corpses (Gilbert, 1950; Stover & Nightingale, 1985).

There is little doubt that a number of physicians and dentists in the Nazi regime enjoyed their work and believed in the aims of the movement. In a broader context, however, some provocative questions arise: What possesses professionals to become participants in crime when they are ethically and technically trained to promote physical and mental health and help those in distress? What procedures are acceptable versus those which are not? Does obtaining informed consent justify the use of noxious stimuli? To what extent are we obligated to render assistance to colleagues who have become participant–victims of such activities?

Withholding treatment from the sick; diagnosing to ensure confinement; falsifying or withholding records; employing sensory and sleep deprivation; and administering mind altering drugs, electric shock, deafening sounds, blinding light, aqueous submersion, fearful threats, and coercion are examples of methods used to assist repressive authorities with maltreatment and terrorism. Participation by professionals is always rationalized and compartmentalized in their thinking. Although many of these procedures have been employed principally by physicians, others are in the domain of psychologists.

Although documentation of actual participation is needed, the following is a hypothetical case. Suppose that a psychologist serving a military regime or employed by a government hospital or clinic is asked to diagnose and treat a severely depressed and suicidal patient who is a terrorist or political insurgent deemed dangerous to our government. Without attempting to answer such questions, several provocative issues come into focus. Should there be doubt that when human life or health is in serious jeopardy professional services ought to be provided analogous to medical intervention? On humanitarian grounds, is that person entitled to the same treatment given to a wounded enemy soldier who is a prisoner of war? Suppose those colleagues maintain that if the psychologist refuses to cooperate, other patients will be even more severely maltreated or killed? What should be our response to the plight of victim colleagues? Should one accept the face validity of a foreign colleague's dilemma? Is there justifiable difference between active participation and passive acceptance? How heinous must behavior be to become totally unacceptable? The gradual assimilation and rationalization of unpalatable political and humanitarian beliefs is not uncommon. Hostage victims do not simply accept or endorse their captors' beliefs because of identification with the aggressor stemming from fear but out of gratitude to the captors for not treating them any worse and for allowing them to remain alive. Under what conditions might such a syndrome be applicable in this context?

Following the Nuremberg trials in 1948, when it was disclosed that Nazi physicians had overseen practices at the concentration camp ovens and showers and injected live typhus into their patients, the World Medical Association inserted a phrase into its Hippocratic oath stating that physicians would "not permit considerations of race, religion, nationality, party politics, or social standing" to intervene between duty and patient (Goldstein & Breslin, 1986). As seen from examples cited, this provision is not inviolate. Amnesty International has reported that torture of political prisoners occurs in about one country out of three.

Psychic Trauma in Children

My work encompasses the effects of psychic stressors on children in the principal spheres of child molestation, physical abuse, suicide in significant others, and witnessing homicide. Inasmuch as the focus of this chapter is criminal behavior, it will suffice to note, en passant, that I have addressed the topic of suicide elsewhere (Frederick, 1977a, 1977b, 1981b, 1985a, 1985b). Other studies of children and trauma include the following:

- effects of war on children (Burt, 1943; Carey-Trefzer, 1949; D. Dulicai, personal communication, March, 1987; Gakman, 1987; Ziv, Kruglanski, & Shulman, 1974)
- children of holocaust survivors (Danieli, 1981)
- victims of natural disasters (Newman, 1976)
- children who witness violence (Pynoos & Eth, 1984)
- victims of hostage-taking (Terr, 1983, 1984; van der Ploeg, 1983)
- physically abused children (Eitinger, 1983; George & Main, 1979; Green, 1978a, 1978b; Pelton, 1982)
- sexually abused children (Burgess, Hartman, MacCausland, & Powers, 1984; Frederick, 1986a; Linn, 1980; Lukianowicz, 1972; Renvoize, 1978; Sadock, 1980a, 1980b; Summit, 1983).

Sexual Abuse

In the discussion pertinent to Table 4, the term *sexual abuse* incorporates rape as well as other forms of child molestation and other forms of sexual abuse. For the data cited in Tables 2 and 3 the 300 subjects were adults. In another study (Frederick, 1985a), I did examine the psychological effects of child molestation. Of the 50 subjects in the sample all disclosed unmistakable evidence of PTSD. Although there are notable differences in violence and aggression as manifested in rape, as opposed to certain other forms of sexual abuse such as child molestation, the psychological symptoms are found in both and show rather significant similarities. My work indicates that the people most psychologically vulnerable to sexual abuse are children and older adults.

Boys are subjected to similar situations, customarily by a bisexual stepfather, relative, family friend, or trusted member of the community such as a scout master, physician, or clergyman. In my experience with respect to sexual abuse among children (Frederick, 1985a), boys are more likely to become victims in late childhood and adolescence from a person outside the family. Girls, on the other hand, are more likely to be sexually molested at a younger age by a parent, stepparent, or other family member. Although victims hope that the trauma will not repeat itself, it will remain imbedded in the thought processes. Many adults and children tend to regress in their behavior toward a more infantile and dependent state.

More women are likely to report rape today than they were a decade or two ago, but rape still goes unreported in a remarkable number of instances. Summit (1983) alluded to the fact that the victim of child molestation is in a position rather analogous to adult rape victims of a few years ago. Lacking astute clinical understanding of the adjustment needed for victims of rape, women were seen to be provocative and largely responsible for inviting or exposing themselves to risk of sexual assault. Most women chose not to report their own victimization, which only confirmed the suspicion that they had something to hide. Persons who did report it frequently regretted that decision because they found themselves subjected to criticism and attacks on their credibility and character. An overriding fear among young people, including adolescents, who are victims of sexual abuse is the fear of exposure to their peers. They fear that if their peers found out about it, they would be rejected and accused of being sexual perverts.

An accommodation syndrome clearly delineated by Summit (1983) is characterized by the following components: (1) secrecy, (b) helplessness, (c) entrapment and accommodation, (d) delayed disclosure, and (e) retraction. Younger victims especially will frequently retract an initial statement because of ambivalent feelings of guilt and anger along with the need to preserve acceptance and harmony. Retractions occur in cases of incest because of the potential chaos and tension that is created within the family setting. Following the regression stage, this compliance and anger marks a fourth phase that is consistent with reports by Summit. Victims of rape or other kinds of sexual abuse are routinely assisted through the first four phases, but the fifth phase of trauma mastery is more difficult.

I have found the following specific signs of child molestation (Frederick, 1986a):

• *The need for proximate protection.* A trustworthy parental surrogate or parent may be sought to sleep nearby or remain close to the victim. Anxiety surfaces in the absence of such affection.

• *Confused sexual identity.* Many remarks are often made about sexual identity, especially if the assault is a homosexual one.

• *Fears of being seen nude.* (e.g., avoidance of group bathing when it was not present before).

• *Psychophysiological disturbances.* Headaches, stomachaches, and occasionally enuresis and encopresis are in evidence.

• *Personal discomfiture.* The victim becomes fidgety, uncomfortable, and tense when anything regarding sexual behavior is encountered.

• *Withdrawal.* Victims tend to remain alone and will resist socializing with others. This is in marked contrast, often, to previous behavior. They are pervasively fearful that peers will think negatively about them.

• *Irritability.* Young victims become unruly and fractious and are easily annoyed. This is readily observed by family members.

• *Risk-taking behavior.* These youngsters will engage in hazardous acts, such as climbing and jumping from high places or riding bicycles dangerously through traffic.

• *Self-destructive thoughts or acts.* Suicidal ideation is almost invariably present, and on occasion it might be overtly expressed. It is a symptom which must be carefully observed.

• *Comments about self-abnegation.* Lack of self-worth and self-defeating comments are usually clearly in evidence.

• *Underreporting of the trauma.* A withholding of the entire account surrounding the act of sexual molestation is likely, especially any aspect about the active participation by the victim.

• *Perpetrator harm.* A fear of retribution by the perpetrator for disclosure haunts the victim. This is frequently followed later by a desire for revenge, which may be expressed by a need to inflict harm on the perpetrator. This only follows after an appreciable period of time when the young victim has been supported and is able to begin to work through the conflicts surrounding the trauma. Meyers, Templer, and Brown (1984) conducted a meaningful investigation concerning the coping skills of rape victims and the possibility that some women may be more vulnerable to rape than others.

Witnessing Violence

Some striking findings have been noted by my colleagues and I (Pynoos, Frederick, et al., in press). In one instance, a woman shot herself to death in front of a class of 10-year-olds; in another an adult man killed his estranged wife and two daughters with adult and child parishioners as witnesses; and in another tragedy, a sniper fired a rifle into a school yard of innocent children. The sniper attack occurred on the afternoon of February 24, 1984, when youngsters attending an elementary school in

Los Angeles had just been dismissed for the day. Some were on the playground before making their way homeward, some had not yet left the building, and some were absent or "off tract" as part of a rotating system of attendance designed to accommodate the population served. Within a few minutes after school had been dismissed, a disturbed man, in his 20s, unleashed a series of rifle shots into the playground and the school building from the second story of a house across the street. One young girl and an adult were killed, and 13 others were injured. A state of siege ensued, during which children dropped to the ground, hid behind objects such as trash cans, or ran back into the school building to seek shelter. Most of those still in the building were instructed to lie beneath tables or were closeted behind doors in the classrooms.

It was not until several hours later that a S.W.A.T. team discovered after forcibly entering the house that the sniper had killed himself with a gunshot to the head. The young assassin himself had been traumatized by the loss of his parents and several siblings in the Jonestown, Guyana, massacre. I performed the psychological autopsy with a colleague and determined that the psychic stress from Jonestown was a principal contributing factor to the assailant's mental state. He had never received any psychological treatment for his condition.

With the permission of the Board of Education and the school principal, my colleagues and I examined a sample of 160 youngsters with the Reaction Index Form C, which is the children's form of a PTSD scale, together with interviews and drawings. These procedures were also used with the youngsters to provide brief intervention and treatment. Following a period in which unstructured drawings in color were elicited, the youngsters were interviewed both by classroom group and individually. Most became phobic about school, playground equipment, the assassin's house, and reprisal. Several teachers wanted the house demolished so that they would not be reminded of the tragedy. Many teachers slept fitfully, had bouts of diarrhea during the night, and verbalized guilt that they had not done more to either prevent the shooting or protect the children, despite the irrationality of such thoughts.

A brief summary of pertinent selected findings are discussed here because detailed and complete results of this study are being reported elsewhere (Pynoos, Frederick, et al., in press). In essence, it became strikingly apparent that the majority of youngsters had suffered PTSD. More than 60% had at least a mild degree of PTSD. The level of exposure to this awesome event took on special meaning in light of the data collected. The Reaction Index Form C proved to be particularly enlightening as a measure of psychic trauma. Youngsters who were actually on the playground at the time of the shooting ($M = 12.0$) revealed mean scores almost twice as high as young subjects who were away from school but in the neighborhood ($M = 6.4$). The analysis of variance computation showed an $F = 16.06$; $df = 6$; $p = .001$. Thus particularly robust findings were disclosed concerning the importance of levels of direct exposure to traumatic events among children who experience violence that results in the homicidal death of another.

Group Treatment

When groups of people have been traumatized, it is helpful to provide both individual and group psychological treatment. Individual treatment should proceed along the lines outlined earlier for individual case examples. Both procedures call for a climate of initial acceptance and encouragement followed by incident-specific treatment related to the trauma. An initial icebreaker in the form of a short questionnaire related to feelings about the trauma can be helpful. A brief sketch of the usefulness of debriefing is necessary at the outset to establish a working climate of encouragement toward open expression of the victim's chaotic feelings.

It is useful to proceed with more than one therapist for a group of more than 15 persons, dividing the participants into smaller units. While one therapist interacts with the victims, another can observe and note significant responses which otherwise may be missed, including unsettling incidents associated with the trauma. I have detailed a group trauma that resulted in multiple homicides treated with appropriate incident-specific treatment (Frederick, 1986b). The treatment relies on sharing and support from other members, a simulation of the event, and, where applicable, returning to the actual scene of the trauma. The following significant aspects of treatment require highlighting:

- Timing is important. The most efficacious period involves the sensitivity of the therapist with corroboration by victims.
- Simple, understandable analogies can be invaluable (e.g., reentry into an automobile after a serious accident) and underscore the necessity of engagement at the scene.
- Any emotion should be supported.
- Age-appropriate techniques should be used (e.g., drawings and puppets for young children).
- Immediate crash training courses for treatment personnel should be given.
- Follow-up personnel should have proven mental health backgrounds in order to initiate skilled and sensitive approaches to both subtle and obvious issues associated with the trauma.

After a brief descriptive outline of the purpose of the meeting, short trauma assessment questionnaires can be distributed to provide information and serve as icebreakers. Encouragement and reinforcement of ventilated feelings must follow. Distressing scenes may be reviewed narratively in the group followed by the imaginary camera technique in individual supplementary sessions. The camera method, emphasizing stop action of traumatic images, is used very selectively in a group setting because some victims are less comfortable than others. With such victims, individual sessions are the procedure of choice.

However, even in a group, open disclosure of troubled feelings from psychic pain tend to emerge because of the need for tension release. Children also will discuss their perceptions of trauma in an atmosphere of acceptance and support. Its irrationality notwithstanding, self-blame is often expressed for not preventing the tragedy.

Conclusion

Rendering emergency mental health services as soon as possible after the trauma is most important. I have seen countless instances wherein long-term chronic problems have developed in both psychological and physiological spheres as a consequence of little or no treatment or unskilled treatment. On the other hand, it has been strikingly evident that when well-delineated and appropriately focused treatment have been provided, problems have soon abated to the point where they have resolved or are no longer handicapping. The value of the incident-specific treatment approach cannot be overemphasized in both the in vitro and in vivo aspects of the procedure.

It is important to train personnel who have proven professional backgrounds in mental health in order to attune them to diagnostic and treatment subtleties. At least several hours of ad hoc training must be provided to qualified personnel in situ. Giving skillful, appropriate emergency treatment to psychic traumas is as crucial as treating severe physical emergencies. Untold harm can be done by untrained or nonprofessional interveners. Any wound must be properly debrided in order to heal. Unhealed or infected psychic wounds often produce distorted and deeply scarred emotions which can last a lifetime and in some instances may result in injury or death by a suicide attempt.

References

American Psychiatric Association. (1980). *Diagnostic and statistical manual of mental disorders* (3rd ed.). Washington, DC: Author.

American Psychiatric Association. (1987). *Diagnostic and statistical manual of mental disorders* (revised 3rd ed.). Washington, DC: Author.

Andriukin, A. A. (1961). Influence of sound stimulation on the development of hypertension. *Cor Et Vasa, 3,* 285–293.

Application of psychological assessment instruments in treatment programs for PTSD. (1986). *VA Practitioner, 3*(5), 41–51.

Bard, M., & Sangrey, D. (1979). *The crime victim's book.* New York: Basic Books.

Bart, P. B., & O'Brien, P. H. (1985). *Stopping rape: Successful survival strategies.* New York: Pergamon Press.

Bastiaans, J. (1982). Consequences of modern terrorism. In L. Goldberger & S. Breznitz (Eds.), *Handbook of stress: Theoretical and clinical aspects* (pp. 644–655). New York: Free Press.

Black, H. C. (1951). *Black's law dictionary* (4th ed.). St. Paul, MN: West.

Blank, A. S. (1982a). Apocalypse terminable and interminable: Operation outreach for Vietnam veterans. *Hospital and Community Psychiatry, 33,* 913–918.

Blank, A. S. (1982b). Stresses of war: The example of Vietnam. In L. Goldberger & S. Breznitz (Eds.), *Handbook of stress: Theoretical and clinical aspects* (pp. 631–643). New York: Free Press.

Burgess, A. W., Hartman, C. R., MacCausland, M. P., & Powers, P. (1984). Response patterns in children and adolescents exploited through sex rings and pornography. *American Journal of Psychiatry, 141,* 656–662.

Burgess, A. W., & Holmstrom, L. L. (1978). *Rape: Crisis and recovery.* Bowie, MD: Robert J. Brady.

Burt, C. (1943). War neuroses in British children. *Nervous Child, 2,* 324–337.

Cannon, W. B. (1942). "Voodoo" death. *American Anthropologist, 44,* 169–181.

Carey-Trefzer, C. (1949). The results of a clinical study of war-damaged children who attended the Child Guidance Clinic, the Hospital for Sick Children, Great Ormand Street, London. *The Journal of Mental Science, 95,* 535–559.

Carmen, E. H., Rieker, P. O., & Mills, T. (1984). Victims of violence and psychiatric illness. *American Journal of Psychiatry, 141*(3), 378–383.

Cline, R. S., & Alexander, Y. (1986). *Terrorism as state-sponsored covert warfare.* Fairfax, VA: Hero Books.

Cohen, R. E., & Ahearn, F. L. (1980). *Handbook for mental health care of disaster victims.* Baltimore: Johns Hopkins University Press.

Corley, K. C., Mauck, H. P., Shiel, F. O., Barber, J. H., Clark, T. S., & Blocher, C. R. (1979). Myocardial dysfunction and pathology associated with environmental stress in squirrel monkey: Effect of vagotomy and propranolol. *Psychophysiology, 16,* 554–560.

Dalton, J. E., Garter, S. H., Lips, O. J., & Ryan, J. J. (1986). Psychological assessment instrument in PTSD treatment problems. *VA Practitioner, 3*(5), 41–51.

Dalton, J. E., Pederson, S. L., Blom, B. E., & Besyner, J. K. (1986). Neuropsychological screening for Vietnam veterans with PTSD. *VA Practitioner, 3*(7), 37–47.

Dane, L. F. (1986). The Iran hostage wives: Long-term crisis coping (Doctoral Dissertation, University of Michigan, Ann Arbor, 1986). (University Microfilms)

Danieli, Y. (1981). Differing adaptational styles in families of survivors of the Nazi Holocaust: Some implications for treatment. *Child Today, 10,* 6–10, 34–35.

Danieli, Y. (1985). The treatment and prevention of long-term effects and intergenerational transmission of victimization: A lesson from Holocaust survivors and their children. In C. R. Figley, *Trauma and its wake* (pp. 295–313). New York: Brunner/Mazel.

Dohrenwend, B. S., Krasnoff, B. L., Askenasy, A. R., & Dohrenwend, B. P. (1978). Exemplification of a method for scaling life events: The PERI Life Events Scale. *Journal of Health and Social Behavior, 19,* 205–229.

Dubek, J. P. (1969). *Sensory deprivation, 15 years of research.* New York: Appleton-Meredith.

Egendorf, A., Kadushin, C., Laufer, R. S., Rothbart, G., & Sloan, L. (Eds.). (1981).

Legacies of Vietnam: Comparative adjustment of veterans and their peers (Vol. 1). New York: Center for Policy Research.

Eichelman, B., Soskis, D. A., & Reid, W. H. (1984). *Terrorism: Interdisciplinary perspectives*. Washington, DC: American Psychiatric Association.

Eitinger, L. (1961). Pathology of the concentration camp syndrome. *Archives of General Psychiatry, 5,* 367–375.

Eitinger, L. (1962). Concentration camp survivors in the post war world. *American Journal of Orthopsychiatry, 32,* 367–375.

Eitinger, L. (1965). Concentration camp survivors in Norway and Israel. *Israel Journal of Medical Sciences, 1,* 883–895.

Eitinger, L. (1971). Acute and chronic psychiatric and psychosomatic reactions in concentration camp survivors. In L. Levi (Ed.), *Society, stress and disease* (Vol. 1, pp. 219–230). London: Oxford University Press.

Eitinger, L. (1978). On being a psychiatrist and a survivor. In A. Rosenfield and I. Greenberg (Eds.), *Holocaust: The impact of the Wiesel*. Bloomington: Indiana University Press.

Eitinger, L. (1980). Concentration camp syndrome and its late sequelae. In J. E. Dimsdale (Ed.), *Survivors, victims, and perpetrators: Essays on the Nazi Holocaust* (pp. 127–162). New York: Hemisphere.

Eitinger, L. (1981). Studies on concentration camp survivors: The Norwegian and global contexts. *Journal of Psychology and Judaism, 6,* 23–32.

Eitinger, L. (1983). Psychological consequences of war disturbances. In H. A. van Geuns (Ed.), *Helping victims of violence* (pp. 47–56). The Hague, Netherlands: Ministry of Welfare, Health, and Cultural Affairs.

Federal Bureau of Investigation. (1985). *FBI uniform crime reports, U.S. Department of Justice*. Washington, DC: U.S. Government Printing Office.

Fields, R. M. (1976). *Society under siege*. Philadelphia: Temple University Press.

Figley, C. R. (Ed) (1978). *Stress disorders among Vietnam veterans: Theory, research, and treatment*. New York: Brunner/Mazel.

Figley, C. R. (Ed.). (1985). *Trauma and its wake: The study and treatment of post-traumatic stress disorder*. New York: Brunner/Mazel.

Foy, D. W., Sipprelle, R. C., Rueger, D. B., & Carroll, E. M. (1984). Etiology of posttraumatic stress disorder in Vietnam veterans: Analysis of premilitary, military, and combat exposure influences. *Journal of Consulting and Clinical Psychology, 52,* 79–87.

Frederick, C. J. (1977a). Crisis intervention and emergency mental health. In W. R. Johnson (Ed.), *Health in action* (pp. 376–411). New York: Holt, Rinehart & Winston.

Frederick, C. J. (1977b). Current thinking about crisis and psychological intervention in United States disasters. *Mass Emergencies, 2,* 43–50.

Frederick, C. J. (1978). An overview of dangerousness: Its complexities and consequences. In C. J. Frederick (Ed.), *Dangerous behavior: A problem in law and mental health* (pp. 3–19). (DHEW Publication No. ADM 78–563). Washington, DC: U.S. Government Printing Office.

Frederick, C. J. (1980). Effects of natural vs. human-induced violence upon victims. In L. Kivens (Ed.), *Evaluation and change: Services for survivors* (pp. 71–75). Minneapolis, MN: Minneapolis Medical Research Foundation.

Frederick, C. J. (1981a). *Aircraft accidents: Emergency mental health problems*. (DHHS Publication No. ADM 81–956). Washington, DC: U.S. Department of Health and Human Services.

Frederick, C. J. (1981b). Suicide prevention and crisis intervention in mental health emergencies. In C. E. Walker (Ed.), *Clinical practice of psychology* (pp. 189–213). New York: Pergamon Press.

Frederick, C. J. (1983). Violence and disasters: Immediate and long-term consequences. In H. A. van Geuns (Ed.), *Helping victims of violence* (pp. 32–46). The Hague, Netherlands: Ministry of Welfare, Health, and Cultural Affairs.

Frederick, C. J. (1985a). Children traumatized by catastrophic situations. In S. Eth & R. S. Pyroos (Eds.), *Post-traumatic stress disorders in children* (pp. 73–99). Washington, DC: American Psychiatric Press.

Frederick, C. J. (1985b). Selected foci in the spectrum of post-traumatic stress disorders. In S. Murphy & J. Laube (Eds.), *Perspectives on disaster recovery* (pp. 110–130). New York: Appleton-Century-Crofts.

Frederick, C. J. (1986a). Post-traumatic stress disorder and child molestation. In A. Burgess & C. Hartman (Eds.), *Sexual exploitation of clients by mental health professionals* (pp. 133–142). New York: Praeger.

Frederick, C. J. (1986b). Treatment for post-traumatic stress disorder: An incident-specific approach. In M. J. Goldstein, B. L. Baker, & K. R. Jamison (Eds.), *Abnormal psychology* (pp. 465–468). Boston: Little, Brown.

Frederick, C. J. (1987, March). Hostage taking and captivity: Psychosocial and physiological aspects. Paper presented at the conference *The hostages: Family, media and government: The human side of terrorism,* University of Maryland Center for International Development and Conflict Management, the International Society for Political Psychology, and the Association of American Foreign Service Women, Washington, DC.

Futterman, S., & Pumpian-Mindlin, E. (1951). Traumatic war neuroses five years later. *American Journal of Psychiatry, 108,* 401–408.

Gakman, D. (1987, February 24). Terror's children: Mending mental health wounds. *The New York Times,* pp. C-1, C-12.

Garbarino, J., & Sherman, D. (1980). High-risk neighborhoods and high-risk families: The human ecology of child maltreatment. *Child Development, 51,* 188–198.

Gelles, R. J. (1974). *The violent home: A study of physical aggression between husbands and wives.* Beverly Hills, CA: Sage.

George, C., & Main, M. (1979). Social interactions of young abused children: Approach, avoidance, and aggression. *Child Development, 50,* 306–318.

Gil, D. G. (1970). *Violence against children.* Cambridge, MA: Harvard University Press.

Gil, D. G. (Ed.). (1985). *Child abuse and violence.* New York: AMS Press.

Gilbert, G. M. (1950). *The psychology of dictatorship.* New York: Ronald Press.

Giles-Sims, J. (1983). *Wife battering, a systems theory approach.* New York: Guilford Press.

Goldstein, R. H., & Breslin, P. (1986). Technicians of torture. *The Sciences, 26,* 14–19.

Green, A. H. (1978a). Psychiatric treatment of abused children. *American Academy of Child Psychiatry Journal, 17,* 356–371.

Green, A. H. (1978b). Self-destructive behavior in battered children. *American Journal of Psychiatry, 134,* 579–582.

Green, A. H. (1983). Psychological trauma in abused children. *American Academy of Child Psychiatry Journal, 22,* 231–237.

Green, B. L., Grace, M. C., & Gleser, G. C. (1985). Identifying survivors at risk:

Long-term impairment following the Beverly Hills supper club fire. *Journal of Consulting and Clinical Psychology, 53*(5), 672–678.

Greer, J. H. (1965). The development of a scale to measure fear. *Behavior Research and Therapy, 3,* 45–53.

Grinker, R. R., & Spiegel, J. P. (1945). *Men under stress.* Philadelphia: Blakiston.

Hanson, J. D., Larson, M. E., & Snowdon, C. T. (1976). The effects of control over high intensity noise on plasma cortisol levels in rhesus monkeys. *Behavioral Biology, 16,* 333–340.

Harris, A. H., Gilliam, W. J., Findley, J. D., & Brady, J. V. (1973). Instrumental conditioning of large-magnitude, daily, 12-hour blood pressure elevations in the baboon. *Science, 182,* 175–177.

Harris, A. H., & Turkkan, J. S. (1981a). Generalization of conditioned blood pressure elevations: Schedule and stimulus control effects. *Physiology and Behavior, 26,* 935–940.

Harris, A. H., & Turkkan, J. S. (1981b). Performance characteristics of conditioned blood pressure elevation in the baboon. *Biofeedback and Self-regulation, 6,* 11–24.

Hathaway, S. R., & McKinley, J. C. (1967). *Minnesota multiphasic personality inventory: Manual for administration and scoring.* New York: Psychological Corporation.

Hilberman, E. (1977). Rape. In B. J. Wolman (Ed.), *International encyclopedia of psychiatry, psychology, psychoanalysis and neurology* (Vol. 9, pp. 360–364). New York: Aesculapius.

Hilberman, E. (1980). Overview: The "wife-beater's wife" reconsidered. *American Journal of Psychiatry, 137,* 1336–1347.

Hillman, R. G. (1981). The psychopathology of being held hostage. *American Journal of Psychiatry, 138,* 1193–1197.

Hocking, F. (1970). Extreme environmental stress and its significance to psychopathology. *American Journal of Psychotherapy, 24,* 4–26.

Holmes, T. H., & Rahe, R. H. (1967). The social readjustment rating scale. *Journal of Psychosomatic Research, 2,* 213–218.

Horowitz, M. J. (1982). Stress response syndromes and their treatment. In L. Goldberger & S. Breznitz (Eds.), *Handbook of stress: Theoretical and clinical aspects* (pp. 711–732). New York: Free Press.

Houston, K. (1986). Psychological variables and cardiovascular and neuroendocrine reactivity. In K. A. Matthews, S. M. Weiss, T. Detre, T. M. Dembroski, B. Faulkner, S. B. Manuck, & R. B. Williams (Eds.), *Handbook of stress reactivity and cardiovascular disease* (pp. 207–229). New York: Wiley.

Howard, S. J., & Gordon, N. S. (1972). *Final progress report: Mental health intervention in a major disaster* (Research grant MH 21649-01). Van Nuys, CA: San Fernando Valley Child Guidance Clinic.

Howells, W. H. (1948). *The heathens.* Garden City, NY: Doubleday.

Jacobsen, D. (1987, March 1). My life as a hostage. *Los Angeles Times,* pp. 10–15, 34, 35.

Jenkins, B. M. (Ed.). (1985). *Terrorism and personal protection.* Stoneham, MA: Butterworth Publishers.

Keane, T. M., & Fairbank, J. A. (1983). A survey analysis of combat-related stress disorders in Vietnam veterans. *American Journal of Psychiatry, 140,* 348–350.

Keane, T. M., & Kaloupek, D. G. (1982). Imaginal flooding in the treatment of a post-traumatic stress disorder. *Journal of Consulting and Clinical Psychology, 50,* 138–140.

Keane, T. M., Malloy, P. F., & Fairbank, J. A. (1984). Empirical development of an MMPI subscale for the assessment of combat-related posttraumatic stress disorder. *Journal of Consulting and Clinical Psychology, 5,* 888–891.

Kempe, C. H., & Helfer, R. E. (Eds.). (1972). *Helping the battered child and his family.* Philadelphia: J. B. Lippincott.

Kennedy, M. (1986). *The Ayatollah in the cathedral—Reflections of a hostage.* New York: Hill & Wang.

Laingen, P. (1987, March). On the human side of terrorism. Paper presented at the conference *The hostages: Family, media and government: The human side of terrorism,* University of Maryland Center for International Development and Conflict Management, the International Society for Political Psychology, and the Association of American Foreign Service Women, Washington, DC.

Lawler, J. E., Barker, G. F., Hubbard, J. W., & Allen, M. T. (1980). The effects of conflict on tonic levels of blood pressure in the genetically borderline hypertensive rat. *Psychophysiology, 17,* 363–370.

Lazarus, R. S. (1966). *Psychological stress and the coping process.* New York: McGraw-Hill.

Lifton, R. J. (1986). *Nazi doctors.* New York: Basic Books.

Lifton, R. J., & Olson, E. (1976). The human meaning of total disaster: The Buffalo Creek experience. *Psychiatry, 39,* 1–17.

Lindemann, E. (1944). Symptomatology and management of acute grief. *American Journal of Psychiatry, 101,* 141–148.

Linn, L. (1980). Other psychiatric emergencies. In H. I. Kaplan, A. M. Freedman, & B. J. Sadock (Eds.), *Comprehensive textbook of psychiatry: Vol. 2.* (3rd ed.) (pp. 2098–2112). Baltimore: Williams & Wilkins.

Lipkin, J. O., Blank, A. S., Parson, E. R., & Smith, J. (1982). Vietnam veterans and post-traumatic stress disorder. *Hospital and Community Psychiatry, 33,* 909–912.

Lipson, G. S., & Dubner, J. S. (1985). San Ysidro massacre: Impact on police officers. San Diego, CA: San Diego Police Department.

Lukianowicz, N. (1972). I Paternal incest; II Other types of incest. *British Journal of Psychiatry, 120,* 303–313.

Lynn, E. J., & Belza, M. (1984). Factitious post-traumatic stress disorder: The veteran who never got to Vietnam. *Hospital and Community Psychiatry, 35*(7), 697–701.

Malloy, P. F., Fairbank, J. A., & Keane, T. M. (1983). Validation of a multi-method assessment of post-traumatic stress disorder in Vietnam veterans. *Journal of Consulting and Clinical Psychology, 51,* 488–494.

Marks, I. M., Viswanathan, R., Lipsedge, M. S., & Gardiner, R. (1972). Enhanced relief of phobias by flooding during waning diazepam effect. *British Journal of Psychiatry, 121,* 493–505.

Mason, J. W. (1968). Organization of the multiple endocrine responses to avoidance in the monkey. *Psychosomatic Medicine, 30,* 744.

Mason, J. W., Brady, J. V., & Sidman, M. (1957). Plasma 17-hydroxycorticosteroid levels and conditioned behavior in the rhesus monkey. *Endocrinology, 60,* 741–752.

Mason, J. W., Brady, J. V., & Tolliver, G. A. (1968). Plasma and urinary 17-hydroxycorticosteroid responses to 72-hour avoidance sessions in the monkey. *Psychosomatic Medicine, 30,* 608–630.

Mason, J. W., Brady, J. V., & Tolson, W. W. (1966). Behavioral adaptations and endocrine activity. In R. Levine (Ed.), *Proceedings of the Association for Re-*

search in Nervous and Mental Disease (pp. 45–59). Baltimore: Williams & Wilkins.

McCarty, R., & Kopin, I. J. (1978). Changes in plasma catecholamines and behavior of rats during the anticipation of foot shock. *Hormones and Behavior, 11,* 248–257.

McGee, R. (1984). Flashbacks and memory phenomena. *Journal of Nervous and Mental Diseases, 172*(5), 273–278.

Melick, M. E., Logue, J. N., & Frederick, C. J. (1982). Stress and disaster. In L. Goldberger & S. Breznitz (Eds.), *Handbook of stress: Theoretical and clinical aspects* (pp. 613–630). New York: Free Press.

Meyers, M. B., Templer, D. I., & Brown, R. (1984). Coping ability of women who become victims of rape. *Journal of Consulting and Clinical Psychology, 52,* 73–78.

Modlin, H. C. (1986). Post-traumatic stress disorder: No longer just for war veterans. *Post Graduate Medicine, 70*(3), 26–44.

Newberger, C. M., & Cook, S. J. (1983). Parental awareness and child abuse: A cognitive–developmental analysis of urban and rural samples. *American Journal of Orthopsychiatry, 53,* 512–524.

Newman, C. J. (1976). Children of disaster: Clinical observations at Buffalo Creek. *Annual Progress in Child Psychiatry and Child Development, 10,* 149–161.

Niehous, W. F. (1985). Surviving captivity II: The hostage's point of view. In B. M. Jenkins (Ed.), *Terrorism and personal protection* (pp. 423–433). Stoneham, MA: Butterworth Publishers.

Ochberg, F. M. (1978). The victim of terrorism: Psychiatric considerations. *Terrorism: An International Journal, 1*(2), 147–167.

Pelton, L. H. (1982). Child abuse and neglect: The myth of classlessness. In L. H. Pelton (Ed.), *The social context of child abuse and neglect* (pp. 23–38). New York: Human Sciences Press.

Peterson, E. A., Augenstein, J. S., Tanis, D. C., & Augenstein, D. G. (1981). Noise raises blood pressure without impairing auditory sensitivity. *Science, 211,* 1450–1452.

President's Task Force on Victims of Crime. (1982, December). *Final report.* Washington, DC.

Pynoos, R., & Eth, S. (1984). The child as witness to homicide. *Journal of Social Issues, 40,* 87–108.

Pynoos, R. S., Frederick, C. J., Nader, K., Arroyo, W., Steinberg, A., Eth, S., Nunez, F., & Fairbanks, L. (in press). Life threat and posttraumatic stress in school age children. *Archives of General Psychiatry.*

Rahe, R. H. (1968). Life-change measurement as a predictor of illness. *Proceedings of the Royal Society of Medicine, 61,* 1124–1126.

Rathbone-McCuan, E., & Voyles, B. (1982). Case detection of abused elderly patients. *American Journal of Psychiatry, 139,* 189–192.

Renvoize, J. (1978). *Web of violence.* London: Routledge & Kegan Paul.

Richardson, L. D. (1985). Surviving captivity I: A hundred days. In B. M. Jenkins (Ed.), *Terrorism and personal protection* (pp. 407–422). Stoneham, MA: Butterworth Publishers.

Rofe, Y., & Lewin, I. (1980). Daydreams in a war environment. *Journal of Mental Imagery, 4,* 59–75.

Rofe, Y., & Lewin, I. (1982). The effect of war environment on dreams and sleep habits. In C. D. Spielberger, I. G. Sarason, & N. A. Milgram (Eds.), *Stress and anxiety, Vol. 8* (pp. 67–79). Washington, DC: Hemisphere.

Rosenfeld, A. A. (1979). Incidence of history of incest among 18 female psychiatric patients. *American Journal of Psychiatry, 136,* 791–795.

Rosenfeld, A. A. (1981). Treating victims of incest. *British Journal of Sexual Medicine, 8,* 5, 10.

Sadock, V. A. (1980a). Normal human sexuality and psychosexual disorders: Special areas of interest. In H. I. Kaplan, A. M. Freedman, & B. J. Sadock (Eds.), *Comprehensive textbook of psychiatry: Vol. 2.* (3rd ed., pp. 1090–1096). Baltimore: Williams & Wilkins.

Sadock, V. A. (1980b). Rape. In H. I. Kaplan, A. M. Freedman, & B. J. Sadock (Eds.), *Comprehensive textbook of psychiatry: Vol. 2.* (3rd ed., pp. 1803–1805). Baltimore: Williams & Wilkins.

Saldana, T. (1986). *Beyond survival.* New York: Bantam Books.

Schoettle, U. C. (1980). Treatment of the child pornography patient. *American Journal of Psychiatry, 137,* 1109–1110.

Segal, J., Hunter, E. J., & Segal, Z. (1980). Universal consequences of captivity: Stress reactions among divergent populations of prisoners of war and their families. *International Social Sciences Journal, 27,* 593–609.

Seigel, R. K. (1984). Hostage hallucinations. *Journal of Nervous and Mental Diseases, 172*(5), 264–272.

Sgroi, S. M. (1982). *Handbook of clinical intervention in child sexual abuse.* Lexington, MA: Lexington Books.

Spielberger, C. D., Gorsuch, R. L., & Lusbene, R. E. (1970). *Manual for the state-trait anxiety inventory (self-evaluation questionnaire).* Palo Alto, CA: Consultant Psychologists Press.

Stern, R., & Marks, I. (1973). Brief and prolonged flooding: A comparison in agoraphobic patients. *Archives of General Psychiatry, 28,* 270–276.

Stone, F. H. (1980). Child battering. *Medicine, 36,* 1862–1865.

Stover, E., & Nightingale, E. O. (Eds.). (1985). *The breaking of bodies and minds.* New York: W. H. Freeman.

Straus, M. A. (1977, March). *Normative and behavioral aspects of violence between spouses: Preliminary data on a nationally representative USA sample.* Paper presented at the *Symposium on Violence in Canadian Society,* Simon Fraser University, Burnaby, British Columbia, Canada.

Straus, M. A., Gelles, R., & Steinmetz, S. (1980). *Behind closed doors: Violence in the American family.* New York: Doubleday.

Stretch, R. H., Vail, J. D., & Maloney, J. P. (1985). Posttraumatic stress disorder among army nurse corps Vietnam veterans. *Journal of Consulting and Clinical Psychology, 53*(5), 704–708.

Summit, R. C. (1983). The child sexual abuse accommodation syndrome. *Child Abuse and Neglect, 7,* 177–193.

Symonds, M. (1975). Victims of violence: Psychological effects and after-effects. *American Journal of Psychoanalysis, 35,* 19–26.

Symonds, M. (1980). The "second injury" to victims. In L. Kivens (Ed.), *Evaluation and change services for survivors* (pp. 36–38). Minneapolis: Minneapolis Medical Research Foundation.

Terr, L. C. (1981). Psychic trauma in children: Observations following the Chowchilla school bus kidnapping. *American Journal of Psychiatry, 138,* 14–19.

Terr, L. C. (1983). Time sense following psychic trauma: A clinical study of 10 adults and 20 children. *American Journal of Orthopsychiatry, 53,* 244–261.

Terr, L. C. (1984). Time and trauma. *Psychoanalytic Study of the Child, 39,* 633–665.

Titchener, J. L., & Kapp, F. T. (1976). Family and character change at Buffalo Creek. *American Journal of Psychiatry, 133,* 295–299.

Turkkan, J. S., Brady, J. V., & Harris, A. H. (1982). Animal studies in stressful interactions. In L. Goldberger & S. Breznitz (Eds.), *Handbook of stress: Theoretical and clinical aspects* (pp. 153–182). New York: Free Press.

U.S. Congress. (1980). *Elder abuse: The hidden problem.* Briefing by the Select Committee on Aging, U.S. House of Representatives, June 23, 1979, Boston, MA, Comm. Pub. No. 96–220. Washington, DC: U.S. Government Printing Office.

U.S. Department of Justice. (1984). Crimes. *Crime & Delinquency,* 4–5.

van der Ploeg, H. M. (1983). Identification of victims, with special reference to hostages. In H. A. van Geuns (Ed.), *Helping victims of violence* (pp. 102–115). The Hague, Netherlands: Ministry of Welfare, Health, and Cultural Affairs.

Van Rappard, M. E. (1983). Battered women. In H. A. van Geuns (Ed.), *Helping victims of violence* (pp. 73–82). The Hague, Netherlands: Ministry of Welfare, Health, and Cultural Affairs.

Ziv, A., Kruglanski, A., & Shulman, S. (1974). Children's psychological reactions to wartime stress. *Journal of Personality and Social Psychology, 30,* 24–30.

IRENE HANSON FRIEZE

THE FEMALE VICTIM: RAPE, WIFE BATTERING, AND INCEST

I rene Hanson Frieze is a professor of psychology, business administration, and women's studies and is chair of the Women's Studies Program at the University of Pittsburgh. She is a former president of APA's Division 35, Psychology of Women, and was a member of the APA Task Force on Victims of Crime and Violence. She was also a member of the Project Advisory Panel for the National Evaluation of the Family Violence Program of the Law Enforcement Assistance Administration and a member of the review panel for the National Institute of Justice solicitation for research grants on reactions of victims.

Frieze's research has included studies of women who are victims of marital rape and battering as well as other forms of victimization. She is the author of numerous publications and articles on victimization and domestic violence. She is the associate editor of *Violence and Victims*, and in 1983 she was an editor of a *Journal of Social Issues* volume on reactions to victimization. Her other research includes studies of professional women and cognitive factors in career decision making, as well as more theoretical research on causal attributions for success and failure.

IRENE HANSON FRIEZE

THE FEMALE VICTIM: RAPE, WIFE BATTERING, AND INCEST

V ictimization can take many forms. One can be physically hurt by others or have property stolen or damaged, or one may be victimized by an accident or a natural or technological disaster. Such experiences typically cause some types of emotional reactions ranging from mild distress to severe psychiatric symptoms that last a lifetime. Victims (whether they label themselves in this way or not) attempt to deal with these reactions through various coping strategies.

In this chapter I will deal with some of the special forms of victimization of most concern to women and girls, those resulting from criminal acts such as rape or violence in the family. They involve interpersonal assault and often have a sexual component. There are other forms of chronic victimization resulting from discrimination that also are of special relevance for women, but I will not directly address these here. Although such forms of enduring victimization are pervasive and have strong negative consequences for their victims, the research on these types of victimization suggests that their dynamics may be different from those associated with the traumatic events that are the focus of this chapter.

The Victimization of Women and Girls

When asked to describe a typical victim, many people think of the person's sex as being female. Women are believed to be victimized more often and the victimization experience itself is perceived as feminine (Howard, 1984). In spite of this common perception, men are more often the victims of traumatic events than women if one considers all forms of victimizing events. Men are nearly twice as likely as women to be robbed or assaulted (Zawitz, 1983). Data from the National Crime Survey from 1983 show that although men have a one or two chance out of a hundred of being victimized by an attempted or completed violent crime, women's chances are less than one (U.S. Department of Justice, 1985). Men are victimized more often by crimes of property as well, although here the differences are not as great. Both sexes experience other forms of victimization caused by severe weather conditions or technologically related trauma at equal rates.

Certain types of victimization put women more at risk than men. More women than men are victimized by a relative (Timrots & Rand, 1987). In addition, women are more frequently victimized than men by sexual violence, physical violence within the home, and nonviolent sexual intimidation or harassment (Sheffield, 1984). Such events happen frequently. According to the National Crime Survey (U.S. Department of Justice, 1986) there were nearly 200,000 rapes or rape attempts in 1984. Most of the victims are female. A comprehensive national survey suggests that 1.8 million wives are beaten by their husbands in any one year (Straus, Gelles, & Steinmetz, 1980). Although wives may also be violent to husbands, the degree of physical injury is far greater for women (Pagelow, 1981). Incest and sexual victimization of children more commonly involves girls than boys (Finkelhor, 1980). Another form of victimization of particular concern for women is sexual harassment in work or school settings (Farley, 1978; MacKennon, 1975; Till, 1980). In a review of research on sexual harassment of college students, Kenig and Ryan (1986) estimated that 15% to 35% of college women experience at least one form of such harassment.

There are other forms of victimization that are even more hidden. Every day, women are victimized by exhibitionists, voyeurs, obscene telephone callers, and harassers on the street. Statistics on the frequency of such events are not regularly collected nor are many of these events reported. In my own survey of college students at the University of Pittsburgh, 85% of the women reported receiving harassing telephone calls (Frieze, 1985). Another study of adult women in Albuquerque asked women to describe some type of sexual incident that "either bothered you at the time or has left some sort of lasting impression" (DiVasto et al., 1984). The most commonly described events included being a victim of an exhibitionist or being sexually harassed. Victims in both situations described themselves as being stressed by the events (although rape generated the highest degree of reported stress in the victims).

The Effect of Socialization in Women's Victimization

Considering all forms of victimization, women are actually less likely to be victims than are men. But, at the same time, women appear to be more fearful than men about being victimized by others (e.g., Riger, Gordon, & Le Bailly, 1978). They also take more precautions in their daily lives to avoid becoming victims. Two reasons have been suggested for this. First, women may be more fearful generally, and this is simply one of many manifestations of this general tendency. Such an interpretation has been questioned by Riger et al. (1979). Instead, they support a second explanation, that women may be especially fearful of crimes such as rape (to which they are in fact more vulnerable). In support of this argument are data showing that crime fears are in fact greatest in the most vulnerable groups: the elderly, members of ethnic minorities, and those with low incomes (Riger & Gordon, 1981).

Other writers have suggested that one reason women feel at risk is because they are actually more vulnerable now than they had been before 1970 (Alexander, 1984; Wilson, 1985). As increasing numbers of women enter the labor force and are therefore more often away from the home alone, they are more likely to be raped or otherwise assaulted (Alexander, 1984). A similar argument is made by Alexander about the increasing percentage of women living alone or in female-headed households. Wilson adds another variable to this analysis by pointing out that poverty levels are also increasing for women (in relation to men) and that poverty in turn increases the vulnerability of women.

Traditional patterns of socialization for men and women may also contribute to increased vulnerability to victimization in women. Russell (1984a) and Walker and Browne (1985) have suggested that by encouraging "feminine" traits in girls and women such as passivity, submissiveness, politeness, and helpfulness, the socialization process may unwittingly increase the probability of their becoming victims (Russell, 1984; Walker & Browne, 1985). Women may also be encouraged to think of themselves as potential victims. Women are not expected to respond aggressively when experiencing minor forms of victimization; they have been taught not to respond to minor offenses such as street harassment and exhibitionism. When the harassment is more serious, they may still not react, at least not at first (Kidder, Boell, & Moyer, 1983). This can have serious consequences. It has been found that women sometimes escape rape by becoming rude and assertive when faced with a threatening and potentially dangerous situation. Although not as effective as this early reaction, displaying even low levels of resistance, such as running or screaming, may distinguish rape victims from women who were assaulted but escaped (Bart, 1981; Queen's Bench Foundation, 1976).

In spite of their socialization, some women do take action when being victimized (Bowker, 1980). In one national crime survey, it was found that women were about as likely as men to take self-protective measures during the commission of a crime against them (Zawitz, 1983). This same national data showed, though, that the sexes differ in the ways in which they attempt to protect themselves. Men were more likely to use physical force to protect themselves, whereas women were more likely to try to get help or frighten off the offender.

Unfortunately, women's defensive actions may not be as effective as they might be. Most girls have not learned how to physically defend themselves. As adults, women's muscles are not developed, and they are usually not skilled in the techniques of fighting (Kidder et al., 1983). In addition, women wearing fashionable, restrictive clothing and high heels may have additional problems in being effective fighters or even in running away.

Violence in Men's Roles and the Victimization of Women

From a young age, boys are trained to be more aggressive than girls. Being male means being successful and being tough, strong, and aggressive (David & Brannon, 1976). Boys are expected to know how to fight and defend themselves physically if attacked by another child. As they grow older, men are more likely than women to respond to frustration or aggressive provocation with violence (Frodi, Macaulay, & Thome, 1977). On a broader level, men are expected to be assertive and dominant, especially in their relationships with women (Cherry, 1983). In addition to being more violent, men also appear to be more accepting of violent or physically aggressive behaviors in others. In one large survey of U.S. men, Blumenthal, Kahn, Andrews, and Head (1972) found that the majority of the men in his sample favored the use of violence as a means of social control of deviant or criminal behavior; however, the majority of the men were not in favor of using violence for social change.

Two types of activities in which violent behavior is most directly reinforced for men are sports and military activities. Contact sports such as football, basketball, baseball, and hockey allow for the most use of aggression, and it is these sports that are viewed as more masculine (David & Brannon, 1976). Many of the descriptive terms used in football have clear aggressive referents (Farrell, 1974). For example, the special team brought in for the kickoff is called the suicide squad. They will determine on whose grounds the ball (battle) will be played (fought) on. The ball carriers are known for slamming face masks and kicking other players. Athletes in general tend to be more aggressive than nonathletes (Thirer, 1977/1978). Fans of these types of violent sports also tend to be more aggressive personally and are less conforming to societal rules of behavior (Sysler, 1977/1978).

By definition, the military endorses aggressive behavior. Many of the training rituals emphasize aggression and train recruits to value aggression (Arkin & Dobrofsky, 1978). Arkin and Dobrofsky suggest that military training makes people more violent. However, a national survey by Blumenthal et al. (1972) failed to find a relation between having military experience and acceptance of aggression. Thus military service alone does not seem to lead to more tolerance of violence and can cause participants to be less tolerant.

All of this suggests that men would be more tolerant of male–female aggression than women. Although society has a general prescription that men should not hit women, it also has a long history of tolerance of marital violence (Dobash & Dobash, 1978). During much of the history of Western civilization, men were expected to keep their wives in line through the "appropriate" use of physical punishment. It has only been in the last century that legal codes have begun to change so that the degree of violence a man is able to inflict on his wife is limited. Today, different states have different rules about this, but generally wife beating is no longer legally acceptable. Given this history, and men's greater tolerance overall for violence, it is not surprising that empirical studies have found men to be more accepting of rape (Feild, 1978), marital violence (Greenblat, 1985), and sexual harassment (Kenig & Ryan, 1986). Furthermore, it is the most traditional men who are most accepting (Greenblat, 1985; Hall, Howard, & Boezio, 1986; Muehlenhard, Friedman, & Thomas, 1985).

Violence and Male Sexuality

In addition to a general glorification of violence in our society and the association of violence with masculinity, there is also an association between aggression and sexuality (Cherry, 1983). Certainly in the animal world, males have to fight other males for sexual access, and physical aggression and sexuality are closely linked. For humans, assertion rather than aggression is tied to sexuality. Within the sexual script in our culture, men more than women initiate dating and other forms of potentially sexual relationships (McCormick & Jesser, 1983). It is most often up to the man to initiate overt sexual behavior in dating and marital relationships. Men who are able to successfully initiate sexual relationships with attractive women are viewed positively by their male peers. Other manifestations of the association of aggression and sexuality for men are their stronger interests in sadomasochistic sex and in pornography of all types, especially violent pornography (Hunt, 1974). There is also evidence that men's sexual fantasies often center around themes of power and aggressiveness (Crepault & Couture, 1980).

This association between sexuality and aggression for men may lead to misunderstandings about sexual initiation (Kenig & Ryan, 1986; Powell, 1986; Russell, 1984a). Men are more likely to blame women who say they receive "annoying sexual attention" and to perceive women's complaints of harassment as overreactions (Kenig & Ryan, 1986). Especially in an ongoing relationship, a very assertive demand for sexual relations may be seen as reasonable by the man and as coercion by the woman. However, women have been socialized to accept advances in marriage and may not label forced sexuality from their husbands as rape, even if the act meets all other definitions of rape (Frieze, 1983).

What Types of Men Are Violent?

Although there is a general tendency for men to be more violent and more sexually aggressive than women, not all men are equally violent. Those who are the most violent are the most likely to be arrested or to otherwise come to the attention of the legal system. Such offenders often have long histories of juvenile and adult violence. These men tend to have low self-esteem and poor impulse control. Some studies also suggest that men who are violent outside the home are likely to be violent toward family members as well (Fagan & Wexler, 1984; Frieze, Knoble, Washburn, & Zomnir, 1980). Similar patterns have been found in rapists (Russell, 1984a). Malamuth (1986) reports that men who admitted to more sexually aggressive acts toward women tended to be generally hostile toward women and were more tolerant of others' aggression toward women. A number of studies have analyzed the childhood backgrounds of adult male sexual offenders. They have often been victims of sexual abuse and exploitation and have low self-esteem and poor interpersonal relations (Groth, 1979).

Societal Reactions to the Victim

Given these patterns of socialization, it is not surprising that our society shows a general tolerance of violence toward women (Schur, 1984). Jokes about wife beating are as common as movies about rape. Pictures of sexually assaulted women are seen on record covers and other advertisements. But this lack of sympathy for female victims should be placed in the broader societal context. Society tends to have rather negative views of victims of both sexes (Janoff-Bulman & Frieze, in press). There are many explanations for this phenomenon. First, we tend to feel that things are generally fair: Bad things do not happen to good people (Lerner, 1980). Perceiving others as victims is threatening, particularly if the choice of a victim is believed to be random or if the person is similar to ourselves (Shaver, 1970). When we learn that someone has been victimized, our world view is threatened (Janoff-Bulman & Frieze, in press). Another concern is the thought that we ourselves might be victimized. Very few people believe that they are potential victims before a victimizing event occurs (Perloff, 1983; Perloff & Fetzer, 1986). Instead, people generally see themselves as less likely than others to have bad things happen.

But, as mentioned earlier, many women feel especially vulnerable to crime and harassment; they feel weak and helpless and unable to defend themselves physically. One way in which women respond to these fears is to develop protective strategies or rules designed to reestablish their sense of invulnerability (Frieze & McHugh, 1986). For example, my students have reported using strategies such as "I won't wear jewelry on the street to tempt muggers," "I won't wear tight pants," or "I'll put strong locks on all my doors." By following such rules, women can again feel safe. But by developing and following rigid safety rules, women may find that their life-styles are restricted in many ways (Burt & Katz, 1985; Riger & Gordon, 1981).

When we learn about someone being victimized, our sense of security is violated. Even reading newspaper accounts of crimes can increase our fears for our own safety (Heath, 1984). If the victim is similar to ourselves, there are concerns that we too might become victims. Our sense of justice is questioned if the victim did not seem to deserve his or her fate. We can respond to such concerns in a number of ways (Frieze & McHugh, 1986); we may reassess what we have learned through denial or trivialization, or we can seek explanations for why this particular person deserved to be a victim.

Denial is a common response to any form of victimization. This applies to female and male victims. Most people underestimate the frequency with which women in our society are victimized (Schur, 1984). This is partly because female victimization is often hidden, "behind closed doors"; many crimes of sexual violence are not reported to the police. Underreporting is common in all crimes against women (Sheffield, 1984). At the same time, there may be an even greater tendency to deny certain forms of victimization in men, especially sexual assaults (Janoff-Bulman & Frieze, in press). It is especially threatening to societal beliefs about male gender roles to see a man in a helpless victim role.

Trivialization is another response to learning about the victim of a negative event. This trivialization occurs for both female and male victims, although possibly more for female victims. Trivialization or laughter is an especially common response to female victim's reports of exhibitionism, obscene telephone calls, and street harassment (Frieze & McHugh, 1986). Women learn to respond to such events as if they did not matter or were funny (Medea & Thompson, 1974). Jokes about sexual harassment, rape, wife abuse, and the sexual assault of children appear in daily conversations. Physical violence between husbands and wives is a common theme of comic strips in newspapers, and jokes about child molestation are found in mass media magazines for men. Such trivialization can also occur with other forms of victimization.

Victim blame. One of the first questions people ask when they learn of someone being raped, beaten, robbed, harassed, or murdered is "Why?" Such attributional questions appear generally when we are confronted with any type of negative or unexpected event (Weiner, 1985a; 1985b). In order to make sense of the event, people create an elaborate causal scenario about how and why it happened to this particular person (Read, 1987). By finding specific things the victim did and then avoiding doing these things ourselves, we can once again feel secure. At the same time, if we find that the victim could have prevented his or her fate, we are more likely to feel anger than sympathy (Reisenzein, 1986; Weiner 1985a). If the victim was not to blame, our world view of a just world is shaken. This is even more problematic if the victim is similar to us in some way. We need to find ways in which we differ from the victim, either in the things we do or in other personal characteristics so that we can be secure that we will not suffer the same fate.

Reactions of the Victim

Although by definition the victim has experienced a material loss or a physical injury, the emotional consequences of the experience may be far more serious. Like someone else learning about the victim of a crime or other injury, the victim must cope with the anxiety associated with any victimization. But now the reaction is much more severe. The victim's assumptions of safety and fairness are shattered. The victim now faces an uncertain and threatening world. Victims are faced with the task of understanding why the event occurred to them and trying to feel safe again.

Typical Emotional Reactions

Studies of victims of crimes, accidents, environmental disasters, and harassment have all found common emotional stress reactions (Janoff-Bulman & Frieze, 1983). Victim reactions include feelings of anger, shock, disbelief, confusion, fear, anxiety, helplessness, and insecurity (Frieze, Hymer, & Greenberg, in press). Sexual problems are a frequent consequence of being victimized by any form of sexual assault (Becker, Skinner, Abel, & Cichon, 1986). Other research has shown that crime victims have higher rates of "nervous breakdowns," suicidal fantasies, and suicide attempts than do nonvictims (Kilpatrick, Best, et al., 1985). Lower levels of positive affect (joy, contentment, vigor, and affection) and more negative affect (anxiety, depression, guilt, and hostility) also characterized crime victims in several samples (Davis & Friedman, 1985). Fear of being victimized again was also a frequent concern in the Davis and Friedman samples.

Psychiatrists have identified these victim reactions in the DSM-III as "posttraumatic stress disorder" (American Psychiatric Association, 1980). Some of the posttraumatic stress disorder (PTSD) criteria include the existence of an external stressor that would evoke anxiety in everyone, reexperiencing the trauma in memories and dreams, numbed responsiveness (detachment from others, lessened affect, diminished interest in significant activities), and at least two of the following: exaggerated startle response, sleep disturbance, feelings of guilt, memory impairment or difficulties in concentrating, phobias about activities relating to the original stressful event, or the intensification of symptoms when exposed to stimuli related to the event.

Although common reactions to various types of events have been noted, there are also differences in victim reactions as a function of previctimization characteristics of the victim and of the nature of the victimizing event. Although more research is needed on such variables, it does appear that PTSD symptoms are greater for traumatic events that are more life-threatening (Wilson, Smith, & Johnson, 1985). Crime victims who are injured also exhibit more negative emotional reactions (Davis & Friedman, 1985; Sales, Baum, & Shore, 1984). Other studies have not shown a strong situation effect and suggest that the crucial distinctions concern the characteristics of the victim (Ellis, 1983). Victims who had had psychiatric problems before the victimizing event tended to have more symptoms afterwards (Ellis, 1983; Sales, Baum, & Shore, 1984). Hymer (1984) suggests that the important question is how well consolidated the victim's sense of self is before the event. Victimization is seen as reevoking earlier repressed conflicts concerning powerlessness and frustration. There is also some evidence that women are more likely than men to have severe emotional reactions following victimization (Davis & Friedman, 1985), which corresponds with a general tendency on the part of women to use more emotion-focused coping strategies than men when dealing with stress (e.g., Stone & Neale, 1984).

Changing Reactions Over Time

Several researchers have suggested that victim reactions follow a predictable sequence (e.g., Bard & Sangrey, 1979; Burgess & Holmstrom, 1979). First is shock or disbelief. After a few hours or days, these reactions change. Mood swings, from sadness to elation or from guilt and self-pity to a desire for retaliation, are typical at this point. Rape victims sometimes shift from feeling confident about their abilities to cope to feeling unable to deal with their lives, and from fears about the past rape to fears of future attacks. Within weeks or months, these alternating feelings are resolved, or long-term reactions begin. Continuing reactions such as severe depression, decreased interest in social and sexual relations, recurrent nightmares, drug abuse, and other symptoms persist (Kilpatrick, Veronen, & Resick, 1979; Notman & Nadelson, 1976). For example, several months after the eruption of Mount Saint Helens, local residents showed increases in illness, alcohol abuse, family stress, violence, and aggression (Adams & Adams, 1984).

Studies of rape and incest victims in particular have documented the existence of negative emotional consequences of victimization for years after the event and sometimes for a lifetime (Silver, Boon, & Stones, 1983). Long-term reactions are also seen in other types of victims. In one study, victims of a flood are still experiencing a variety of symptoms up to 2 years later, and so were victims of a nuclear power plant accident (Baum, Fleming, & Singer, 1983; Green & Gleser, 1983).

Coping With the Stress of Victimization

How distressed is the victim? How should the victim ideally react to his or her experience? Presently, such questions are impossible to answer. There is a good deal of debate about how to measure the degree of stress one experiences as a result of any environmental stressor (Dohrenwend & Shrout, 1985; Lazarus, DeLongis, Folkman, & Gruen, 1985). Without a measure of distress, it is hard to assess the effectiveness of any coping strategy. There is also more basic disagreement about what it means to cope successfully (Silver & Wortman, 1980). Does successful coping mean that there are few if any negative emotional symptoms present? We expect victims to be upset. Perhaps such negative feelings are necessary for the victims' recovery. But we have no clear guidelines about how intense the victims' reactions "should" be or how long they "should" last. This ambiguity makes it difficult for victims to assess the normalcy of their own reactions. Victims' feelings that their reaction is more extreme than is typical or that they are deviant further increases their distress (Coates & Winston, 1983). There may also be differences in the most adaptive reactions at different points in the recovery process (Schultz & Decker, 1985). Even less is known about this, though. In this section, I discuss some of the major coping strategies of victims. In practice, it has been shown that people often use a variety of coping strategies, and they may use different strategies at different points in time (Folkman & Lazarus, 1985).

Emotion-Focused Coping

As has just been described, the experience of victimization generates a host of emotions. Gaining some control over these feelings is the most important goal of many victims. Methods of achieving this include looking on the brighter side, trying to forget about the event, thinking about other things, trying to relax, or attempting to gain catharsis through expressing the emotions relating to the event (Folkman, 1984; Stone & Neale, 1984).

The goal of most of these emotion-based coping strategies is to decrease the intensity of negative feelings, although this does not always happen. Emotional discharge (i.e., "letting out your feelings"), a popular coping strategy among women, tends to produce continued upset (Billings & Moos, 1984; Stone & Neale, 1984). These stress-management researchers argue that focusing more on solving problems that may eliminate the sources of stress is more effective in the long run in reducing negative emotions.

But many victims are confronted with a situation that cannot be changed or modified. Folkman reports that emotion-based coping is more common when the stressful event cannot be changed (as would be the situation for the typical victim). In such cases, there may be few alternative coping strategies. Meyer and Taylor (1986) found reduced fear and depression in rape victims who reported that they coped with the rape by thinking positive thoughts and by trying to reduce their feelings of stress.

Redefinition of the Event

Whether or not the individual feels victimized depends in part on an assessment of what happened (Folkman, 1984). Many interpretations are possible. One of the first responses of the victim is to analyze the event that has occurred to decide how serious it was. My own work has suggested that people are reluctant to label themselves as "victims." When asked why they would not consider themselves victims after experiencing events that would typically be identified as victimizing, college students usually answered that the event "was not serious enough" or that "it was an accident." Such responses seem very much like the denial mentioned earlier as a response of others to the victim.

Taylor (1983) has identified three processes by which the victim copes with a threatening event: restoration of self-esteem through self-enhancing evaluations, a search for meaning, and an attempt to regain mastery over one's life. Cancer patients, for example may compare themselves with others who are less fortunate (Wood, Taylor, & Lichtman, 1985). Burgess and Holmstrom (1979) call this "minimization" and cite it as one of several adaptive responses to rape. Another example of this comes from a study of rape victims (Scheppele & Bart, 1980). In these cases, some of the victims were able to dissipate some of the negative reactions they may have felt by redefining the experience. Although all these women were victims of acts legally classified as rape, those who had been forced to perform sexual acts other than those involving the penis defined themselves as "escaping" rape, and they did not label themselves as victims. Conversely, most of those who were penetrated vaginally, orally, or anally did define the crime as rape. This second group had the most negative reactions to the crime and were the most likely to report it to the police. Another way of redefining the event is to look at the experience as having a greater meaning, perhaps a test of personal strength and character or a message from God. This search for meaning is a common response in incest victims (Silver et al., 1983). These data suggest that some form of denial can be an effective coping strategy for the victim. However, if such denial results in the victim not receiving needed treatment, it can cause even more serious problems (Roth & Cohen, 1986).

Self-Blame

Research on the reactions of all types of victims reveals a general tendency for victims to ask why they had become victims and, in the process of answering this question, to find things that they might have done differently (e.g., Burgess & Holmstrom, 1979; Frieze et al., 1987). It is not uncommon, for example, for a victim of an unprovoked sexual assault or battering to take some responsibility for the crime. Thus a battered woman may say to herself, "If only I had gotten dinner ready on time." A rape victim may focus on the clothing she was wearing or on not being vigilant enough in observing others around her. Even victims of natural disasters tend to blame themselves, saying things such as, "We should have left the area sooner."

Common sense might dictate that blaming oneself for one's victimization would be self-defeating and maladaptive. However, there is some research indicating that such self-blame can be quite functional (Burgess & Holmstrom, 1979; Janoff-Bulman, 1979). This is especially true if the self-blame is behavioral rather than characterological. Characterological self-blame attributes one's victimization to relatively permanent aspects of one's personality. Such characterological attributions give a woman little confidence that she can avoid future victimization and can produce feelings of depression and helplessness. In an empirical test of these ideas, Janoff-Bulman (1979) found that rape counselors reported that rape victims who made characterological attributions also tended to feel they deserved the rapes. Not only did these women see themselves as the type of woman who gets raped, but also as the type of person who should be raped. In this same study, counselors reported that rape victims who attributed their rapes to behavioral factors were more confident about avoiding future attacks. By perceiving their own actions or behavior as "responsible" for the rape (such as saying they should have been more careful about going out alone at night or dating someone they did not know well), victims were able to psychologically take control of the event. Other evidence for self-blaming is seen in the actions of crime victims who put locks on doors, buy a gun, or take other crime prevention measures (Davis & Friedman, 1985).

Other research has suggested that self-blaming may not always be adaptive. In Meyer and Taylor's (1986) study of rape victims, those who blamed themselves were more likely to experience sexual dissatisfaction and depression after the rape. This was true for two types of self-blaming (that were similar to the Janoff-Bulman typology). In another study Katz and Burt (in press) found that rape victims who blamed themselves had a longer recovery period. There was more negative symptomatology in the self-blamers, and they rated themselves as less recovered. However, this study did not differentiate types of self-blame. Schulz and Decker (1985) also failed to find that self-blaming was adaptive for victims of spinal cord injuries.

Gilbert and Mangelsdorff (1979) provide a possible explanation for these discrepancies. They found that people who feel that they have more control over their daily lives tended to feel more stress. Perhaps self-blaming is adaptive only if it truly gives the victim a sense that he or she can control their lives in the future and can prevent another victimization.

Behavioral Reactions

In addition to trying to manage one's emotions and thinking about what has happened, victims also take actions that may be maladaptive. They may turn to drugs or alcohol (Burgess & Holmstrom, 1979). They may withdraw from contact with friends or acquaintances. As a response to their fear or shock, female victims are especially likely to retreat into their homes, not going out and not seeing others. Other victims move to a new residence or change their telephone numbers. Such forms of withdrawal do not appear to be adaptive, although they are not uncommon responses, especially in rape victims (Burgess & Holmstrom, 1979; Meyer & Taylor, 1986). Some victims become aggressive and hostile, lashing out at others. Aggressive responses such as trying to find and punish one's assailant or becoming violent toward family members are especially common in male victims (Carmen, Riecker, & Mills, 1984; Singer, 1986). Other types of aggressive responses more typical of women include feeling anger toward men, buying a gun and learning to use it, or enrolling in a self-defense class.

Many victims turn to others for help—for medical assistance, emotional support, information, or assistance with physical tasks resulting from the victimization (Frieze et al., in press). Not all victims seek help, and those who do may not receive the assistance they want. Friends and acquaintances as well as bystanders may ignore victims because they see them as "losers" or because they fear guilt by association (Bard & Sangrey, 1979). Others avoid victims because they are so often depressed, and most people prefer not being around unhappy people (Coates, Wortman, & Abbey, 1979).

For many victims, though, positive social support aids in successful coping (e.g., Schulz & Decker, 1985). This is especially true for female victims (Holahan & Moos, 1985). Janoff-Bulman and her associates (Janoff-Bulman, 1985; Janoff-Bulman, Madden, & Timko, 1983) argue that positive social support is of special importance to women because being victimized by another human being has weakened their belief that the world is benevolent and caring. This part of their world view has to be rebuilt over time with the help of others who care.

The first people many victims go to for help are their families and friends. They may seek this help immediately after the victimization, after a few days, or much later. In a study of abused wives, two-thirds relied on family or friends for emotional help or shelter (Flynn, 1977); in a Milwaukee study, 43% of the abuse victims received help from family members and 52% from friends (Bowker, 1984). Victims may also seek help from the criminal justice system. Overall, about one-third of all crimes are reported to the police (Zawitz, 1983). Notifying the police reduces the victim's stress in several ways. The victim's sense of injustice, outrage, or offense can be reduced by reporting the crime, and a sense of control may be restored if the police catch the offender, especially if the person is convicted, punished, or forced to make restitution (Frieze et al., in press).

However, the low rate of reporting to the police suggests that they are not seen as a source of help by many victims. Indeed, two of the most frequently cited reasons that victims give for not calling the police are that "nothing can be done" and that "the police would not want to be bothered" (Zawitz, 1983). Abused wives often have difficulties with the police. In two studies, abused wives rated the police as the least helpful of available sources of help (Bowker, 1983; Frieze, 1980). Police officers may not define battered women as the victims of violent crime, and they may refuse to arrest the abusive husband even when the wife requests them to do so (Bowker, 1983). On the positive side, the victim will often feel comforted and reassured when the police are responsive to her needs. Many rape victims do have positive experiences with the police, who, they report, are helpful and make them feel better (Sales et al., 1984). Moreover, arrest has been shown to be effective in keeping violent husbands from further beating their wives; when the police do agree to intervene, they can be very effective (Sherman & Berk, 1984).

Many female victims turn to self-help groups, an intermediate step between professional services and friends, for assistance. Support groups exist for rape victims, battered women, and incest victims in many areas of the country. Self-help groups have a formal structure and serve specific types of victims. Operating on the assumption that people who have experienced a similar traumatic situation are the best experts on how to cope with it, these groups offer victims the opportunity to meet and talk with others who have been through the same thing (Silverman, 1980).

Coates and Winston (1983) found that participation in peer support groups helps the victim to feel less deviant, to find meaning in the victimizing experience, and to reach better long-term adjustment. But groups may not help victims overcome depression or other symptoms; exposure to other victims who are coping better than oneself can be quite upsetting.

Finally, victims may seek formal psychotherapy. Until recently, there has been little formal attention devoted to the special needs of victims of crime and other traumatic events (American Psychological Association, 1984). I will discuss special techniques that have been developed for victims of rape, battering, and incest in the following sections of this chapter.

*   *   *

Three forms of victimization are particularly relevant to women: rape, wife battering, and incest. As shown in Table 1, all three forms of victimization involve similar assumptions about the victim and the assailant. The first of these beliefs is consistent with the societal response of trivialization discussed earlier. The victimization of women is not considered to be serious. An even more common belief is the idea that the woman or girl provoked the assault, parallel with the belief that the assailant was overcome by his feelings and could not help himself. It is assumed that a woman wearing seductive clothing is "asking for" rape or that a wife who argues with her husband is provoking him. By reversing such assumptions, we see how rooted they are in our stereotypic assumptions. Do we assume that if a husband argues with his wife, she is justified in harming him with a gun or some other weapon (that would allow her to hurt him in the way he could harm her with his fists)? Or do we think a

Table 1
Common Myths About Female Victims and Their Assailants

The Victim

1. Nothing really happened. She is only trying to get the guy in trouble.
2. She provoked it.
3. She is a "bad" woman (or girl) who deserves it.
4. If she were a moral, traditional woman (or girl) who kept her place, this would never have happened to her.
5. She likes it. She allows herself to be victimized.

The Assailant

1. He was overcome with sexual (or aggressive) feelings at the time and could not help himself.
2. He comes from a poor or disadvantaged background and should be pitied.
3. He was drinking at the time.

man who wears shorts in the park was asking to be raped by a group of men? For no other crimes is there so much suspicion of the victim and her behavior.

Related to the provocation belief is the notion that the woman somehow deserves her fate because she is immoral or is acting out of role. Such explanations are part of the victim-blaming phenomenon discussed earlier that is applied to all victims, but perhaps with more emphasis on gender-role expectations for the female victim. Another belief is the idea that women are inherently masochistic, that they like being victimized, or at least that they seek it out or accept it (see Shainess, 1984, for a relatively modern version of this belief). Such conceptualizations have little empirical validity (Caplan, 1985).

Rape: The Prototypic Victimization

The issue of rape is a complex one that relates to many of our stereotypic beliefs about men and women (Brownmiller, 1976; Medea & Thompson, 1974). As is probably apparent already, one of the most commonly studied victims is the female rape victim. Perhaps the crime of rape is the prototypic exemplar of all forms of victimization, because the assailant is the stereotypic aggressive man and the victim is the stereotypic helpless woman. Schur (1984) argues that sexual harassment and even rape are tolerated in our society as natural extensions of our expectations for men to be assertive in relations between men and women.

Social Attitudes About Rape Victims

Much confusion exists about what sequences of events constitute a rape and when such acts are justifiable on the part of the man (Muehlenhard, Friedman, & Thomas, 1985). In our society, a woman is expected to restrict sexual access (to everyone except her spouse or lover) and to make it clear by her overt behavior that she is not interested in sex. If women hitchhike, wear suggestive clothing, get drunk, or otherwise step out of the bounds of what is considered proper behavior for women, many feel that rape is justifiable (Burt, 1980). In a recent study of college students, it was found that simply by asking a man out for a date, a woman was seen as justifying her date raping her (Muehlenhard et al., 1985).

Assumptions about natural forms of sexual activity further complicate the situation in regard to rape in marriage. It is widely believed that a woman should not refuse to have sex with her husband, or even with a man she has previously engaged in sexual relations with. Even today, according to the law in many states a woman cannot be raped by her husband even if he physically forces her to have sex. Actions that would be defined as rape if done by a stranger are often not considered rape if done by one's spouse (Frieze, 1983). Instead, the wife may be blamed for refusing to engage in sexual relations when requested to do so by her husband.

Who Are the Rapists and Their Victims?

Like other forms of victimization, it is impossible to accurately know how many women are raped, especially when the rape occurs between couples who are already acquainted, dating, or married. Many rapes or attempted rapes are not reported to authorities, and some rapes may not even be identified as such by their victims. This reluctance to report is especially likely if the rape involves people who are acquainted or have previously had sexual relations (Koss, 1985). Such cases are almost impossible to successfully prosecute.

In one recent telephone interview study of over 2,000 women in South Carolina, 9% reported having been the victim of a rape or attempted rape, as compared with 5% reporting ever being robbed (Kilpatrick, Best, et al., 1985). In another analysis of these same data, 6% of the women were found to have been sexually assaulted by an acquaintance, whereas 2% reported a sexual assault by a family member (Kilpatrick & Amick, 1984). This is lower than Johnson's (1980) "conservative estimate" that 20% of all women are raped in their lifetime. Zawitz's (1983) analysis of National Crime Survey data shows a rate of 2 rapes per 1,000 adult women per year (as compared with a rate of 7 robberies per 1,000 adults). Clearly, estimates of rape vulnerability are affected by the method of data collection.

Keeping these qualifications in mind, we can still look at the existing data on stranger and acquaintance rapes to determine who is the most likely target of rape. National Crime Survey data from 1983 indicate that there are 4.2 rapes of girls between the ages of 16 to 19 for every 1,000 female adults. The rate drops to 3.6 for those aged 20 to 24 and to 2.1 for those 25 to 34. Even lower rates of 0.3 for those aged 35 to 49 and 0.1 for women over 65 can be contrasted with the 2.0 rate for 12- to 15-year-olds. These data suggest that nearly all rapes are committed against young women. Rates drop dramatically after the age of 35. Rapists, too, tend to be under 35 (Russell, 1984a), and thus they may simply be selecting target victims from the age group with whom they would normally have sexual relations.

Groth (1979) has done extensive clinical work with convicted rapists. He has classified rapes into three basic categories: power, anger, and sadistic rapes. Power rapes appear to be more sexually motivated and involve the least force of the three types. Rapists in this category find the idea of rape sexually stimulating and may assume that their victim does too. They may return to the same victim and rape her again, assuming that she enjoys this type of sexuality. Anger rapes appear to be motivated primarily by hostility or anger toward women. During the rape, the rapist may force the victim to engage in unpleasant acts and may use more force than necessary. The rapist may not even be sexually aroused. Finally, sadistic rapists torture or even murder their victims. Here, the crime is definitely an aggressive rather than a sexual act.

Reactions to Being Raped

Two types of reactions appear to be especially common in rape victims: depression (Frank & Stewart, 1984; Frank, Turner, & Duffy, 1979) and sexual problems (Burt & Katz, 1985; Norris & Feldman-Summers, 1981). All of the other victim reactions discussed earlier are also frequently reported. These include fear; anxiety; somatic symptoms such as headaches, sleep disturbances, and startle responses; and social withdrawal (Burgess & Holmstrom, 1974; Kilpatrick, Resick, & Veronen, 1981). Victims of attempted rape often report the same symptoms (Becker, Skinner, Abel, Howell, & Bruce, 1983). Burgess and Holmstrom have labeled these reactions as "rape trauma syndrome." Many now identify rape trauma syndrome as an example of PTSD (Kilpatrick, Veronen, & Best, 1985).

Help for Rape Victims

Women who are raped by a stranger or by an acquaintance are often blamed for their role in the act. This makes positive social support especially important for rape victims (Sales et al., 1984). Such victims need to be accepted by their friends and family. Victim blaming can be especially problematic if it comes from a husband or lover. Rape victims typically react to the crime with fear and guilt, or with anger and hostility toward men. Whereas the female victim is experiencing these types of reactions, her spouse or lover is more likely to feel angry. Many male partners of rape victims have recurrent fantasies of going after the rapist and harming or even killing him (Holmstrom & Burgess, 1979). It is also hard for the victim's lover to be supportive of her when she is expressing negative feelings toward men generally and is not interested in sex. Such differences in responses in the victim and her lover may cause additional strains on ongoing relationships.

As mentioned earlier, rapes are often not reported to the police or other agencies. This may be because victims doubt that they will be believed or that the offender will be punished. To some extent such fears are realistic. In 1983, arrests were made of about half of the reported rapes nationally. In the same year, federal courts convicted and sentenced 76% of the rape defendants who came to trial. But many cases never came to trial (McGarrell & Flanagan, 1985). Thus, if we assume that about half of all rapes are reported, there is less than a 20% chance of the rapist actually being convicted. Court appearances are stressful too, because testifying forces the victim to relive the experience, and it may also evoke fears of retaliation from the criminal (Sales et al., 1984).

Probably the most common form of formal psychological help for rape victims today comes from rape crisis centers. These ideally provide an array of services including hotlines, crisis intervention counseling, and advocates who accompany the victim in her interactions with the criminal justice system. Educational programs are also provided for victims and the general public (Harvey, 1985).

Clinical work with rape victims suggests that they may show very long-term, delayed reactions (Koss, 1983). This may make them especially difficult to treat. Different types of treatment have been studied to see how effective they are in moderating rape victim symptoms. These include biofeedback and relaxation training to manage the emotions resulting from the experience. Systematic desensitization, cognitive behavior therapy, and stress innocuation have also been tried (Ellis, 1983; Turner & Frank, 1981; Veronen & Kilpatrick, 1983). All of them appear to be successful, at least for some victims. However, because of the changes in victim reactions over time, even when there is no intervention, it is difficult to assess the effects of any of these techniques (Ellis, 1983). Some victims have no need of formal intervention at all and others may have multiple problems as a result of trauma brought on by the rape (Veronen & Kilpatrick, 1983).

Wife Battering

Special problems exist for the battered woman, because the victimization is often repeated and the victim is intimately involved with the victimizer (Miller & Porter, 1983). Estimates of the percentage of marriages with violence range from 25% to 60% (Pagelow, 1984). However, such figures include marriages with relatively low levels of violence. Extremely violent relationships constitute a much lower figure. But, because marital violence does tend to increase over time, marriages with low levels of violence today may turn out to be severely violent relationships tomorrow.

Certain predictable patterns have been identified in battered women's marriages (Frieze et al., 1980; Pagelow, 1984). These are outlined in Table 2. Typically the man initiates the violence, but over time, the wife will fight back (Saunders, 1986). Thus both partners may be fighting, but even so, the more severe violence typically comes from the husband. Other correlates of violence include high levels of alcohol use by the husband (but, not by the wife), a controlling style in the husband where he

Table 2
Typical Pattern of the Violent Marriage

1. Husband (or boyfriend) is violent for the first time to his wife.
2. She is shocked. He is very apologetic.
3. She forgives him.
4. He is violent again.
5. He is again forgiven by the wife.
6. Violence occurs again and increases in intensity.
7. Wife fights back on one or more occasions.
8. Wife withdraws from others and becomes isolated. She has little, if any, power in the relationship.
9. Sexual relationship worsens. Marital rape may occur.
10. Wife tries to leave, but returns because she has nowhere to go or feels too inadequate to make it on her own.
11. Wife finally leaves when the violence is so severe she fears for her life or the lives of her children.

closely monitors the wife's whereabouts and makes all major decisions, disrupted sexual relations, and possibly, marital rape. The battered woman feels socially isolated and has control of few resources. Within these violent marriages, there is often physical or sexual abuse of children as well. Although either the wife or the husband may be physically abusive toward the children, husbands are more often the highly abusive parent.

Reactions to Being Battered

Like other types of victims, battered women respond emotionally, cognitively, and behaviorally to violence. The responses of battered women, labeled as "Battered Woman Syndrome," are a form of PTSD (Walker, 1985). Specific symptoms include anxiety, hypersensitivity to potential violence, passivity and helplessness, or aggressive fighting as a form of self-defense (Saunders, 1986). With repeated unsuccessful attempts to control the battering, some battered women begin to demonstrate many of the signs of learned helplessness (Walker, 1979, 1984). As this occurs, they become less and less able to change their situations for the better.

Battered women have often been cited as blaming themselves for the violence, but this does not mean that they feel that they alone have caused the violence (Frieze, 1979; Miller & Porter, 1983). Rather than asking "Why me?" as other victims do, they may ask instead, "What did I do tonight that set him off?" Once they answer this question, battered women may go to great ends to attempt to change their behaviors so that they will not initiate the violence again. Unfortunately, these efforts are rarely successful in stopping the battering and, instead, make it even more likely that the violence will escalate over time (Frieze, 1980; Hilberman & Munson, 1978; Walker, 1978, 1984). However, many battered women do continue to hope that their husbands will be able to stop the violence in the future (Pagelow, 1984).

Given the abusiveness of violent marriages, many ask why battered women remain in such relationships. Reasons are complex and depend upon the individual (Chandler, 1986). Some of the common factors that keep women in these marriages are outlined in Table 3. The battered wife may fear that her husband will retaliate against her, their children, or her family if she tries to leave. Such fears are often justified because women who have left abusive husbands have been followed by them and harassed or even killed (Browne, 1987; Jones, 1980). Having no money or no place to go can also keep the battered woman from leaving. She may also value her marriage and want to keep it going (Chandler, 1986).

In spite of all these factors, some battered women are able to leave. The severely battered woman may leave her husband because she is in fear of her life or that of her children if she stays (Frieze, 1979; Walker, 1978). Women who are battered *and* raped by their husbands suffer some of the strongest reactions and are most likely to leave (Frieze, 1983).

Table 3
Reasons Battered Women Stay in Violent Marriages

Beliefs of Battered Women

- The violence is temporary. Whatever the problem that set off the violence in the past, it has now been resolved.
- Her violent husband needs her. He has serious problems that would be made even worse if she left him.
- She values her marriage and wants to do everything she can to keep it together.
- All men are violent toward others in the family. Leaving would accomplish nothing because any other man would treat her in the same way.
- She would never be able to get along on her own. She is not a very competent person (as her husband has told her so many times).

Lack of External Resources

- She has no monetary resources to draw upon to support herself and her children. (Even women earning good incomes have had no control of the money they earn.)
- She has no way to protect herself against very violent retaliation from her battering husband if he comes after her or her family.
- She has no friends or family who can help her.
- There is no shelter for battered women accessible to her or she feels that she cannot go to such a shelter.

Some women feel so trapped in a violent marriage that they may resort either to killing or attempting to kill their battering husbands (Browne, 1987).

Help for Battered Women

Most battered women do seek help for the violence or, more generally, for marital problems (Frieze, 1979; Pagelow, 1981). As with other victims, social support can be quite important for the battered woman in trying to cope with her victimization and in avoiding future battering (Mitchell & Hodson, 1982). Most battered women have also sought help from therapists, social service agencies, or ministers. A number of therapeutic programs have been developed to help them (e.g., Gillman, 1980), however, in many cases, battered women do not feel that institutional help of any type solves their problems.

Self-help groups are now readily available for battered women. They are often conducted as part of the services of battered women's shelters. However, not all women know about these groups even in areas where they are available. A study of wife-abuse victims in southwestern Wisconsin revealed that only 10% of the women went to a shelter after the first incidence of abuse but, with repeated abuse, 29% sought their help (Bowker, 1983). Along with self-help groups, most shelters also offer emergency housing and practical help for the woman who wants to leave her abuser.

One reason why therapy is so often cited as not being helpful for battered women is that it appears that it is the battering men rather than the women who need the most help (Rosenbaum & O'Leary, 1981; Walker & Browne, 1985). Even court-mandated treatment for the men can be highly successful in ending the violence and helping them cope with other problems (Dutton, 1986). Arrest can also constitute effective treatment (Sherman & Berk, 1984).

Incest

Another type of victimization is sexual molestation of children (Finkelhor, 1979). This can occur within the family or outside of it. More than other forms of victimization, the sexual abuse of children is rarely reported to authorities. Like marital violence, child sexual abuse can involve close family members as abusers. It is often repeated, sometimes over a period of years. It is predictable, but not controllable by the victim; the child can expect the abuse to occur whenever left alone with the offender. There is typically no one whom the child can confide in about the abuse. Secrecy is maintained through bribes or threats (Conte, 1985).

Estimates of the frequency of child sexual abuse are highly unreliable. In his major survey of sexual activity, Kinsey (Kinsey, Pomeroy, Martin, & Gebhard, 1953) reported that 24% of the women in his sample had been sexually approached as children by a male adult. About half of these approaches were by men known to the victim. Exhibitionism was the major form of activity. In a more recent study of a normal population of college students, Finkelhor (1980) found that 19% of the women and 9% of the men reported some form of sexual victimization as children. The majority of these cases involved some male adult whom they were acquainted with. Nine percent of the women had had such experiences with a family member. Similar percentages are reported in other studies (Herman, 1981). In about half the cases, the abuse was from the father or stepfather. However, Kilpatrick and Amick (1984) reported that less than 1% of women surveyed by telephone said that they had been forced to have sex with fathers, stepfathers, or other relatives. Differences here may well reflect the methodology used for data collection as well as the definition being used for sexual abuse.

Looking more closely at sexual abuse within the family, stepfathers appear to be much more likely than fathers to seek sexual relations with daughters (Finkelhor, 1980; Russell, 1984b). In one survey, 17% of the women who had had a stepfather as a principal figure in their homes while growing up were sexually abused by him (Russell, 1984b). The comparable percentage for biological fathers was only 2%. Although girls are more often victimized than boys, boys are also sexually abused by male adults. In one study 33% of the case load of sexual abuse of children consisted of young male victims (Swift, 1977).

Reactions to Being Sexually Abused as a Child

Sexual victimization by a family member appears to have some of the most severe and long-term consequences for the victim than for victims of any form of victimization (e.g. Courtois & Watts, 1982; Tsai & Wagner, 1978). However, even with this type of experience, some of the victims do not show impaired functioning as adults (Conte, 1985). Variables affecting the impact of the victimization include how long the abuse lasted and whether sexual intercourse or oral or anal sex occurred. The longer and more frequent the abuse, the more traumatic it was for the young victim. Genital sexual activities were also found to be more traumatic (Browne & Finkelhor, 1986).

As adults, many female incest victims often have difficulty relating to men, inadequate social skills, and difficulties in sexual functioning (Silver, Boon, & Stones, 1983; Tsai & Wagner, 1978). Male incest victims have also been reported as having sexual problems as adults (Groth, 1979). Male patients admitted to hospitals for psychiatric problems often had a pattern of physical or sexual abuse as children and aggressive acting out behavior as adults (Carmen et al., 1984). Female patients also had a history of abuse, but they more often responded with depression or suicidal behavior. A high percentage of borderline personality problems was found in a sample of women with a history of father–daughter incest who were seeking psychiatric help (Barnard & Hirsch, 1985). The long-term effects of sexual molestation from men outside the family are not as severe, although they are still seen as highly unpleasant by the victims (Becker, Skinner, Abel, & Treacy, 1982; Finkelhor, 1980).

At the time of the sexual abuse, these young victims feel isolated and alienated from their peers, are distrustful of adults, and feel guilt and shame (Pagelow, 1984). Incest may occur in the context of a violent marriage where the husband is abusive toward his wife as well as his children. Mothers may also be schizophrenic or highly depressed (Herman, 1981). In such a situation, the wife has little power to prevent the sexual abuse of her children. Not surprisingly, the female incest victim often feels alienated from her mother. Any affectionate relationships she has with her parents are with her father. She may take on other aspects of her mother's role as a wife in addition to having sexual relations with her father. At the same time, her father may attempt to control her by preventing her from having outside social contacts and from developing normal sexual relationships with her male peers (Tisza, 1982). With all of these negative elements, it is not surprising that incest victims may demonstrate depression, suicidal thoughts, and physical self-mutilation (Knittle & Tuana, 1980). If there are supportive adults available to these young victims of sexual molestation, their adjustment tends to be better (Tsai, Feldman-Summers, & Edgar, 1979).

Although young children can do little to stop physical or sexual abuse, as they reach preadolescence or adolescence, a common reaction of victimized children is to run away from home (Bolton, Reich, & Gutierres, 1977). Although this may free them from victimization in the home, it does expose them to a variety of other forms of potential victimization. Early marriage may also be a form of escape for the victimized girl. Unfortunately, some of these marriages are themselves violent, and there is no escape from violence for the woman (Walker, 1979).

Help for Incest Victims

Because of problems of reporting and identification, most of the victims who present themselves for treatment are adults. Two problems that appear with some frequency are sexual dysfunctions that are treated directly (McGuire & Wagner, 1978) and questions about "why?" (Conte, 1985). As adults, many former incest victims continue to be concerned with this experience and seek to find meaning in the event, trying to determine why it happened. Perhaps this is their attempt to reestablish a positive world view (Silver et al., 1983). Other therapeutic techniques are more general approaches to management of the emotional distress. One method of treatment that has shown some success is implosive therapy. Clients are given repeated exposure to the incest scene through imagery until it becomes less stressful (Rychtarik, Silverman, Van Landingham, & Prue, 1984).

Conclusion

As we have seen, women are frequently victimized in our society, although their patterns of victimization differ somewhat from the victimization of men. Men are more exposed to crimes of violence and to property crimes. Women are more often sexually victimized and assaulted by family members or acquaintances. No matter what the sex of the victim, the victimizer is almost always male.

Reactions to all forms of victimization are similar and involve many forms of emotional reactions. To successfully cope with their experience, victims need to feel in control of their life and also feel a sense of personal safety. This may occur with the aid of friends or through counseling or therapy. Presently we do not know enough about how to help them. Better therapeutic techniques are needed. Perhaps these need to be more targeted to specific types of victims.

This chapter has dealt with three of the most researched forms of victimization of women. We also need more basic research to better understand the dynamics of other forms of victimization such as sexual harassment in the workplace and the physical abuse of elderly women in the home (e.g., Pierce & Trotta, 1986). Such work may also help us to more clearly identify the ways in which female victims are different from male victims in their reactions and in their needs.

References

Adams, P. R., & Adams, G. R. (1984). Mount Saint Helens's ashfall: Evidence for a disaster stress reaction. *American Psychologist, 39*(3), 252–260.

Alexander, C. S. (1984). Women as victims of crime. In E. B. Gold (Ed.). *The changing risk of disease in women: An epidemiologic approach* (pp. 81–87). Lexington, MA: Heath.

American Psychiatric Association. (1980). *Diagnostic and statistical manual of mental disorders* (3rd ed.). Washington, DC: Author.

American Psychological Association. (1984). *Final report. Task force on the victims of crime and violence.* Washington, DC: Author.

Arkin, W., & Dobrofsky, L. (1978). Military socialization and masculinity. *Journal of Social Issues, 34*(1), 151–168.

Barnard, C. P., & Hirsch, C. (1985). Borderline personality and victims of incest. *Psychological Reports, 57,* 715–718.

Bard, M., & Sangrey, D. (1979). *The crime victim's book.* New York: Basic Books.

Bart, P. (1981). A study of women who both were raped and avoided rape. *Journal of Social Issues, 37*(4), 123–137.

Baum, A., Fleming, R., & Singer, J. E. (1983). Coping with victimization by technological disaster. *Journal of Social Issues, 39*(2), 117–138.

Becker, J. V., Skinner, L. J., Abel, G. G., & Cichon, J. (1986). Level of postassault sexual functioning in rape and incest victims. *Archives of Sexual Behavior, 15*, 37–50.

Becker, J. V., Skinner, L. J., Abel, G. G., Howell, J., & Bruce, K. (1983). The effects of sexual assault on rape and attempted rape victims. *Victimology, 7*, 106–113.

Becker, J. V., Skinner, L. J., Abel, G. G., & Treacy, E. C. (1982). Incidence and types of sexual dysfunctions in rape and incest victims. *Journal of Sex and Marital Therapy, 1*, 65–74.

Billings, A. G., & Moos, R. H. (1984). Coping, stress, and social resources among adults with unipolar depression. *Journal of Personality and Social Psychology, 46*, 877–891.

Blumenthal, M. D., Kahn, R. L., Andrews, F. M., & Head, K. B. (1972). *Justifying violence: Attitudes of American men.* Ann Arbor: University of Michigan, Institute for Social Research.

Bolton, F. G., Jr., Reich, J. W., & Gutierres, S. E. (1977). Delinquency patterns in maltreated children and siblings. *Victimology, 2*(2), 349–357.

Bowker, L. H. (1984). Coping with wife abuse: Personal and social networks. In A. R. Roberts (Ed.), *Battered women and their families* (pp. 168–191). New York: Springer.

Bowker, L. H. (1980). Women as victims: An examination of the results of LEAA's national crime survey program. In L. H. Bowker (Ed.), *Women and crime in America* (pp. 158–179). New York: Macmillan.

Bowker, L. H. (1983). *Beating wife-beating.* Lexington, MA: Lexington Books.

Browne, A. (1987). *When battered women kill.* New York: Free Press.

Browne, A., & Finkelhor, D. (1986). Impact of child sexual abuse. A review of the research. *Psychological Bulletin, 99*, 66–77.

Brownmiller, S. (1976). *Against our will: Men, women, and rape.* New York: Bantam Books.

Burgess, A. W., & Holmstrom, L. L. (1974). Rape trauma syndrome. *American Journal of Psychiatry, 131*, 981–986.

Burgess, A. W., & Holmstrom, L. (1979). Adaptive strategies and recovery from rape. *American Journal of Psychiatry, 136*(10), 1278–1282.

Burt, M. (1980). Cultural myths and supports for rape. *Journal of Personality and Social Psychology, 38*, 217–230.

Burt, M. R., & Katz, B. L. (1985). Rape, robbery, and burglary: Responses to actual and feared criminal victimization, with special focus on women and the elderly. *Victimology, 10*, 325–358.

Caplan, P. J. (1985). *The myth of women's masochism.* New York: Dutton.

Carmen, E. H., Riecker, P. P., & Mills, T. (1984). Victims of violence and psychiatric illness. *American Journal of Psychiatry, 141*(3), 378–383.

Chandler, S. (1986). *The psychology of battered women.* Unpublished doctoral dissertation, University of California, Berkeley.

Cherry, F. (1983). Gender roles and sexual violence. In E. R. Allgeier & N. B. McCormick (Eds.), *Changing boundaries: Gender roles and sexual behavior* (pp. 245–260). Palo Alto, CA: Mayfield.

Coates, D., & Winston, T. (1983). Counteracting the deviance of depression: Peer support groups for victims. *Journal of Social Issues, 39*(2), 169–194.

Coates, D., Wortman, C. B., & Abbey, A. (1979). Reactions to victims. In I. H. Frieze, D. Bar-Tal, & J. S. Carroll (Eds.), *New approaches to social problems: Applications of attribution theory.* San Francisco: Jossey-Bass.

Conte, J. R. (1985). The effects of sexual abuse on children: A critique and suggestions for future research. *Victimology, 10*, 110–130.

Courtois, C. A., & Watts, D. L. (1982). Counseling adult women who experienced incest in childhood or adolescence. *Personnel and Guidance Journal, 60*(5), 275–279.

Crepault, C., & Couture, M. (1980). Men's erotic fantasies. *Archives of Sexual Behavior, 9*, 565–582.

David, D., & Brannon, R. (1976). *The forty-nine percent majority: The male sex role.* Reading, MA: Addison-Wesley.

Davis, R. C., & Friedman, L. N. (1985). The emotional aftermath of crime and violence. In C. R. Figley (Ed.), *Trauma and its wake: The study and treatment of post-traumatic stress disorder* (pp. 90–112). New York: Brunner/Mazel.

DiVasto, P. V., Kaufman, A., Rosner, L., Jackson, R., Christy, J., Pearson, S., & Burgett, T. (1984). The prevalance of sexually stressful events among females in the general population. *Archives of Sexual Behavior, 13*, 59–67.

Dobash, R. E., & Dobash, R. P. (1978). Wives: The "appropriate" victims of marital violence. *Victimology, 2*, 426–442.

Dohrenwend, B. P., & Shrout, P. E. (1985). "Hassles" in the conceptualization and measurement of life stress variables. *American Psychologist, 40*, 780–785.

Dutton, D. (1986). The outcomes of court mandated treatment for wife assault: A quasi-experimental evaluation. *Violence and Victims, 1*, 163–176.

Ellis, E. M. (1983). A review of empirical rape research: Victim reactions and response to treatment. *Clinical Psychology Review, 3*, 473–490.

Fagan, J. A., & Wexler, S. (1984, October). *Crime at home and in the streets: The relation between family and stranger violence.* Paper presented at the National Conference on Family Violence as a Crime and Justice Problem, National Institute of Justice, Washington, DC.

Farley, L. (1978). *Sexual shakedown: The sexual harassment of women on the job.* New York: McGraw-Hill.

Farrell, W. (1974). *The liberated man.* New York: Random House.

Feild, H. S. (1978). Attitudes toward rape: a comparative analysis of police, rapists, crisis counselors, and citizens. *Journal of Personality and Social Psychology, 36*, 156–179.

Finkelhor, D. (1979). *Sexually victimized children.* New York: Free Press.

Finkelhor, D. (1980). Risk factors in the sexual victimization of children. *Child Abuse and Neglect, 4*, 265–273.

Flynn, J. P. (1977). Recent findings related to wife abuse. *Social Casework, 58*, 13–20.

Folkman, S. (1984). Personal control and stress and coping processes: A theoretical analysis. *Journal of Personality and Social Psychology, 46*(4), 839–852.

Folkman, S., & Lazarus, R. S. (1985). If it changes it must be process: Study of emotion and coping during three stages of a college examination. *Journal of Personality and Social Psychology, 48*, 150–170.

Frank, E., & Stewart, B. D. (1984). Depressive symptoms in rape victims: A revisit. *Journal of Affective Disorders, 7*, 77–85.

Frank, E., Turner, S. M., & Duffy, B. (1979). Depressive symptoms in rape victims. *Journal of Affective Disorders, 1,* 269–277.

Frieze, I. H. (1979). Perceptions of battered wives. In I. H. Frieze, D. Bar-Tal, & J. S. Carroll (Eds.), *New approaches to social problems: Applications of attribution theory.* San Francisco: Jossey-Bass.

Frieze, I. H. (1980). *Causal attributions as mediators of battered women's responses to battering* (In final report NIMH Grant No. 1 R01 MH30193). Pittsburgh, PA: University of Pittsburgh.

Frieze, I. H. (1983). Investigating the causes and consequences of marital rape. *Signs: Journal of Women in Culture and Society, 8,* 532–553.

Frieze, I. H. (1985). *Female and male reactions to potentially victimizing events.* Paper presented at the Tenth National Conference of the Association for Women in Psychology, New York, NY.

Frieze, I. H., Hymer, S., & Greenberg, M. S. (in press). Describing the crime victim: Psychological reactions to victimization. *Professional Psychology.*

Frieze, I. H., Knoble, J., Washburn, C., & Zomnir, G. (1980). *Types of battered women.* Paper presented at the Annual Research Conference of the Association for Women in Psychology, Santa Monica, CA.

Frieze, I. H., & McHugh, M. C. (1986). When disaster strikes. In C. Tavris (Ed.), *Everywoman's emotional well-being* (pp. 349–370). New York: Nelson Doubleday.

Frodi, A., Macaulay, J., & Thome, P. (1977). Are women always less aggressive than men? A review of the experimental literature. *Psychological Bulletin, 84,* 634–660.

Gilbert, L. A., & Mangelsdorff, D. (1979). Influence of perceptions of personal control on reactions to stressful events. *Journal of Counseling Psychology, 26,* 473–480.

Gillman, I. S. (1980). An object–relations approach to the phenomenon and treatment of battered women. *Psychiatry, 43*(4), 346–358.

Green, B. L., & Gleser, G. C. (1983). Stress and long-term psychopathology in survivors of the Buffalo Creek disaster. In D. F. Ricks & B. S. Dohrenwend (Eds.), *Origins of psychopathology: Problems in research and public policy* (pp. 73–90). New York: Cambridge University Press.

Greenblat, C. S. (1985). "Don't hit your wife . . . unless": Preliminary findings on normative support for the use of physical force by husbands. *Victimology: An International Journal, 10,* 221–241.

Groth, A. N. (1979). *Men who rape: The psychology of the offender.* New York: Plenum.

Hall, E. R., Howard, J. A., & Boezio, S. L. (1986). Tolerance of rape: A sexist or antisocial attitude. *Psychology of Women Quarterly, 10,* 110–118.

Harvey, M. R. (1985). *Exemplary rape crisis programs: a cross-site analysis and case studies.* Washington, DC: National Institute of Mental Health.

Heath, L. (1984). Impact of newspaper crime reports on fear of crime: Multimethodological investigation. *Journal of Personality and Social Psychology, 47,* 263–276.

Herman, J. L. (1981). Father–daughter incest. *Professional Psychology, 12,* 76–79.

Hilberman, E., & Munson, K. (1978). Sixty battered women. *Victimology, 2,* 460–471.

Holahan, C. J., & Moos, R. H. (1985). Life stress and health: Personality, coping, and family support in stress resistance. *Journal of Personality and Social Psychology, 49,* 739–747.

Holmstrom, L. L., & Burgess, A. W. (1979). Rape: The husband's and boyfriend's initial reactions. *The Family Coordinator, 28,* 321–330.

Howard, J. A. (1984). The "normal" victim: The effects of gender stereotypes on reactions to victims. *Social Psychology Quarterly, 47,* 270–281.

Hunt, M. (1974). *Sexual behavior in the 1970's.* Chicago: Playboy Press.

Hymer, S. (1984). The self in victimization: Conflict and developmental perspectives. *Victimology, 9,* 142–150.

Janoff-Bulman, R. (1979). Characterological versus behavioral self-blame: Inquiries into depression and rape. *Journal of Personality and Social Psychology 37,* 1798–1809.

Janoff-Bulman, R. (1985). Criminal vs. non-criminal victimization: Victims' reactions. *Victimology, 10,* 498–511.

Janoff-Bulman, R., & Frieze, I. H. (1983). A theoretical perspective for understanding reactions to victimization. *Journal of Social Issues, 39*(2), 1–17.

Janoff-Bulman, R., & Frieze, I. H. (in press). The role of gender in reactions to criminal victimization. In R. Barnett, L. Biener, & G. Baruch (Eds.), *Women in stress.* Free Press.

Janoff-Bulman, R., Madden, M. E., & Timko, C. (1983). Victims' reactions to aid: The role of perceived vulnerability. *New Directions in Helping, 3,* 21–42.

Johnson, A. G. (1980). On the prevalance of rape in the United States. *Signs: Journal of Women in Culture and Society, 6,* 136–146.

Jones, A. (1980). *Women who kill.* New York: Fawcett Columbine Books.

Katz, B. L., & Burt, M. R. (in press). Self-blame: Help or hinderance in recovery from rape? In A. Burgess (Ed.), *Rape and sexual assault.* New York: Garland Press.

Kenig, S., & Ryan, J. (1986). Sex differences in levels of tolerance and attribution of blame for sexual harassment on a university campus. *Sex Roles, 15,* 535–549.

Kidder, L. H., Boell, J. L., & Moyer, M. M. (1983). Rights consciousness and victimization prevention: Personal defense and assertiveness training. *Journal of Social Issues, 39*(2), 153–168.

Kilpatrick, D. G., & Amick, A. E. (1984). *Intrafamilial and extrafamilial sexual assault: Results of a random community survey.* Paper presented at the Second National Family Violence Research Conference, Durham, NH.

Kilpatrick, D. G., Best, C. L., Veronen, L. J., Amick, A. E., Villeponteaux, L. A., & Ruff, G. A. (1985). Mental health correlates of criminal victimization: A random community survey. *Journal of Consulting and Clinical Psychology, 53,* 866–873.

Kilpatrick, D. G., Resick, P. A., & Veronen, L. J. (1981). Effects of a rape experience: A longitudinal study. *Journal of Social Issues, 37*(4), 105–122.

Kilpatrick, D. G., Veronen, L. J., & Best, C. L. (1985). Factors predicting psychological distress among rape victims. In C. R. Figley (Ed.), *Trauma and its wake: The study and treatment of post-traumatic stress disorder* (pp. 113–141). New York: Brunner/Mazel.

Kilpatrick, D., Veronen, L., & Resick, P. (1979). The aftermath of rape. Recent empirical findings. *American Journal of Orthopsychiatry, 49,* 658–669.

Kinsey, A. C., Pomeroy, W. B., Martin, C. E., & Gebhard, P. H. (1953). *Sexual behavior in the human female.* Philadelphia, PA: Saunders.

Knittle, B. J., & Tuana, S. J. (1980). Group therapy as primary treatment for adolescent victims of intrafamilial sexual abuse. *Clinical Social Work Journal, 8*(4), 236–242.

Koss, M. P. (1983). The scope of rape: Implications for the clinical treatment of victims. *Clinical Psychologist, 36*(4), 88-91.

Koss, M. P. (1985). The hidden rape victim: Personality, attitudinal, and situational characteristics. *Psychology of Women Quarterly, 9,* 193–212.

Lazarus, R. S., DeLongis, A., Folkman, S., & Gruen, R. (1985). Stress and adaptational outcomes: The problem of confounded measures. *American Psychologist, 40,* 770–779.

Lerner, M. J. (1980). *The belief in a just world.* New York: Plenum.

MacKennon, C. (1979). *Sexual harassment of working women: A case of sex discrimination.* New Haven, CT: Yale University Press.

Malamuth, N. M. (1986). Predictors of naturalistic sexual aggression. *Journal of Personality and Social Psychology, 50,* 953–962.

McCormick, N. B., & Jesser, C. J. (1983). The courtship game: Power in the sexual encounter. In E. R. Allgeier & N. B. McCormick (Eds.), *Changing boundaries: Gender roles and sexual behavior* (pp. 64–86). Palo Alto, CA: Mayfield.

McGarrell, E. F., & Flanagan, T. J. (1985). *Sourcebook of criminal justice statistics: 1984.* Washington, DC: U.S. Department of Justice, Bureau of Justice Statistics.

McGuire, L. S., & Wagner, N. N. (1978). Sexual dysfunction in women who were molested as children: One response pattern and suggestions for treatment. *Journal of Sex and Marital Therapy, 4,* 11–15.

Medea, A., & Thompson, K. (1974). *Against rape.* New York: Farrar, Straus & Giroux.

Meyer, C. B., & Taylor, S. E. (1986). Adjustment to rape. *Journal of Personality and Social Psychology, 50,* 1226–1234.

Miller, D. T., & Porter, C. A. (1983). Self-blame in victims of violence. *Journal of Social Issues, 39*(2), 139–152.

Mitchell, R. E., & Hodson, C. A. (1982). *Battered women: The relationship of stress, support, and coping to adjustment.* Paper presented at the meeting of the American Psychological Association, Washington, DC.

Muehlenhard, C. L., Friedman, D. E., & Thomas, C. M. (1985). Is date rape justifiable? The effects of dating activity, who initiated, who paid, and men's attitudes toward women. *Psychology of Women Quarterly, 9,* 297–310.

Norris, J., & Feldman-Summers, S. (1981). Factors related to the psychological impacts of rape on the victim. *Journal of Abnormal Psychology, 90,* 562–567.

Notman, M., & Nadelson, C. (1976). The rape victim: Psychodynamic considerations. *American Journal of Psychiatry, 133,* 408–412.

Pagelow, M. D. (1981). *Women-battering: Victims and their experiences.* Beverly Hills, CA: Sage.

Pagelow, M. D. (1984). *Family violence.* New York: Praeger.

Perloff, L. S. (1983). Perceptions of vulnerability to victimization. *Journal of Social Issues, 39*(2), 41–62.

Perloff, L. S., & Fetzer, B. K. (1986). Self–other judgments and perceived vulnerability to victimization. *Journal of Personality and Social Psychology, 50,* 502–510.

Pierce, R. L., & Trotta, R. (1986). Abused parents: A hidden family problem. *Journal of Family Violence, 1,* 99–110.

Powell, G. N. (1986). Effects of sex role identity and sex on definitions of sexual harassment. *Sex Roles, 14,* 9–19.

Queen's Bench Foundation. (1976). *Rape: Prevention and resistance.* San Francisco, CA: Author.

Read, S. J. (1987). Constructing causal scenarios: A knowledge structure approach to causal reasoning. *Journal of Personality and Social Psychology, 52,* 288–302.

Reisenzein, R. (1986). A structural equation analysis of Weiner's attribution–affect model of helping behavior. *Journal of Personality and Social Psychology, 50,* 1123–1133.

Riger, S., & Gordon, M. T. (1981). The fear of rape: A study in social control. *Journal of Social Issues, 37*(4), 71–92.

Riger, S., Gordon, M. T., & Le Bailly, R. (1978). Women's fear of crime: From blaming to restricting the victim. *Victimology, 3*(3–4), 274–284.

Rosenbaum, A., & O'Leary, K. D. (1981). Marital violence. Characteristics of abusive couples. *Journal of Consulting and Clinical Psychology, 49,* 63–71.

Roth, S., & Cohen, L. J. (1986). Approach, avoidance, and coping with stress. *American Psychologist, 41,* 813–819.

Russell, D. E. H. (1984a). *Sexual exploitation: Rape, child sexual abuse, and workplace harassment.* Beverly Hills, CA: Sage.

Russell, D. E. H. (1984b). The prevalence and seriousness of incestuous abuse: stepfathers vs. biological fathers. *Child Abuse and Neglect, 8,* 15–22.

Rychtarik, R. G., Silverman, W. K., Van Landingham, W. P., & Prue, D. M. (1984). Treatment of an incest victim with implosive therapy: A case study. *Behavior Therapy, 15,* 410–420.

Sales, E., Baum, M., & Shore, B. (1984). Victim readjustment following assault. *Journal of Social Issues, 40*(1), 117–136.

Saunders, D. G. (1986). When battered women use violence: Husband-abuse or self-defense? *Victims and Violence, 1,* 47–60.

Scheppele, K. L., & Bart, P. B. (1983). Through women's eyes: Defining danger in the wake of sexual assault. *Journal of Social Issues, 39*(2), 63–80.

Schulz, R., & Decker, S. (1985). Long-term adjustment to physical disability: The role of social support, perceived control, and self-blame. *Journal of Personality and Social Psychology, 48,* 1162–1172.

Schur, E. M. (1984). *Labeling women devient: Gender, stigma, and social control.* New York: Random House.

Shainess, N. (1984). *Sweet suffering: Woman as victim.* New York: Bobbs-Merrill.

Shaver, K. (1970). Defensive attribution: Effects of severity & relevance on the responsibility assigned for an accident. *Journal of Personality and Social Psychology, 14,* 101–113.

Sherman, L. W., & Berk, R. A. (1984). The specific deterrent effects of arrest for domestic assault. *American Sociological Review, 49,* 261–272.

Silver, R. L., Boon, C., & Stones, M. H. (1983). Searching for meaning in misfortune: Making sense of incest. *Journal of Social Issues, 39*(2), 81–102.

Silver, R. L., & Wortman, C. B. (1980). Coping with undesirable life events. In J. Garber & M. E. P. Seligman (Eds.), *Human helplessness: Theory and applications* (pp. 279–340). New York: Academic Press.

Silverman, P. R. (1980). *Mutual self help groups: Organization and development.* Beverly Hills, CA: Sage.

Singer, S. I. (1986). Victims of serious violence and their criminal behavior: Subcultural theory and beyond. *Victims and Violence, 1,* 61–70.

Stone, A. A., & Neale, J. M. (1984). New measure of daily coping: Development and preliminary results. *Journal of Personality and Social Psychology, 46,* 892–906.

Straus, M. A., Gelles, R. J., & Steinmetz, S. K. (1980). *Behind closed doors: Violence in the American family.* Garden City, NY: Doubleday.

Swift, C. (1977). Sexual victimization of children: An urban mental health center survey. *Victimology, 2*(2), 322–327.

Sysler, B. (1977). An analysis of the relationship between aggressive sport fan behavior and personality. *Dissertation Abstracts, 38*(1), 159a.

Taylor, S. E. (1983). Adjustment to threatening events: A theory of cognitive adaptation. *American Psychologist, 38,* 1161–1173.

Thirer, J. (1977). Changes in aggression of various classifications of athletes and nonathletes as influenced by type of film viewed. *Dissertation Abstracts, 38*(4), 2015a.

Till, F. J. (1980). *Sexual harassment: A report on the sexual harassment of students.* Washington, DC: National Advisory Council on Women's Educational Programs.

Timrots, A. D., & Rand, M. R. (1987). Violent crime by strangers and nonstrangers. *Bureau of Justice Statistics Special Report.* Washington, DC: U. S. Department of Justice.

Tisza, V. (1982). Incest. In C. C. Nadelson & M. T. Notman (Eds.), *The woman patient: Aggression, adaptations and psychotherapy* (Vol. 3, pp. 65–94). New York: Plenum.

Tsai, M., Feldman-Summers, S., & Edgar, M. (1979). Childhood molestation: Variables related to differential impacts on psychosexual functioning in adult women. *Journal of Abnormal Psychology, 88,* 407–417.

Tsai, M., & Wagner, N. N. (1978). Therapy groups for women sexually molested as children. *Archives of Sexual Behavior, 7*(5), 417–427.

Turner, S. M., & Frank, E. (1981). Behavior therapy in the treatment of rape victims. In L. Michelson, M. Hersen, & S. Turner (Eds.), *Future perspectives in behavior therapy* (pp. 269–291). New York: Plenum.

U. S. Department of Justice. (1985). *Criminal victimization in the United States, 1983: A national crime survey report.* Washington, DC: U. S. Government Printing Office.

U. S. Department of Justice. (1986). *Criminal victimization in the United States, 1984.* Washington, DC: Author.

Veronen, L. J., & Kilpatrick, D. G. (1983). Stress management for rape victims. In D. Meichenbaum & M. E. Jaremko (Eds.), *Stress reduction and prevention* (pp. 341–374). New York: Plenum.

Walker, L. E. (1978). Battered women and learned helplessness. *Victimology, 3,* 525–534.

Walker, L. E. (1979). *The battered woman.* New York: Harper & Row.

Walker, L. E. (1984). *The battered woman syndrome.* New York: Springer.

Walker, L. E. (1985). Psychological impact of the criminalization of domestic violence on victims. *Victimology, 10,* 281–300.

Walker, L. E., & Browne, A. (1985). Gender and victimization by intimates. *Journal of Personality, 53*(2), 179–194.

Weiner, B. (1985a). An attributional theory of achievement motivation and emotion. *Psychological Review, 92,* 548–573.

Weiner, B. (1985b). "Spontaneous" causal thinking. *Psychological Bulletin, 97,* 74–84.

Wilson, J. P., Smith, W. K., & Johnson, S. K. (1985). A comparative analysis of PTSD among various survivor groups. In C. R. Figley (Ed.), *Trauma and its* wake: The study and treatment of post-traumatic stress disorder (pp. 142–172). New York: Brunner/Mazel.

Wilson, N. K. (1985). "Venerable bedfellows:" Women's liberation and women's victimization. *Victimology, 10,* 206–220.

Wood, J. V., Taylor, S. E., & Lichtman, R. R. (1985). Social comparison in adjustment to breast cancer. *Journal of Personality and Social Psychology, 49*(5), 1169–1183.

Zawitz, M. W. (Ed.). (1983). *Report to the nation on crime and justice: The data.* Washington, DC: U. S. Department of Justice.

Suggested Reading

Adams-Tucker, C. (1984). Early treatment of child incest victims. *American Journal of Psychotherapy, 38*(4), 505–516.

Bart, P. B., & O'Brien, P. H. (1985). *Stopping rape: Successful survival strategies.* New York: Pergamon Press.

Caplan, P. J. (1985). *The myth of women's masochism.* New York: Dutton.

Finkelhor, D. (1979). *Sexually victimized children.* New York: Free Press.

Frieze, I. H. (1983). Investigating the causes and consequences of marital rape. *Signs: Journal of Women in Culture and Society, 8,* 532–553.

Frieze, I. H., & McHugh, M. C. (1986). When disaster strikes. In C. Tavris (Ed.), *Everywoman's emotional well-being* (pp. 349–370). New York: Nelson Doubleday.

Groth, A. N. (1979). *Men who rape: The psychology of the offender.* New York: Plenum.

Hymer, S. (1984). The self in victimization: Conflict and developmental perspectives. *Victimology, 9,* 142–150.

Janoff-Bulman, R., & Frieze, I. H. (1983). A theoretical perspective for understanding reactions to victimization. *Journal of Social Issues, 39*(2), 1–17.

Koss, M. P. (1983). The scope of rape: Implications for the clinical treatment of victims. *Clinical Psychologist, 36*(4), 88–91.

Pagelow, M. D. (1984). *Family violence.* New York: Praeger.

Russell, D. E. H. (1982). *Rape in marriage.* New York: Macmillan.

Russell, D. E. H. (1984). *Sexual exploitation: Rape, child sexual abuse, and workplace harassment.* Beverly Hills, CA: Sage.

Schur, E. M. (1984). *Labeling women deviant: Gender, stigma, and social control.* New York: Random House.

Sonkin, D. J., Martin, D., & Walker, L. E. A. (1985). *The male batterer: A treatment approach.* New York: Springer.

Walker, L. E. (1984). *The battered woman syndrome.* New York: Springer.

EDWIN S. SHNEIDMAN

A PSYCHOLOGICAL APPROACH TO SUICIDE

E dwin S. Shneidman, PhD, is Professor of Thanatology at the University of California at Los Angeles School of Medicine. He was formerly codirector (and cofounder) of the Los Angeles Suicide Prevention Center and was the charter director of the Center for the Study of Suicide Prevention at the National Institute of Mental Health, Bethesda, Maryland. He has been a Public Health Service Special Research Fellow and Visiting Professor at Harvard University, Visiting Professor at the Ben Gurion University of the Negev (Beersheva), Clinical Associate at the Massachusetts General Hospital and the Karolinska Hospital (Stockholm), and a Fellow at the Center for Advanced Study in the Behavioral Sciences at Stanford University. He has been president of the Division of Clinical Psychology (Division 12) and the Division of Psychologists in Public Service (Division 18) of the American Psychological Association (APA) and was Founder–President of the American Association of Suicidology.

Shneidman has edited books including *Thematic Test Analysis, Essays in Self-Destruction, On the Nature of Suicide, Death and the College Student, Suicidology: Contemporary Developments,* and *Death: Current Perspectives.* He is author of *Deaths of Man* (nominated for the 1973 National Book Award in Science), *Voices of Death,* and *Definition of Suicide,* as well as over 150 articles and chapters on suicide in various publications, including the *Encyclopaedia Britannica, Comprehensive Textbook of Psychiatry,* and *Encyclopaedia of Psychology.* He is the recipient of the APA Award for Distinguished Professional Contributions to Public Service.

A PSYCHOLOGICAL APPROACH TO SUICIDE

I t is the dream of every proprietor of ideas to have the opportunity to discuss a topic which has been the benign obsession or unity thema of one's intellectual and professional life. My abiding focus for almost 40 years has been suicide and suicide prevention.

For me, it began in 1948 while on an assignment given to me by a superintendent of a mental hospital. I came upon several thousand genuine suicide notes tucked among the hundreds of thousands of folders of coroner's cases filed away in an underground vault. My first thought—megalomaniac in its association—was that, like Freud's conception of dreams as the royal road to the unconscious, suicide notes could be the regal highway to the thinking and reasoning styles, the personality, and the emotional states of suicide. Later, I discovered that there were potholes and washouts in that road, but that is the story of a life-long odyssey, much of it on blue highways.

The moment I saw the suicide notes it seemed imperative that I not read them then but rather put them aside, gather comparable data (i.e.,

Portions of this chapter are adapted from "Suicide and Suicide Prevention" by E. S. Shneidman, in R. J. Corsini and B. D. Ozaki (Eds.), 1984, *Encyclopedia of Psychology* (Vol. 3, pp. 383–386), New York: Wiley. Copyright 1984 by John Wiley and Sons. Other portions are adapted from *Definition of Suicide* by E. S. Shneidman, 1985, New York: Wiley. Copyright 1985 by E. S. Shneidman. Adapted by permission of John Wiley and Sons.

suicide-like notes written by matched non-suicidal persons), and invoke Mill's Method of Difference in order to conduct the natural experiment latent in the materials (i.e., to exhibit the differences between genuine suicide notes and their simulated counterparts to see what particularly accrued to suicide). I also called in a colleague, with the commonsense notion that at some junctures two heads may be better than one, and so my long-term association with Norman Farberow was begun. That intense collaboration lasted until 1966, when I left the Los Angeles Suicide Prevention Center, which we cofounded, to head the new Center for the Study of Suicide Prevention at the National Institute of Mental Health.

Approaches to Suicide

It is almost banal to say that the topic of suicide is a complicated one. Suicidal phenomena *are* enormously complex. A dozen individuals can end their lives by shooting bullets through their heads and arrive at that seemingly same unit-of-behavior by means of very different routes, pathways, and histories. In order to understand suicide one, ideally, has to be a personologist; to understand suicide one must understand human behavior and mentation and the multiple reasons (e.g., biological, socio-cultural, interpersonal, cognitive, affective, and unconscious) that lie behind or accompany a suicidal event.

This brief statement itself contains several implications. One implication is that suicidal phenomena can best be understood through multidisciplinary approaches. In suicidology, no one specialty has a stranglehold on truth. Each specialty may represent legitimate aspects, but any sensible scientist should take warranted umbrage if an associate claims that a particular specialty represents the whole field.

Allow me to share a visual image. I see *suicide* as a circle, a large encompassing concept. This circle is made up of several sectors. Researchers have yet to conceptualize whether or not there is a special core or essence at the center of this circle. There is such a conceptual circle for each instance of suicide. The size, density, and importance of the various sectors vary from case to case of individual suicide. The common labels of these several sectors are as follows: (a) literary and personal document; (b) philosophical and theological; (c) demographic; (d) sociocultural; (e) sociological; (f) dyadic and familial; (g) psychodynamic; (h) psychological; (i) psychiatric or mental illness; (j) constitutional and genetic; (k) biological and biochemical; (l) legal and ethical; (m) preventional; (n) systems theory; and (o) political, global, or supernational.

Another implication (still having to do with multiplicity) is that both bench-work and fieldwork are needed; one cannot disregard either Virchow or Freud; one should be as precise, scientific, statistical, and nomothetical as possible but should not eschew the great power of the idiographic, clinical, intensive, and longitudinal single-case approach. It is a mistake to trade specious precision for indispensable relevance. As a prolix introduction to my central remarks, I shall briefly discuss each of the sectors of suicide (or approaches to suicide; Shneidman, 1973b).

The Literary and Personal Document Approach

If you believe, as I do, that the great novelists and playwrights (e.g., Dostoevsky, Melville, and Ibsen) offer enormous insights into the human condition and its vicissitudes (including suicide), then it is their works that one should study. For example, one could learn about the psychology and sociology of suicides of women in the 19th century by a close study of Edna's drowning in Kate Chopin's *The Awakening* (1899), Anna's death in Tolstoy's *Anna Karenina* (1877), Emma's poisoning in Flaubert's *Madame Bovary* (1856), Lucy and Isabel's deaths in Melville's *Pierre* (1852), or Hedda's suicide in Ibsen's *Hedda Gabler* (1890).

In addition, in this same idiographic and literary tradition, there are those rare diaries of individuals who ruminated and wrote for years about their own suicidal thoughts and then, in a tragic validation of their own beliefs and urgings, committed suicide. These diaries hold nuggets of insight and implication for any careful and patient miner. I have assembled a number of 20th century diaries of people who committed suicide and wish to give an account of them. (Rosenblatt's 1983 consideration of 19th century diarists and 20th century grief theories was a similar endeavor.) Here are some of them:

Writers and artists: Virginia Woolf (1882–1941), English writer; Cesare Pavese (1908–1950), Italian novelist and poet; and Sylvia Plath (1932–1963), American poet and novelist.

Students and young adults: Joseph Windrow (1956–1972), high school student; Doris Schaffer (1938–1963), American flower-child of the 1960s; and Wallace Baker (1891–1913).

Recluses and rejects: Arthur Crew Inman (1895–1963); Rachel Roberts (1926–1980), English actress and ex-wife of actor Rex Harrison; and Doris Carrington (1899–1932), friend of Lytton Strachey.

Displaced persons and victims of persecution: Andrew Bihaly (1910–1946), Hungarian survivor of the Holocaust; Klaus Mann (1907–1949), author and son of Thomas Mann; and Adam Czerniakow (1880–1942), who presided over the Warsaw ghetto under the Nazis.

Crusaders and reformers: Charlotte Perkins Gilman (1860–1935), American suffragette, lecturer, and activist; and Vachel Lindsay (1879–1931), American poet, orator, crusader, and friend of Sara Teasdale (an American poet who also committed suicide).

One diary that I would like to mention separately is *The Inman Diary* (1985), a 2-volume set edited by Aaron from Inman's original 155 volumes. Inman was a conspicuously unattractive character: He was querulous, acerbic, pro-Nazi, a child molester, and a hypochondriac, but this diary is an undeniably rich document and is perfect grist for a multidisciplinary mill. What a joy it would be someday to have an intensive assessment of this one rich and fascinating documentation of a suicide conducted by several experts representing several different specialties (a procedure Murray described in *Explorations in Personality*, 1938).

From a somewhat different angle, Alvarez, a contemporary English poet, critic, and author (and a failed suicide himself) has written a book, *The Savage God* (1971), about suicide in literature or "the power that the act of suicide has exerted over the creative imagination" (p. 141). In this context, Alvarez discussed the impact of the idea of suicide on the works of Beckett, Chatterton (who committed suicide), Coleridge, Cowper, Dante, Donne, Dostoevsky, Eliot, Goethe, Kafka, Mann, Pasternak, and Yeats. (Lester, Sell, & Sell [1980, pp. 113–142] listed authors who have committed suicide and literary works dealing with the theme of suicide; Cutter [1983] included similar information for artists.)

But I want to emphasize the power of having members of a first-rate multidisciplinary team independently examine individual suicides in depth. The meaning of any individual suicide is not a sum, an abstract, nor a synthesis of these proceedings; it is, rather, everything that all the experts will have said, with multiple wisdoms, insights, and implications.

Philosophical and Theological Approaches

Philosopher Choron, in his book *Suicide* (1972), outlined the position of the major Western philosophers in relation to death and suicide. In general, the philosophers of suicide never meant their written speculations to be prescriptions for action but simply reflections of their own inner intellectual debates on this ubiquitous and fascinating topic.

Many famous philosophers have touched upon the topic of suicide: Pythagorus, Epictitus, Montaigne, Descartes, Spinoza, Voltaire, Montesquieu, Rousseau, Hume, Kant, Schopenhauer, and Neitzsche). The existential philosophers of our own century—Kierkegaard, Jaspers, Camus, Sartre, and Heidigger—have made the pointlessness and meaninglessness of life (and the topic of suicide) a central issue. Camus begins *The Myth of Sisyphus* by saying that the topic of suicide is the central problem for philosophy.

The indispensable reference for anyone who wishes to explore the larger view of philosophic and theological matters is Pepper's book, *World Hypotheses* (1942). This book organized my thoughts and answered my questions on these important topics in a totally satisfying way. (It is not at all about suicide, but it is one of the half-dozen most important books that I have read in my own suicidological career.)

In theological terms, neither the Old nor the New Testament directly forbids suicide. However, contemporary Western attitudes are highly colored by Christian doctrine. Historically, the excessive martyrdom of the early Christians frightened the church elders sufficiently for them to introduce a serious deterrent; they related suicide to sin. In the 4th century, Saint Augustine (345–430) stated that suicide violated the Sixth Commandment (related to killing) and precluded the possibility of repentance. In the 7th century, the Council of Toledo proclaimed that an individual who attempted suicide was to be excommunicated. When Saint Thomas (1225–1274) emphasized that suicide was a mortal sin in that it usurped God's power over man's life and death, the notion of suicide as sin took firm hold. For hundreds of years the notion has continued to play an important part in Western society's view of self-destruction. (See Battin, 1982, for a discussion of the church's view of suicide.)

The discussion of suicide is lively among theological circles to this day and, in general, suicide is condemned, especially in the fundamentalist regions of this country. However, it can be noted (with approving compassion) that in 1986, when a conservative southern U.S. Senator committed suicide, the eulogies on that occasion never mentioned the word sin.

The Demographic Approach

The demographic approach relates to various statistics on suicide. The medieval English coroners began to keep rolls, that is, documents that incorporated death (and birth) records. In England, from the 11th century on, the determination of whether or not the property of a deceased individual could be kept by the heirs or had to be forfeited to the Crown depended on whether or not the death was judged by the coroner to be an act of God or a felony. Suicide was the latter, a felony against the self or *felo de se;* thus the way in which a death was certified was of enormous importance to the survivors. (A historical consideration of penal laws and suicide may be found in Guernesy, 1883/1963.)

In 1662, Graunt published a small book of observations on the London bills of mortality that listed all deaths, which had great social and medical significance (see Shneidman, 1976). Graunt devised categories of information (i.e., sex, locale, and type of death) and made mortality tables. He was the first to demonstrate that regularities could be found in mortality phenomena and that these regularities were important data to be used in policy making and planning by the government and business.

In 1741, the science of statistics—the "istics" of the state—evolved from the work of a Prussian clergyman, Süssmilch. He called his efforts *political arithmetic*—what we now call vital statistics. From his studies came the "laws of large numbers," which permitted long-range planning (for food and supplies and potential tax income based on the size of the population) in Europe as well as in the American colonies. Cassedy (1961), writing about colonial America, said that Süssmilch's "exhaustive analysis of vital data from church registers . . . became the ultimate scientific demonstration of the regularity of God's demographic laws" (p. 110). The traditions about statistics on suicide stem from Graunt and Süssmilch.

Some fairly recent data show that from 1970 to 1980, 272,322 suicides were recorded in the United States. The suicide rate is around 12 per 100,000 population (12.4 in 1984; National Center for Health Statistics [NCHS], 1986). Except for those over 65, it ranks as one of the 10 leading causes of death in all age groups. Suicide rates gradually rise among those in adolescence, increase sharply in the early adult age group, and parallel advancing age up to ages 75–84, in which it reached a rate of 22.0 suicides per 100,000 in 1984 (NCHS, 1986). Male suicides outnumber female suicides at a ratio of 3 to 1 (3.4:1 in 1984; NCHS, 1986). More Whites than non-Whites commit suicide (27,002 vs. 2,284, respectively, in 1984; NCHS, 1986). Suicide is more prevalent among single, widowed, separated, and divorced people. The modal method is firearms.

The suicide activities of youth and young adults have recently been of particular interest. In relation to those data Holinger and Offer (1986) wrote:

> Among the young, 20–24 year olds are at highest risk of suicide, followed by 15–19 and 10–14 year olds. White males have the highest suicide rates in all youthful age groups. However, suicide rates for the young are lower than the adult and older age groups. Time trends for adolescents show high rates during the 1930s, decreases throughout the 1940s and 1950s, dramatic increases from the late 1960s to the late 1970s with a recent levelling off of suicide rates. (abstract)

Nonetheless, suicide among the young is considered to be a special problem. (For reviews of youth suicide see, e.g., Peck, Farberow, & Litman, 1985; Seiden, 1969). As a reflection of this, organizations concerned with suicide, notably the National Institute of Mental Health, the American Association of Suicidology, and the National Committee for Youth Suicide Prevention have made youth suicide a focus for study and concern.

The Sociocultural Approach

In the sociocultural approach, two facts are obvious: Everyone is born into and develops within a sociocultural matrix, and the act of suicide itself has different integral meanings for both perpetrator and survivor among different cultures. In this chapter, I discuss suicide primarily within the United States; although I believe that my model also applies to Western Europe, it is not as easily extrapolated to South America, the Arab world, and the Orient. There are some universals, some transcultural elements, and many particulars.

My definition of suicide emphasizes what I believe to be the essentially relativistic and contextual nature of suicide when considered in global and omni-historical terms. My definition is the following: "Currently in the Western world, suicide is a conscious act of self-induced annihilation, best understood as a multidimensional malaise in a needful individual who defines an issue for which the suicide is perceived as the best solution" (Shneidman, 1985, p. 203). The several implications of this definition—its contextualism, the role of intention, its multidimensional nature, the strong belief that suicide is a malaise and not a disease (and should not be confused with affective disorders), that the key is pain attendant to frustrated psychological needs, and that this pain is compounded by perceptual constriction—are expanded upon later in this chapter.

There are, of course, many sociocultural studies (e.g., Hendin's *Suicide and Scandinavia,* 1964). One especially fine, recent one, written by a rare bicultural scholar, is Iga's *The Thorn in the Chrysanthemum: Suicide and Economic Success in Modern Japan* (1986). Iga wrote of an ancient culture dramatically transmuted by its foreign victor, of recovery in the context of its old and new values, and of suicide as one especially onerous price of recovery and success.

The Sociological Approach

Durkheim's giant book, *Le Suicide* (1897/1951) demonstrated the power of the sociological approach. As a result of his analysis of French data on suicide, Durkheim proposed that there are four kinds of suicides, all of them emphasizing the strength or weakness of the person's relationships or ties to society. *Altruistic* suicides are literally required by society. Here, the customs or rules of the group demand suicide under certain circumstances (e.g., hara-kiri and suttee). *Egoistic* suicide occurs when the individual has too few ties with his community; demands to live do not reach him or her. *Anomic* suicides are those that occur when the accustomed relationship between an individual and society is suddenly shattered, such as the shocking, immediate loss of a loved one, a close friend, a job, or even a fortune. *Fatalistic* suicides derive from excessive regulation (e.g., persons whose futures are piteously blocked, such as slaves or prisoners).

For years, sociologists did not make major changes in Durkheim's theory. Henry and Short (1954) added the concept of internal (superego) restraints to that of Durkheim's external restraint, and Gibbs and Martin (1964) sought to operationalize Durkheim's concept of social integration.

In a major break with Durkheim, sociologist Douglas (1967) pointed out that the social meanings of suicide vary greatly and that the more socially integrated a group is, the more effective it may be in disguising suicide. Furthermore, social reactions to stigmatized behaviors can themselves become a part of the etiology of the various actions the group seeks to control.

Maris (1981) believed that a systematic theory of suicide should be composed of at least four categories of variables: those concerning the person, the social context, biological factors, and *temporality,* a concept that he expanded into the idea of suicidal careers. It seems that after an extended hiatus, the sociological theories vis-à-vis suicide, are in a period of development and 20th century modernization.

Dyadic and Familial Approaches

Especially when one reads suicide notes (which are written by approximately 15% of those who commit suicide), one gets the keenest impression that suicide is literally a two-person event (see, e.g., Shneidman, 1980). Phrases in the notes such as "It was not your fault . . . I love you . . . I hate you . . . forgive me" all make the dyadic point. The concept of the significant other has its sharpest operational meaning in a case of suicide, in which another person seems to be both the life-sustainer and the last straw, both the focus of the victim's life and the precipitating reason for the death.

Quite recently, Pfeffer (1986) described the family characteristics that can support (and that abandon and even encourage) suicide within that setting. Pfeffer found that:

> Studies consistently have reported that families of suicidal children are disorganized by parental separations, divorce, and stresses of living in a one-parent family . . . the suicidal children were distinguishable from [others] . . . by the seriousness of family stresses [in which] losses were the predominant type of stress . . . [and by] parental violent and sexual abusive patterns . . . and [other] parental psychopathology. (p. 125)

Inman's diary, noted earlier, is filled with his fear, hatred, and fantasies of revenge on his father. One can hardly disconnect his suicide from his relationships to his father and, later, to his wife.

The Psychodynamic Approach

As Durkheim detailed the sociology of suicide, Freud fathered the psychodynamic explanations of suicide (Friedman, 1967). To Freud, suicide was a drama within the mind, mainly of unconscious hostility directed toward the introjected love object. Menninger (1938) delineated the psychodynamics of hostility and asserted that suicide is made up of three skeins: the wish to kill, the wish to be killed, and the wish to die.

Zilboorg (1937) refined Freud's psychoanalytic hypothesis and stated that every suicidal case contained not only unconscious hostility but also an unusual lack of the capacity to love others. He extended the concern solely from intrapsychic dynamics to include the external world, specifically citing the role of the broken home in suicidal proneness.

In an important exegesis of Freud's thoughts on suicide from 1881 to 1939, Litman (1967) concluded that there is more to the psychodynamics of suicide than hostility. These factors include several emotional states (e.g., rage, guilt, anxiety, and dependency) as well as a great number of specifically predisposing conditions. Feelings of abandonment and particularly of helplessness and hopelessness are important in his model.

Thus the locus of blame for suicide has shifted. The early Christians made suicide a personal sin, Rousseau transferred sin from the individual to society, Hume tried to secularize and decriminalize suicide entirely, Durkheim focused on the inimical effects of society on people, and Freud—eschewing both the notions of sin and crime—gave suicide back to the individual, but put the locus of action in the unconscious mind.

The Psychological Approach

The psychological approach can be distinguished from the psychodynamic approach in that a set of dynamics or a universal unconscious scenario is not posited, but, rather, certain general psychological features that seem to be necessary for a lethal suicide event to occur are emphasized. I have noted the following four features: (1) acute *perturbation*, that is, an increase in the individual's state of general upset; (2) heightened *inimicality*, an increase in self-abnegation, self-hate, shame, guilt, self-blame, and in behaviors that are overtly against one's own best interests; (3) a sharp and almost sudden increase of *constriction* of intellectual focus, a tunnelling of thought processes, a narrowing of the mind's content, and a truncating of the capacity to see viable options that would ordinarily occur to the mind; and (4) the idea of *cessation*, which is the insight that it is possible to end suffering by stopping the unbearable flow of consciousness. The last is the igniting element that explodes the mixture of the previous three components. In this context, suicide is best understood not as a movement toward cessation but rather as flight from the intolerable emotion—psychological pain.

The psychological approach to suicide cannot afford to ignore psychological needs, especially the needs that are felt to be unacceptably unfulfilled, thwarted, or blocked. A lexicon of psychological needs is presented by Murray (1938). In my own work with suicidal patients, I have found Murray's need system indispensable for understanding and reducing the patient's psychological pain and the perturbations that drive suicidal impulses.

Suicidologists following the psychological approach believe that human thoughts, feelings, and behaviors (e.g., a phobia, an irrational prejudice, or a desperate transient feeling that one would be better off dead) are in the mind and not in the brain. Of course, the mind is located in the brain, but these feelings are functions of the mind, and no indications of them can be found, as structures, on autopsy in the brain. There is no question that certain experiences such as a defeat in an athletic contest or an election, or rejection, or the loss of a loved one do produce concurrent changes in blood chemistry and a hundred other physiological processes, but for researchers to convert suicide into "depression" alone may mix cause and effect. It does not address what the person is hurting from. Many people have been "down," blue, dysphoric, depressed, dispirited, and bereft, but no one dies of these conditions. Many people, however, have died of suicide. Suicide is a human, psychological orientation toward life, not a biological, medical disease. There is no germ, spirochete, coccus, or virus or biochemical storm that causes suicide, for it is not a disease. Suicide is a human malaise tied to what is on one's mind, including one's view of the value of life at that moment. It is essentially hopeless unhappiness and psychological hurt, which is not a medical condition.

The Psychiatric or Mental Illness Approach

Of course I am aware of the scores of studies of affective disorders (manic-depressive disease, bipolar depression, unipolar depression, etc.) and of the scores of studies that indicate what percent of suicides (usually around 90%) have been assigned or could be assigned DSM-III psychiatric diagnostic mental disease labels (see, e.g., Miles, 1977). My own belief is that absolutely 100% of all suicide victims are perturbed, but perturbation itself is not a disease. It is a state of mind with a concomitant, but usually not causative, condition of the brain. Furthermore, it is clear that the vast percentage (I estimate 99%) of individuals diagnosed as schizophrenic do not commit suicide, just as the vast majority of individuals diagnosed with a depressive illness lead relatively long, albeit unhappy, lives (as, unhappily, do their loved ones). Accordingly, I shall forbear citing the plethora of studies relating suicide to psychiatric disorders, except to say that they look formidable, almost overwhelming, until one steps back from them and views them in a broader perspective.

Constitutional and Genetic Approaches

There is a long historical thread of trying to understand a person's behavior in terms of one's constitution or one's inner physiological workings. The ancient Greek physician Galen (130–200) posited four humors: sanguine (blood), phlegmatic (phlegm), choleric (yellow bile), and melancholic (black bile). Burton's *Anatomy of Melancholy* is an explication of dysphoria, filled with all sorts of phrases for the word *suicide,* which had not yet, in 1652, been invented. Earlier in this century, Kretchmer and

Sheldon independently attempted to link somatic, constitutional body types to temperament and, indirectly, to suicide. (I think it is safe to say that that approach has joined phrenology as a serious competitor in the scientific discussion halls.)

However, discussion and research of the topic of genetics and suicide is lively and current. At a conference at the National Institutes of Health, Roy (1986b) reported that there are five lines of evidence relating to genetic factors in suicide: clinical studies, twin studies, the Iowa-500 study, the Amish study, and the Copenhagen adoption studies. He believes these studies provide indirect evidence for genetic factors in suicide.

Roy's (1986b) summary reads as follows:

> Suicide like so much else in psychiatry tends to run in families. The question is what is being transmitted. No doubt in some youthful suicide victims what is being transmitted is not a genetic factor but a psychological factor. . . . However, the family, twin and adoption studies show that there are genetic factors in suicide. In many victims there will be genetic factors involved in the genetic transmission of manic-depression, schizophrenia and alcoholism—the psychiatric disorders most commonly associated with suicide. However, the Copenhagen adoption studies strongly suggest there may be a genetic factor for suicide independent of, or additive to, the genetic transmission of psychiatric disorder. (pp. 14–16)

In a similar paper (Roy, 1986a), he cited another possible reason for this conclusion. He suggested that a family member may serve as a role model. He emphasized that it is not clear which of these factors or what combination of them accounts for suicide running in families.

In response, I ask: Has it been demonstrated that manic-depression, schizophrenia, and alcoholism are genetically transmitted? Are the psychological sequelae of being an adopted child fully understood? Is suicide really a psychiatric disorder? Both the conceptualizations and the evidence in this matter are murky and equivocal.

Kety (1986) stated, "We cannot dismiss the possibility that the genetic factor in suicide is an inability to control impulsive behavior . . . In any case, suicide illustrates better than any of the mental illnesses . . . the very crucial and important interaction between genetic factors and environmental influences" (p. 44).

Researchers should not dismiss the role of any possible relevant sector. But, in my experience with suicidal patients, suicide diaries, and suicide notes, it is quite clear that it is not impulsiveness but planning, calculated behavior, and carefully (but admittedly confused) thought-out behavior that is exhibited. It could hardly be impulsiveness that geneticists would claim to be inherited and then related to suicide. But the major mistake is to conceptualize suicide as a disease in the first place. My reflections may very well be a genetic defect in me, but my inherited skepticism prompts me to say that I doubt it.

Biological and Biochemical Approaches

Before my discussion of the biology of suicide, an introductory caution must be stated: In this chapter I discuss the prevention and treatment of suicide, not the prevention and treatment of depression, or, for that matter, of schizophrenia, alcoholism, addiction, or paresis. Suicide and depression are not synonymous. There is much current research and there are many exciting developments on depression, but eliminating depression—an enormously important goal in its own right—would not eliminate suicide. In this connection, Maris' (1986) edited volume on the biology of suicide merits careful study.

The contemporary line of biochemical studies began in the 1950s with reports of observations of the chemical similarity between the putative neurotransmitters serotonin and LSD and the suggestion that schizophrenia might be caused by abnormal serotonin transmission. (This logic reminds me disturbingly of the original rationale for the use of metrozol, insulin, or electric shock to induce epileptic-like seizures to cure schizophrenia, based on the absolutely erroneous clinical belief that no schizophrenics had epilepsy, and the tortured logic that if one could remit an induced epileptic-like seizure, one might then pull the schizophrenia back with it.) At any rate, in the 1960s it was recognized that the use of reserpine, which depletes brain stores of serotonin, noradrenaline, and dopamine (and was administered to reduce blood pressure), could cause severe depression in some patients. At about the same time, pharmacologists discovered that monoamine oxidase inhibitors and tricyclic compounds of the imipramine type labeled antidepressant drugs (e.g., Elavil and Sinequan) also interfered with turnover of the monamines in the central nervous system. These observations led to two further hypotheses: the noradrenaline and the serotonin hypotheses, in which a relationship between depression and transmission at certain key sites in the central nervous system was posited.

Asberg, Nordstrom, and Traskman-Bendz (1986) indicated that two clusters of biological factors that tend to correlate with suicidal behavior have emerged: variables associated with a serotonergic transmitter (the monamine serotonin, 5-hydroxytryptamine, 5-HT) and certain endocrine functions, particularly the release of cortisol and thryrotropin. Asberg et al. (1986) stated that from 1958 to 1967, there were only 5 among 1,267 titles on the general topic of suicide that dealt with biological subjects, whereas in her 1986 report, that had 18 pages of text, she cited 152 references, mostly on biological aspects of depression and suicide. In her seven post-mortem studies of monamines and their metabolites in the brains of suicide victims, three show no differences and one is equivocal.

There are many studies of different chemicals and different methods involving enormous energy and thought, dozens of investigators and hundreds of subjects, but in summary they are more equivocal than clear.

On a closely related topic, deCatanzaro (1981) wrote a sociobiological perspective of suicide from a neo-Darwinian view, attempting to collate evidence from anthropology, sociology, biology, psychology, and psychiatry into a unified sociological–genetic–evolutionary framework. He proposed a study of the social ecology of suicide and suggested that suicide occurs when an individual's capacity to behave toward his or her inclusive fitness is impaired. I am reminded of Murray's statement (1938) that: "Suicide does not have *adaptive* (survival) value, but it does have *adjustive* value for the organism. Suicide is *functional* because it abolishes painful tension" (p. 15).

Legal and Ethical Approaches

In the United States, only Alabama and Oklahoma consider committing suicide a crime, but inasmuch as punishments are too repugnant to be enforced, there are no effective penalties for breaking these laws. In several states, suicide attempts are misdemeanors, although these laws are seldom, and then rather selectively, enforced. Thirty states have no laws against suicide or suicide attempts, but every state has laws that specify that it is a felony to aid, advise, or encourage another person to commit suicide (see Victoroff, 1983, chapter 15 and Appendix B). There are essays and books about the legal aspects of suicide by Silving (1957), Williams (1957), Shaffer (1976), and Engelhardt and Malloy (1982), among others.

Discussion of the ethics of suicide—an omnipresent topic—has had a recent renaissance. *Suicide: The Philosophical Issues* (Battin & Mayo, 1980), *Ethical Issues in Suicide* (Battin, 1982), and the 1983 issue on suicide and ethics in the journal *Suicide and Life-Threatening Behavior* (Battin & Maris, 1983) provide a sufficiency of thoughts on a number of provocative and vexatious issues. The major subtopics in this area seem to be the role of intention in suicide, the morality of suicide, the rationality of suicide, the right to commit suicide, the responsibility not to commit suicide, and assisted suicide and the related topics of active and passive euthanasia. There are a fair number of individuals—relatively young scholars especially—writing on these lively topics, and I consider these activities a good augury for suicidology.

The Preventional Approach

My colleagues and I (Shneidman, Farberow, & Litman, 1970) approached suicide from a preventive perspective. Under our direction, the Los

Angeles Suicide Prevention Center was established in the 1950s. Early on, we concluded from our research that the vast majority (about 80%) of committed suicides have recognizable presuicidal verbal and behavioral manifestations. Many people now know what these are: speaking of not being around, giving away prized possessions, and the like (see Shneidman, 1965). We reconstructed the events preceding a death by means of a *psychological autopsy,* which is a special interview procedure (developed at the Los Angeles Suicide Prevention Center along with the Los Angeles County Coroner) to help answer the question, What is the most accurate mode of death—natural, accident, suicide, or homicide? (Litman, Curphey, Shneidman, Farberow, & Tabachnick, 1963; Shneidman, 1969, 1977; Weisman & Kastenbaum, 1968).

We concluded that suicidal behavior is often a form of communication, a cry for help born out of pain, with clues and messages of suffering and anguish and pleas for response. If we have not unequivocally demonstrated that we singlehandedly effected a drastic reduction in the suicide rate of Los Angeles (see outcome and prevention studies regarding suicide prevention centers and suicide rates, e.g., Auerback & Kilmann, 1977, pp. 1191–1194) we have at least served thousands of people who are perturbed, undoubtedly saved some lives, indisputably increased the communication among mental health and other agencies in the community, and directly and indirectly raised the consciousness and lowered the taboo about the topic of suicide throughout the country.

A Systems Theory Approach

Systems theory might be the concept that holds the whole conceptual suicidal circle together. Within the last 50 years, there have been important advances in theoretical thinking based on the insight that there is an alternative to the mechanistic theories that have dominated physics, biology, and psychology. This alternative, called *general systems theory,* emphasizes the interconnectedness of parts within cells, the organism or collectivity, and the uniqueness of the whole. (See Bertalanffy, 1969, and Tyler, 1984.)

Miller's *Living Systems* (1978) is an encyclopedia of 20th-century physical, biological, and social sciences organized in a masterful fashion as a brilliantly conceived scheme. More than an encyclopedia, it is an empirically testable scientific theory. In it Miller states:

> The general living systems theory which this book presents is a conceptual system concerned primarily with concrete systems which exist in space–time. Complex structures which carry out living processes can be identified at seven hierarchical levels—cell, organ, organism, group, organization, society and supranational system. My central thesis is that systems at all these levels are open systems

composed of subsystems which process inputs, throughputs and out-
puts of various forms of matter, energy and information. I identify
nineteen critical subsystems whose processes are essential for life,
some of which process matter, energy, or information. Together they
make up a living system (p. 1).

Into this framework Miller places 173 hypotheses, which he discusses
in detail. Several of Miller's hypotheses have possible implications for the
study of self-destruction in the human organism.

My hypothesis formulated in the language of Miller's (1978) systems
theory approach is the following:

When any living system—cell, organ, organism, group, organization,
community, society, or supranation—manifests or displays the following three features: (a) *heightened* stress, disorganization, tension,
chaos, internal antitheses, pathology, or pain (either organizational
pain or, in the sole case of human beings, subjectively felt and report-
able pain); (b) real or perceived limitations in the range of options
that result in a reduction of possible actions; and (c) a fast-growing
push (chemical, physical, social, psychological, or political) for precipitous irreversible action, then the probable result will be the *destruction* of that living system. (See the section on the Cubic Model,
which follows.)

In the human organism this kind of destruction is called *suicide,* but in
other living systems (i.e., from cells to supranational systems) it is necessary to change the concept from suicide (which implies motivation) to the
more objective term *self-destruction.* One obvious implication of this view
is that two models are needed: (1) a *subjectivist* cubic model for the study
of humans, which features subjective psychological pain, perceptual constriction, and an untoward penchant for action (discussion to follow); and
(2) an *objectivist* model for the study of all other living systems, in which
reliably reported, past or present processes and events (e.g., chaos, disorganization, decay, and pathology) that relate to termination furnish the
appropriate data. Four brief examples can be given. At the level of the
cell, "If too much water enters a red cell, it swells up, the internal osmotic
equilibrium is destroyed, and the cell membrane ruptures" (Miller, 1978,
p. 100). At the level of an organization, the failure of a microcomputer
company occurred because of breakdowns within the system of the company (Reynolds, 1987); the third example, at the societal–national level,
was the recent (1986) downfall of the Marcos regime in the Philippines;
and finally, the example that is touching on possible international self-
destruction, what Menninger (1983) called the "exhibitionistic drunken
gesturing of two suicidal giants" (p. 350).

From the suicidological point of view it appears that the main challenge, and the greatest potential, for living systems theory is—after having first identified literal or paradigmatic instances of self-destruction "above" and "below" the human organism, that is, in cells and organs and human collectivities—to formulate some generalizations about self-destruction that are true and relevant for self-destruction in humans. Perhaps human cells, organs, groups, and organizations in their self-destructive activities can give researchers fresh insights into ourselves. What insights and what progress toward prevention a systems theory approach might yield! A priori, the implications of this exciting task are enormous (see Blaker, 1972).

The Political, Global, or Supernational Approach

Murray (1954/1980) said, "There will be no freedom for any exuberant form of life without freedom from atomic war . . . nothing is of signal importance today save those thoughts and actions which, in some measure, propose to contribute to the diagnosis and alleviation of the global neurosis which so affects us" (p. 613). Contemporary, self-disserving national neuroses (amounting to an international insanity) may very well lead to the self-induced death of human life. We live in a death-haunted time.

Overwhelmingly the most important kind of suicide for everyone to know about and to prevent is the global suicide that threatens us all and which, by the very presence of that threat, poisons our lives. Lifton (1979) appropriately urges on our consciousness the fact that we are in great danger—even if the bombs do not explode—of breaking our psychological connections to our own sense of species continuity and generativity, connections that are necessary to sustain human relationships.

Commonalities of Suicide: A Psychological Approach

Given that I am a psychologist, it is only sensible that I stick to my particular specialty and, from the various legitimate approaches to suicide that I have outlined, talk about the one I know best, namely the psychological aspects of suicide. I say again that I do not mean to imply by my presentation the depreciation or denigration of other approaches to this topic, but I leave it to proponents and spokespersons of the other approaches to make their presentations at other times and in other settings. There are ten common psychological characteristics that accrue to most committed suicides (Shneidman, 1985). They are meant to answer the key question, What are the interesting, relevant, common psychological dimensions of committed suicide? (See Table 1.)

Table 1
The Ten Commonalities of Suicide

I. The common purpose of suicide is to seek a solution	VI. The common cognitive state in suicide is ambivalence
II. The common goal of suicide is the cessation of consciousness	VII. The common perceptual state in suicide is constriction
III. The common stimulus in suicide is intolerable psychological pain	VIII. The common action in suicide is egression
IV. The common stressor in suicide is frustrated psychological needs	IX. The common interpersonal act in suicide is communication of intention
V. The common emotion in suicide is hopelessness–helplessness	X. The common consistency in suicide is with life-long coping patterns

Note. Adapted from Shneidman (1985) by permission of John Wiley and Sons. © 1985 by E. S. Shneidman.

Each suicide is an idiosyncratic event. In suicidology, there are no universals or absolutes. I am convinced that the search for a universal formulation for all suicide is a chimera. The best that one can reasonably hope to discover are the most frequent (i.e., common) characteristics that accrue to most suicides and to make this discussion in as commonsensical and ordinary language as possible.

I. The Common Purpose of Suicide Is To Seek a Solution

First of all, suicide is not a random act. It is never done pointlessly or purposelessly. It is a way out of a problem and an unbearable situation. It has an inexorable logic and impetus of its own. It is the answer— seemingly the only available answer—to a real puzzle: How to get out of this? What to do? Its purpose is to seek a situation to a problem that is generating intense suffering.

Fowles, English novelist and essayist, early in his career wrote a brilliant set of aphorisms, called *The Aristos* (1964). (The Greek word *aristos* means the best possible solution to a given situation.) The dozen or so individuals whom I have talked to, who, in one way or another, attempted to commit suicide and fortuitously survived have all said something like this: "It was the only thing I could do. It was the best way out of that terrible situation; it was the answer to the problem I had to solve; I could not see any other way."

In this sense, every suicide is an aristos; every suicide has as its purpose the seeking of a solution to the perceived problem. To understand what a suicide was about, one has to know the problem it was intended to solve. All this ties to my definition of suicide (stated earlier).

II. The Common Goal of Suicide Is the Cessation of Consciousness

In a curious and paradoxical way, suicide is both a moving toward and a moving away from something; the common practical goal of suicide is to stop the painful flow of consciousness. Suicide is best understood not so much as a moving toward the idea of a reified death, as it is in terms of the idea (in the mind of the suicidal person) of cessation, specifically when cessation—the complete stopping of one's consciousness of unendurable pain—is seen by the suffering individual as the solution, indeed the perfect solution, of life's painful and pressing problems. The moment that the idea of the possibility of stopping consciousness occurs to the anguished mind as the perfect answer or the only way out—in the presence of the three essential ingredients of suicide, elevated perturbation, unusual constriction, and high lethality—then the igniting spark has been added, and the active suicidal scenario has begun.

III. The Common Stimulus in Suicide Is Intolerable Psychological Pain

If cessation is what the suicidal person is moving toward, then pain is what that person is seeking to escape. In any close analysis, suicide is best understood as a combined movement toward cessation and a movement away from intolerable emotion, unendurable pain, and unacceptable anguish. No one commits suicide out of joy; no suicide is born out of exaltation. The enemy to life is pain. This is a psychological pain, a metapain, or the pain of feeling pain. Suicide is a human response to psychological pain. The clinical rule is: Reduce the level of suffering, often just a little bit, and the individual can choose to live.

IV. The Common Stressor in Suicide Is Frustrated Psychological Needs

Suicide is best understood not so much as an unreasonable act—every suicide seems logical to the person who commits it given that person's major premises, styles of syllogizing, and constricted focus—as it is a reaction to frustrated psychological needs. A suicide is committed because of thwarted, blocked, or unfulfilled needs.

In order to understand suicide in this context, a much broader question must be asked: What purposes do most human acts in general intend to accomplish? The best answer to that question is that, in general, human acts are intended to satisfy a variety of human needs. There is no compelling a priori reason why a classification of suicidal acts might not parallel a classification of general human needs. Indeed, such a classification of needs exists. In Murray's (1938) list of human needs (e.g., the need for achievement, affiliation, autonomy, counteraction, defendance, harmavoidance, inviolacy, and succorance) is a ready-made, viable, useful taxonomy of suicidal behaviors. Most suicides represent combinations of various needs, so that a particular case of suicide might properly be subsumed under two or more different need categories.

There are many pointless deaths, but there is never a needless suicide. Address the frustrated needs of the person, and the suicide will not occur. The therapist's function is to help the patient in relation to the thwarted needs. Even a little bit of improvement can save a life. In general, the goal of psychotherapy is to increase the patient's psychological comfort. One way to perform this task is to focus on the thwarted needs. Questions such as "What is going on?" "Where do you hurt?" and "What would you like to have happen?" can be asked by a therapist who is helping a suicidal person.

V. The Common Emotion in Suicide Is Hopelessness–Helplessness

At the beginning of life the common emotion is probably random, general excitement. In the suicidal state it is a pervasive feeling of helplessness-hopelessness. Suicidal people feel that "There is nothing that I can do (except to commit suicide) and there is no one who can help me (with the pain that I am suffering)." I believe that this formulation permits suicidologists to withdraw somewhat gracefully from the rival assertions that either hostility, shame, guilt, or depression is the central emotion of them all.

In the 20th century, psychologists believed that hostility was the force that drove people to commit suicide. Stekel, in a speech at the 1910 meeting of the Psychoanalytic Society in Vienna, asserted that no person kills himself except as he fantasizes the death of another; therefore, suicide is essentially hostility directed toward the ambivalently viewed, introjected love object. One would plunge a knife into one's chest in order to expunge or kill the internalized homunculus of the loved–hated father or mother within, a phenomenon I once called murder in the 180th degree.

Today we suicidologists know that there are other deep basic emotions. The early psychoanalytic formulations are seen as a brilliant hypothesis but as more pyrotechnical than universal. But underlying all of these, and others that might be mentioned, is that emotion of active, impotent ennui, the feeling of hopelessness–helplessness.

VI. The Common Cognitive State in Suicide Is Ambivalence

One does not ordinarily think of Freud as a giant in the history of logic, but, in a way, he made as enormous an impact in extending the understanding of cognitive maneuvers as did Bacon, Mill, and Russell. Western logic is Aristotelian. Aristotle's logic is dichotomous; a term is either A or non-A and an inference is either true or false.

Freud realized that something can psychologically be both A and non-A. One can both love and hate the same person. It is an Aristotelian question to say Make up your mind! The response is that a person has two minds, at least. The prototypical suicidal state is one in which an individual cuts his or her throat, cries for help at the same time, and is genuine in both of these acts. This non-Aristotelian ambivalence is the common cognitive state in suicide: One feels that he or she has to do it and, simultaneously, yearns for rescue and intervention. No one univalently wishes to commit suicide. Individuals would be happy not to do it, if they didn't "have to."

It is more useful to discuss this all-too-human conflict in concrete and effective terms and to answer the cruel question, Why not let him or her commit suicide? by asking the practical counter-question: Why not reduce the level of a suicidal person's unbearable stress? In effect, why not be a good Samaritan and *do* some things, quite simple and inexpensive things, such as talking to some people, making some arrangements, contacting some agencies, and persuading some intransigent people in the suicidal person's behalf. The suicidal person's life can thereby be saved by the efforts of a benignant person, a helper, and a compassionate friend.

VII. The Common Perceptual State in Suicide Is Constriction

Suicide is not best understood as a psychosis, a neurosis, or a character disorder, but is much more accurately understood as a transient psychological constriction of affect and intellect. This constriction is a narrowing of the range of options usually available to that individual's consciousness when his or her mind is not panicked into the dichotomous thinking of a suicidal individual: either some total solution or cessation, "Caesar aut nihil," to quote from Binswanger's (1958) famous case of Ellen West.

The usual life-sustaining images of loved ones are not disregarded; much worse, these images are not even within the range of what is in the suicidal person's mind. A person who commits suicide turns his or her back on the past and declares that all memories are unreal. Any attempt at rescue or remediation has to deal from the first with the psychological constriction.

The fact that suicide is committed by individuals who are in a special constricted condition leads to the suggestion that no one should ever commit suicide while disturbed. It is not a thing to do while one is not in one's best mind. Never kill yourself when you are suicidal. It takes a mind capable of scanning a range of options greater than two to make a decision as important as taking one's life. Dichotomous slogans such "Death Before Dishonor," "Live Free or Die," "Give Me Liberty or Give Me

Death," or "Better Dead than Red" all have some patriotic appeal, but they are not sensible or wide-ranged enough to be prescriptions for making it through life.

It is vital to counter the suicidal person's constriction of thought by attempting to widen the mental blinders and to increase the number of options, certainly beyond the two options of either having some magical resolution or being dead. An example may be useful. A teenage college student, who was demure, rather elegant, and somewhat wealthy, was encouraged to come to see me. She was single, pregnant, and suicidal, with a formed suicide plan. Her challenge to me was that I had somehow magically to arrange for her to be the way she was before she became pregnant (virginal, in fact) or she would have to commit suicide. Her being pregnant was such a mortal shame to her, that, combined with strong feelings of rage and guilt, she simply could not bear to live. At that moment suicide was the *only* option for her.

I did several things. I took out a sheet of paper and began to widen her blinders. I said something like, "Now, let's see: You could have an abortion here locally." She responded, "I couldn't do that." (It is precisely terms such as *can't, won't, have to, never, always,* and *only* that are negotiated in psychotherapy.) I continued, "You could go away and have an abortion." "I couldn't do that." "You could bring the baby to term and keep the baby." "I couldn't do that." "You could have the baby and adopt it out." Further options were similarly dismissed. When I said, "You can always commit suicide, but there is obviously no need to do that today," there was no response. "Now," I said. "Let's look at this list and rank them in order of your preference, keeping in mind that none of them is optimal."

My nonjudgmental approach in making this list already had a calming effect on her. Within a few minutes her lethality had begun to de-escalate. She actually rank-ordered the list, commenting negatively on each item. What was of critical importance was that suicide was now no longer ranked first or second. We were then simply "haggling" about life, a perfectly viable solution.

The point is not how the issue was eventually resolved or what interpretations were made as to why she permitted herself to become pregnant or about other aspects of her relationships with men. What is important is that it was possible to achieve the assignment of that day: to lower her lethality by reducing her perturbation, by widening her range of logical and realistic options from only the choice between suicide and one other untenable choice to a wider range of possibilities.

In addition, it is important to keep in mind that there is a latent syllogism in every suicide. In working with a suicidal person, it is vital not to accept his or her major premise. However, one should not argue or dispute the premise directly. Just as one does not collude with a suicidal person in fact, one should not collude with a suicidal person in thought and logic.

VIII. The Common Action in Suicide Is Egression

Egression is a person's intended departure from a region of distress. Suicide is the ultimate egression, beside which running away from home, quitting a job, deserting an army, or leaving a spouse are relatively pale actions. Goffman spoke of "unpluggings": having a good read, darting into a movie, or going for a weekend to Las Vegas or Atlantic City, which are benign egressions. But psychologists must distinguish between one's wish to get away and the need to end the distress forever. The point of suicide is a radical and permanent change of scene; the action to effect it is to leave.

In 1921, Violet Keppel Trefusis wrote to her lover Vita Sackville-West, who was then in the eighth year of her bisexual marriage to Harold Nicolson. "I am dead with grief. I am utterly alone. You cannot want me to suffer so. You had to choose between me and your family, and you have chosen them. I do not blame you. But you must not blame me if one day I seek for what escape I can find" (Nicolson, 1972, pp. 149–150).

That passage is an operational definition of what suicide is from the suicidal person's point of view: "what escape I can find." In that brief quotation from the letter, one can see intimations of several common characteristics of suicide: the wish for cessation, the need to stop pain, the sense of hopelessness, the presence of constriction, and the search for escape, as well as the communication of the intent.

IX. The Common Interpersonal Act in Suicide Is Communication of Intention

One of the most interesting findings from large numbers of psychological autopsies of unequivocal suicidal deaths was that there were clues to the impending lethal event in approximately 80% of the cases studied, (Shneidman, Farberow, & Leonard, 1961). Individuals intent on committing suicide consciously or unconsciously emit signals of distress and pleas for response, in the usually dyadic interplay that is an integral part of the suicidal drama. It is sad and paradoxical to note that the common interpersonal act of suicide is not hostility, rage, destruction, withdrawal, or depression, but communication of intention.

Suicidologists now know the usual verbal and behavioral clues (see Shneidman, 1965). The verbal statements are tantamount to saying, "I am going away" (i.e., egression), "You won't be seeing me," "I cannot endure the pain any longer"; the behavioral signs are such unusual acts as putting affairs in order, giving away prized possessions, and, more generally, behaving in ways that are different from one's usual behaviors.

The communication of suicidal intention is not always a cry for help. First, it is not always a cry; it can be a shout, a murmur, or silence. Second, it is not always for help; it can be for autonomy, inviolacy, or any of a number of other needs. Nonetheless, in most cases of suicide, the common penultimate act is some interpersonal communicative exchange related to that intended final act.

X. The Common Consistency in Suicide Is With Life-long Coping Patterns

People who are dying over weeks or months of a disease (e.g., cancer), are very much themselves, even exaggerations of their normal selves. Contrary to some notions currently popular in paperback thanatology, there is not any standard set of stages in the dying process through which individuals are marched, lock-step, to their deaths (Shneidman, 1973a). In terms of emotions displayed (rage, acceptance, etc.) or mechanisms of psychological defense manifested (projection, denial, etc.), such persons exhibit a full panoply of both of these, arranged in almost every conceivable number and order. What one does see in almost every case, I believe, are certain patterns: displays of emotion and uses of defense mechanisms that are consistent with *that* individual's microtemporal, mesotemporal, and macrotemporal reactions to pain, threat, failure, powerlessness, and duress in earlier episodes of his or her life. People who are dying are emotionally enormously consistent with themselves. So are suicidal people.

Suicide is an act, by definition, that the individual has never done before, so there is no precedent. Yet there are some consistencies with life-long coping patterns. One must look to previous episodes of disturbance, to the capacity to endure psychological pain, and to the penchant for constriction and dichotomous thinking for earlier paradigms of egression. Examples would lie in the details and nuances of how the individual handled such traumas as quitting a job or getting a divorce.

I speak with a sense of conviction that flows from some data I examined (Shneidman, 1971). I studied a group of men who were about 55 years old, each of whom had been studied rather intensively on a continual basis since they were about 6 years old (i.e., the well-known Terman longitudinal study of the gifted, begun in 1920, with 1,528 young men and women and continuing to this date at Stanford University under the direction of Professor Sears). In my study, other than the demonstration that it was possible in a blind study (beyond chance expectation) to select the 5 subjects who had committed suicide from a group of 30 cases, the main finding was that, working from a detailed life-chart that I constructed for each individual, the determination of whether or not the person would commit suicide at around age 55 could be made before the 30th birthday in each man's life. There were already certain psychological consistencies within the person's life (i.e., certain characteristics or habitual patterns of reactions for that person to threat, pain, pressure, and failure) that made dire predictions of a tragic suicidal outcome at 55 an almost straightforward psychological extrapolation from the earlier years.

In light of the enormous unpredictability of life, what impresses and excites me as a psychologist is how much of a person's life, in some of its more important aspects, is reasonably predictable. I feel this way about suicide. It is enormously complicated, but it is not totally random, and it is amenable to some prediction. That is my main approach to prevention.

Cubic Model of Suicide

What are some of the implications of this approach for a possible overarching theoretical model of suicide into which data on a large range of variables might be placed to build an empirical science of suicidology? Briefly, I shall attempt to outline a proposal.

Imagine a cube made up of 125 cubelets, with 25 cubelets on each plane, and 5 cubelets in each row and each column. As we look at the cube, we see three planes, each with 25 small squares. I call these three factors or components of this model *press, pain,* and *perturbation* (see Figure 1).

Murray (1938) might have had the word *pressure* in mind when he decided to use the word *press* to represent those aspects of the inner and outer world, or environment, that move, touch, impinge on, or affect an individual and make a difference. Press refers to the events done to the individual to which he or she reacts. There is positive press (e.g., good genes and happy fortune) and negative press (e.g., conditions and events that perturb, stress, threaten, or harm the individual). It is the latter—even success is negative if it is threatening—that are relevant to suicide. Press includes both actual and imagined events. There are all sorts of negative press: belittlement by an insult, being rejected or humiliated, a real or imagined slight, the loss of a loved one, real or magnified failure, a diagnosed cancer, powerlessness, humiliation, loss of control, poverty, bigotry, oppression, or persecution. But I am referring to the press that comes as the mind mediates, exaggerates, or even imagines the negative press that it perceives or misperceives. In this cubic model, press ranges from positive (in the back row of the top plane) to negative, in the front row of the top plane.

Pain refers to psychological pain resulting from thwarted psychological needs. Pain is the front plane of the cube. The left column of cubelets represents little or no pain; the next column over, some bearable pain, and so on up, until the right column represents intolerable psychological pain.

Murray's (1938) list of psychological needs includes the following, which are especially relevant in suicide: the needs for achievement, autonomy, recognition, succorance, and avoidance of humiliation, shame,

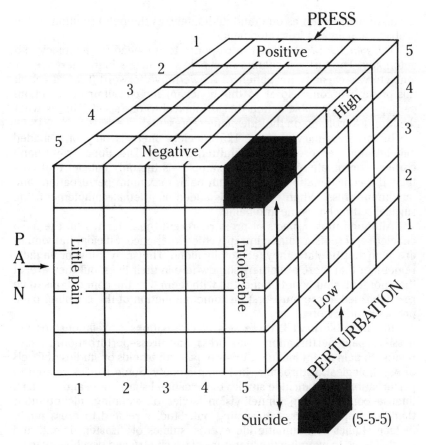

Figure 1. A theoretical cubic model of suicide.

and pain. Redress the thwarted needs of a suicidal person and the willingness to live resurges.

Perturbation, arbitrarily assigned to the side plane of the large cube, is a general term meaning the state of being perturbed or upset. Perturbation, ranked on a nine-point rating scale, includes everything in DSM-III. In relation to suicide, perturbation includes, especially, constriction and the self-harming penchant for precipitous or ill-advised action. *Constriction* is the reduction of the individual's perceptual and cognitive range. At its worst, the individual cuts the viable options down to two, then to one; there is dichotomous thinking. On this plane, the bottom row reflects open-mindedness, wide mentational scope, and clear syllogistic and non-syllogistic reasoning. The top row reflects constriction of thought, tunnel vision, and a narrowing of focus to one or two options, with cessation, death, and egression as one (and, ultimately, as the only) solution to the problem of pain and frustrated needs.

The *penchant for action* is a response to the need for inviolacy and autonomy. The furthest column of cubelets reflects a high tolerance for ambiguity, a capacity for patience. As we move forward (toward us) on this plane, we come closer to this penchant for consummatory action, perhaps an irreversible action that is inimical to one's self. That is what the foremost column on the side plane represents.

In this imaginary cube of 125 cubelets, there is only one shaded cubelet that represents a committed suicide. The upper right-hand corner—coordinates 5-5-5 in this example—is the only cubelet that contains the concatenation of maximum pain, maximum perturbation, and maximum press. When egression is added as a lethal complement, the suicidal setting has come into being.

Although most aspects of press represent the outer world, the 5-5-5 cubelet represents a totally intrapsychic experience. Suicidal individuals are in an autistic state; they feel totally alone. They may know or vaguely remember that there are others somewhere in their lives, but they are, at that moment, simply not connected with them. For the connections to be re-established, there must first be some diminution of the crippling pain, press, or constriction.

In this cubic model, three sets of correlations or relationships are possible: pain–perturbation, pain–press, and press–perturbation. Studies related to pain might include studies of pain thresholds or studies of levels of psychological disturbance, including anxiety. Some studies related to perturbation might include studies of perceptual sharpeners and levelers, intense concentration, tunnel vision, styles of scanning, dichotomous thinking, impulsiveness, and acting out. Studies related to press might include studies of traumatic life events, studies of disaster, defeat, and death. I hope to examine the literature of psychiatry and psychology (e.g., sensation, perception, emotion, learning, and personality) to find non-suicide studies that have related one of these aspects with another and then ponder the possible implications of those *general* findings for this suicide model. Of course, I invite others to do the same.

These three aspects of suicide—press, pain, and perturbation—are closely interconnected. One can address either the topic of suicide or an individual case of suicide by beginning with any of the three planes of the cubic model. Conceptually, the three separate aspects are, in some ways, synonymous with each other. For instance, pain grows out of perturbation, perturbation makes for pain, there is neither pain nor perturbation without negative press, and some negative press grows out of perturbation. One can come in on the concatenating suicidal drama during any one of its three linked acts. Even so, I believe the central feature of suicide is pain, and the key to suicide prevention lies in the reduction of that individual's psychological pain. All else—demographic variables, family history, previous suicidal history—is peripheral except as those factors bear on the presently felt pain. Ultimately, suicide occurs when there is the co-existence of intolerable pain, intense negative press, and extreme perturbation with perceptual constriction and an irresistable penchant for life-ending action. It is the future task of a scientific suicidology to explicate—with empirical studies on intrapsychic variables (thoughts, feelings, bodily sensations), on interpersonal aspects, and on situational stressors—the several cubelets of this larger model. The goal is to stitch suicide into the body of academic psychology—perception, memory, cognition, conation, emotion, motivation, and consciousness.

Treatment Implications

One can hardly fail to infer the implications for treatment in the real life-and-death situation of a suicidal crisis. They follow logically from the explication of the suicidal state of mind. Thus, psychologically speaking, the simply stated prescriptions are (a) reduce the hurt, (b) lift the blinders, (c) pull back from action, and (d) lighten the pressure, even just a little bit. (Get the person out of the 5-5-5 cubelet.) Any of these actions can save a life. In terms of this model, that is how suicide is prevented. The underlying rule is: Lower the pain, perturbation, and press, and the lethality will decrease with it.

Following this model, some questions for potential suicide prevention would include: Where do you hurt? What is going on? What do you feel that you have to solve or get out of? Do you have any formed plans to do anything harmful to yourself and what might you do? What would it take (to keep you alive)? Have you ever been in a situation similar to this before, what did you do, what happened, and how was it resolved? The next step is to state (not in a question, because the suicidally constricted mind usually cannot formulate an answer), Let me help you generate more possibilities, to re-think (and re-state) the problem and then look at possible courses of action other than the only one that you have in mind; although these new ideas might not totally solve the problem the way you had conceptualized it, they will provide some solution that you can live with.

For example, a university senior who made straight A's for three and a half years received a B and was determined to kill himself. Friends around him pointed out to him that he still had a 3.98 grade point average. That did not "cut the ice." They were attempting to dissuade him by talking about grades. That was on the phenotypic level and missed the genotypic point. He could have been better addressed by saying, "I understand your anguish, your need for a perfect performance, this blemish on your academic record, and your problem." His problem, like a man who committed suicide after having lost the tip of a finger in an industrial accident, was how to live with a lack of perfection. His pain, perturbation, and press all related to the push of his inner standards, which, at this point, threatened his life. A high suicidal state indicates that the time has come, unfortunately, that the standards themselves must be touched. Simply put, the rule is: Change the *aufgabe* a little bit, and the pain and press will then, hopefully, be redefined. Then the perturbation—which drives the lethality—will be reduced, and the person can live.

Suicide (in Melville's terms) is much more like a damp and dismal November of the mind than it is like an earthquake in the brain. Earthquakes are manifestations of the inexorable forces of nature. But with suicide, "human nature" and potential victims are one and the same. Both the etiology and the remediation are intrapsychic, interpersonal, and sociocultural.

There is no suicide (except possibly jumping) that does not involve the hand. In a figurative sense, suicide is always held within the hand of the individual (which is our way of saying it is within the mind). But also, in this figurative way, the prevention of a suicide is clearly in the hands of others. But I am talking not only of helping hands but also of alert minds that are attuned to signals of lethally oriented distress in a fellow human being.

Suicide and Public Policy

These reflections about suicide and public policy are not necessarily dependent on my theoretical model for suicide. In them, I have followed the lead of Zimmerman in her writings on family policy (in press). Four hypotheses are presented:

1. The more identifiable the risk, the more targeted will be the public response to relieve it. It follows that suicidologists have a clear responsibility to identify, delineate, and disseminate the common clues to suicide in understandable language.

2. The more organized and intense the political activity on behalf of potential victims, the more likely public policy will concern itself with that general problem. Therefore, it makes good tactical sense for us to focus on perhaps the most dramatic and tragic of all suicides (as a group), which is suicide among the young.

3. The more elevated the status of the potential victims, the more intense will be the public policy response, and vice versa. Society is not egalitarian about death; people mourn the death of a talented, beautiful, or young person more than his or her converse. Therefore, there is a strategic point to an emphasis on youth suicide prevention.

4. The more congruent the prevention strategies are with current political and policy trends, the more active will be the public response on that topic. In this connection, suicidologists must keep in mind the cold and sobering socioeconomic fact that more liberal federal leadership

Table 2
Interstate Rankings, Per Capita, for Suicide and
Public Welfare Expenditures

State	Suicide	Welfare Expenditures	State	Suicide	Welfare Expenditures
Alabama	11	21	Montana	43	17
Alaska	26	46	Nebraska	9	8
Arizona	47	1	Nevada	50	4
Arkansas	23	20	New Hampshire	19	33
California	42	45	New Jersey	3	37
Colorado	45	18	New Mexico	49	10
Connecticut	2	38	New York	1	50
Delaware	30	27	North Carolina	34	15
Florida	46	2	North Dakota	12	19
Georgia	33	12	Ohio	22	28
Hawaii	7	42	Oklahoma	40	32
Idaho	39	9	Oregon	41	31
Illinois	6	39	Pennsylvania	13	41
Indiana	15	7	Rhode Island	14	49
Iowa	10	35	South Carolina	16	6
Kansas	18	26	South Dakota	37	23
Kentucky	36	29	Tennessee	29	13
Louisiana	28	24	Texas	25	5
Maine	32	40	Utah	31	11
Maryland	8	30	Vermont	44	34
Massachusetts	5	48	Virginia	38	22
Michigan	24	47	Washington	35	36
Minnesota	17	43	West Virginia	20	14
Mississippi	4	25	Wisconsin	27	44
Missouri	21	16	Wyoming	48	3

Note. Reprinted from Zimmerman (in press) by permission. 1 is lowest; 50 is highest. An inverse relation between public welfare expenditures and suicide (−.44) was found, significant at the .001 level of confidence.

tends, in general, to tolerate and support sociological and psychological approaches to what are called social problems (a category in which suicide is generally included); whereas, conversely, more conservative federal leadership tends to support—albeit at a noticeably reduced level—nonpsychological approaches, specifically in the case of suicide, biological, and medical solutions.

There are solid empirical data on this topic. Zimmerman (in press), in a systematic survey of the United States, using 1980 and 1982 data, correlated the amounts of expenditures for education and public welfare programs with suicide rates and teenage birth rates, state by state (see Table 2). Zimmerman demonstrated a statistically significant negative correlation between per capita state public welfare expenditures and suicide rates. The lower the expenditure for public welfare within the state, the higher the suicide rate; the more generous the expenditure, the lower the rate. I cannot see why this finding from state to state is not true for the national government. To quote the unpublished research report: "One way or another we all must pay. Either we pay to invest in people and thereby make life better for everyone, *or* we pay for our neglect of them through suicide and the personal and social tragedy that that implies . . . [so that] public welfare services might well be considered a measure of a society's connection with and commitment to its people." To this I would add that it is past the time for the present administration to start earning higher marks. One can talk endlessly about suicide prevention, but what is needed is more than a modicum of federal support to effect a significant reduction in suicidal deaths.

The single most haunting question on the topic of public policy and suicide prevention is contained in Pogo's immortal query: "What if we met the enemy and it is us?" What if we are suffering casualties among our own people that stem from our own derelictions and our own misguided priorities. In this regard, we currently seem to be practicing, to paraphrase William James, the immoral equivalent of shameful surrender.

I wish I could conclude on a positive note, but the larger, long-range prospects do not give me reasons for optimism. What comes to mind is Murray's statement about the straits of the world 30 years ago in his essay "This I Believe" (1953/1981). I paraphrase from it: Present conditions however are so extremely unfavorable to an elevating advance of a desired scale and scope that we would be well advised to prepare our sinews for a long and protracted era of fierce neglect and its resultant anguish until our priorities are sensibly redressed and our eyes opened. As Melville said in that great suicidal book, *Moby-Dick*, "Oh, Time, Strength, Cash, and Patience."

References

Aaron, D. (Ed.). (1985). *The Inman diary* (Vols. 1–2). Cambridge, MA: Harvard University Press.

Alvarez, A. (1971). *The savage god.* New York: Random House.

Asberg, M., Nordstrom, P., & Traskman-Bendz, L. (1986). Biological factors in suicide. In A. Roy (Ed.), *Suicide* (pp. 47–71). Baltimore, MD: Williams & Wilkins.

Auerback, S. M., & Kilmann, P. R. (1977). Crisis intervention: A review of outcome research. *Psychological Bulletin, 84,* 1189–1217.

Battin, M. P. (1982). *Ethical issues in suicide.* Englewood Cliffs, NJ: Prentice-Hall.

Battin, M. P., & Maris, R. (Eds.). (1983). Special issues: Suicide and ethics. *Suicide and Life-Threatening Behavior, 13,* 7–129.

Battin, M. P., & Mayo, D. J. (Eds.). (1980). *Suicide: The philosophical issues.* New York: St. Martin's Press.

Bertalanffy, L. (1969). *General systems theory.* New York: Braziller.

Binswanger, L. (1958). The case of Ellen West. In R. May (Ed.), *Existence* (pp. 294–295). New York: Basic Books.

Blaker, K. P. (1972). Systems theory and self-destructive behavior: A new theoretical base. *Perspectives in Psychiatric Care, 10,* 168–172.

Cassedy, J. H. (1961). *Demography in early America.* Cambridge, MA: Harvard University Press.

Choron, J. (1972). *Suicide.* New York: Scribner's.

Cutter, F. (1983). *Art and the wish to die.* Chicago: Nelson-Hall.

deCatanzaro, D. (1981). *Suicide and self-damaging behavior: A sociobiological perspective.* New York: Academic Press.

Douglas, J. D. (1967). *The social meaning of suicide.* Princeton, NJ: Princeton University Press.

Durkheim, E. (1951). *Suicide.* Glencoe, IL: Free Press. (Original work published 1897)

Engelhardt, H. T., Jr., & Malloy, M. (1982). Suicide and assisting suicide: A critique of legal sanctions. *Southwestern Law Journal, 36,* 1003–1037.

Fowles, J. (1964). *The aristos.* Boston: Little, Brown.

Friedman, P. (1967). *On suicide.* New York: International Universities Press.

Gibbs, J. P., & Martin, W. T. (1964). *Status integration and suicide.* Eugene, OR: University of Oregon Press.

Guernesy, R. S. (1963). *Suicide: A history of the penal laws in reflection to it and their legal, social, moral, and religious aspects in ancient and modern times.* New York: Strouse. (Original work published 1883)

Hendin, H. (1964). *Suicide in Scandinavia.* New York: Grune & Stratton.

Henry, A. F., & Short, J. F. (1954). *Homicide and suicide.* Glencoe, IL: Free Press.

Holinger, P. C., & Offer, D. (1986, May). *Sociodemographic, epidemiologic and individual attributes [of youth suicides].* Paper presented at the Department of Health and Human Services Task Force on Youth Suicide. Bethesda, MD.

Iga, M. (1986). *The thorn in the chrysanthemum: Suicide and economic success in modern Japan.* Berkeley and Los Angeles: University of California Press.

Kety, S. S. (1986). Genetic factors in suicide. In A. Roy (Ed.), *Suicide.* Baltimore, MD: Williams & Wilkins.

Lester, D., Sell, B. H., & Sell, K. D. (1980). *Suicide: A guide to information sources.* Detroit: Gale Research Company.

Lifton, R. J. (1979). *The broken connection.* New York: Harper & Row.

Litman, R. E. (1967). Sigmund Freud on suicide. In E. S. Shneidman (Ed.), *Essays in self-destruction.* New York: Science House.

Litman, R. E., Curphey, T. J., Shneidman, E. S., Farberow, N. L., & Tabachnick, N. D. (1963). Investigations of equivocal studies. *Journal of the American Medical Association, 184,* 924–929.

Maris, R. (1981). *Pathways to suicide.* Baltimore, MD: Johns Hopkins University Press.

Maris, R. (Ed.). (1986). *Biology of suicide.* New York: Guilford Press.

Menninger, K. (1938). *Man against himself.* New York: Harcourt, Brace.

Menninger, K. (1983). The suicidal intention of nuclear armament. *Bulletin of the Menninger Clinic, 47*(4), 325–353.

Miles, C. P. (1977). Conditions predisposing to suicide: A review. *Journal of Nervous and Mental Disease, 164,* 231–246.

Miller, J. G. (1978). *Living systems*. New York: McGraw-Hill.

Murray, H. A. (1938). *Explorations in personality*. New York: Oxford University Press.

Murray, H. A. (1948). A conception of personality. In C. Kluckhohn & H. A. Murray (Eds.), *Personality in nature, society, and culture*. New York: Knopf.

Murray, H. A. (1981). This I believe. In E. S. Shneidman (Ed.), *Endeavors in psychology: Selections from the personology of Henry A. Murray*. New York: Harper & Row. (Original work published 1953)

National Center for Health Statistics. (1986). Advance report of final mortality statistics, 1984. *NCHS Monthly Vital Statistics Report, 35* (Suppl. 2), 6.

Nicolson, N. (1972). *Portrait of a marriage*. New York: Atheneum.

Peck, M. L., Farberow, N. L., & Litman, R. E. (1985). *Youth suicide*. New York: Springer Publishing.

Pepper, S. (1942). *World hypothesis*. Berkeley and Los Angeles: University of California Press.

Pfeffer, C. (1986). *The suicidal child*. New York: Guilford Press.

Reynolds, P. (1987, March). Imposing a corporate structure. *Psychology Today*, pp. 33–38.

Rosenblatt, P. C. (1983). *Bitter, bitter tears: Nineteenth-century diarists and twentieth-century grief theories*. Minneapolis: University of Minnesota Press.

Roy, A. (1986a). Genetic factors in suicide. *Psychopharmacology Bulletin, 22*, 666–668.

Roy, A. (1986b, May 8). *Genetics and suicidal behavior*. Paper presented at HHS Task Force on Youth Suicide, National Institute of Mental Health, Bethesda, MD.

Seiden, R. H. (1969). *Suicide among youth: A review of the literature, 1900–1967* (Suppl. to the *Bulletin of Suicidology*). (PHS Publication No. 1971) Washington, DC: U.S. Government Printing Office.

Shaffer, T. (1976). Legal views of suicide. In E. S. Shneidman (Ed.), *Suicide: Contemporary developments* (pp. 404–419). New York: Grune & Stratton.

Shneidman, E. S. (1965). Preventing suicide. *American Journal of Nursing, 65*(5), 111–116.

Shneidman, E. S. (1969). Suicide, lethality and the psychological autopsy. In E. S. Shneidman & M. Ortega (Eds.), *Aspects of depression* (pp. 225–250). Boston: Little, Brown.

Shneidman, E. S. (1981). Suicide among the gifted. In E. S. Shneidman (Ed.), *Suicide thoughts and reflections, 1960–1980* (pp. 62–89). New York: Human Sciences Press. (Reprinted from Perturbation and lethality as precursors of suicide in a gifted group. *Life-Threatening Behavior, 1*, 23–45)

Shneidman, E. S. (1973a). *Deaths of man*. New York: Quadrangle/New York Times Books.

Shneidman, E. S. (1973b). Suicide. In *Encyclopaedia Britannica*. Chicago: William Benton.

Shneidman, E. S. (Ed.). (1976). *Suicidology: Contemporary developments*. New York: Grune & Stratton.

Shneidman, E. S. (1977). The psychological autopsy. In L. I. Gottschalk (Ed.), *Guide to the investigation and reporting of drug abuse death* (pp. 42–56). Washington, DC: U.S. Government Printing Office.

Shneidman, E. S. (1980). *Voices of death*. New York: Harper & Row.

Shneidman, E. S. (1984). Suicide and suicide prevention. In R. J. Corsini & B. D. Ozaki (Eds.), *Encyclopedia of psychology* (Vol. 3, pp. 383–386). New York: Wiley.

Shneidman, E. S. (1985). *Definition of suicide.* New York: Wiley.

Shneidman, E. S., Farberow, N. L., & Leonard, C. (1961). *Some facts about suicide: Causes and prevention.* Bethesda, MD: National Institute of Mental Health. (Publication No. 852)

Shneidman, E. S., Farberow, N. L., & Litman, R. E. (1970). *Psychology of suicide.* New York: Science House.

Silving, H. (1957). Suicide and law. In E. S. Shneidman & N. L. Farberow (Eds.), *Clues to suicide* (pp. 79–95). New York: McGraw-Hill.

Tyler, L. (1984). *Thinking creatively.* San Francisco: Jossey-Bass.

Victoroff, V. M. (1983). *The suicidal patient: Recognition, intervention, management.* Oradell, NJ: Medical Economic Books.

Weisman, A. D., & Kastenbaum, R. (1968). *The psychological autopsy: A study of the terminal phase of life.* New York: Behavioral Publications. (*Community Mental Health Journal* Monograph No. 4)

Williams, G. (Ed.). (1957). *The sanctity of life and the criminal law.* New York: Knopf.

Zilboorg, G. (1937). Considerations on suicide, with particular reference to that of the young. *American Journal of Orthopsychiatry, 7,* 15–31.

Zimmerman, S. (in press). *Approaches to understanding family policy.* Beverly Hills, CA: Sage.

COPING WITH IRREVOCABLE LOSS

C amille B. Wortman was born in a small town outside Pittsburgh, Pennsylvania, in 1947. In 1969, she graduated summa cum laude from Duke University. While in Duke University's social psychology graduate program, she studied under Jack Brehm and Ned Jones. From 1972 to 1979, she taught at Northwestern University, where she won a Distinguished Teaching Award. She is currently a Professor of Psychology at the University of Michigan.

Wortman's major research interest concerns how people react to stressful life events. For the past 10 years, she has studied the predictors of long-term adjustment to a variety of life crises including acute and chronic illness, physical disability, criminal victimization, and loss of a loved one. She has conducted longitudinal, theory-based investigations to determine how such variables as attributions of causality, feelings of control or mastery, and the availability of social support influence the process of adaptation. In 1980, she was the recipient of the APA's Distinguished Scientific Award for an Early Career Contribution in Psychology for this work. Long-term goals of this research program include elaborating the theoretical mechanisms through which stress is defined by its deleterious effects on subsequent health and functioning.

During the past few years, Wortman has focused her attention on the area of bereavement and has recently completed two studies researching the grieving process. One study is a longitudinal investigation of how parents cope with the loss of an infant to the Sudden Infant Death Syndrome, and the second is a case-control study focusing on the long-term effects of the sudden, unexpected loss of one's spouse or child. She is also in the midst of a large-scale prospective longitudinal study of widowhood.

COPING WITH IRREVOCABLE LOSS

L oss is an inevitable part of life. In fact, as people grow older, losses become more frequent occurrences with which they must cope. As Judith Viorst expressed in her book *Necessary Losses* (1986), "We lose not only through death, but also by leaving and being left, by changing and letting go and moving on. . . . Our losses include not only our separations and departures from those we love, but our . . . losses of . . . dreams, impossible expectations, illusions of freedom and power, illusions of safety—and the loss of our own younger self" (p. 2). What do psychologists know about how people cope with such experiences? Active, goal-directed behavior, which is a common response to other stressful situations (cf. Lazarus & Folkman, 1984), is of little use in coping with permanent loss. Clearly, even superb coping abilities cannot alter the finality of aging or death. In fact, the major coping task faced by individuals who encounter such events is to reconcile themselves to a situation that cannot be changed and over which they have little, if any, control.

Camille B. Wortman presented a Master Lecture at the 1986 APA Convention. The lecture was based on this paper, which she wrote in collaboration with her colleague, Roxane Cohen Silver, PhD, from the University of Waterloo, Ontario, Canada.

The research in this paper was supported by USPHS Grant MCR-260470 to both authors, by National Science Foundation Grant BNS78-04743, by National Institute of Aging program project grant A605561, and by a grant from the Insurance Institute for Highway Safety to Camille B. Wortman.

Irrevocable losses provide an excellent arena in which to study basic processes of stress and adaptation to change. In fact, irrevocable losses such as death and physical disability share a number of characteristics that make them particularly interesting to study. Permanent losses often disrupt plans, hopes, and dreams for the future, at least temporarily (cf. Silver & Wortman, 1980). Such losses also challenge individuals' beliefs and assumptions about themselves and their world (see Janoff-Bulman & Frieze, 1983; Wortman, 1983).

In an attempt to advance theoretical development in the rich and complex area of irrevocable losses, in this chapter we will update and expand on our earlier review on reactions to undesirable life events (Silver & Wortman, 1980). This time we will focus on irrevocable loss in particular. Because reactions to bereavement and permanent disability are the most carefully studied examples of how people adapt to loss, we will focus on these two areas. In the sections to follow we begin with a brief review of the theoretical formulations that have been most influential in these areas. Drawing from these theories, and from the literature on grief and loss, we will consider how individuals are assumed to cope with such events. Taken together, theories of loss and clinical lore paint a strong and consistent picture about how individuals should cope following loss. We will identify what we believe are the most prevalent assumptions about what constitutes a normal response to loss. In each case, we will evaluate the validity of the assumption by presenting data recently collected from our own program of research, as well as data from other researchers in the area. In the final sections of the chapter, we will explore the implications of the data we present for further theoretical development, as well as for intervention with those who have endured loss.

Past Theoretical Approaches on Reactions to Irrevocable Loss

Several different kinds of theoretical formulations have been advanced to explain how people react to loss (see Bowlby, 1980; Osterweis, Solomon, & Green, 1984; and Raphael, 1983, for reviews).[1] One of the most influential approaches to loss has been the classical psychoanalytic model of bereavement, which is based on the work of Freud in "Mourning and Melancholia" (1917/1957). Freud maintained that the major task of

---

[1] In this chapter, we have chosen to focus on the classic psychodynamic model, on Bowlby's (1980) attachment model, and on stage models of emotional reaction to loss, because we believe that these approaches have been the most influential in shaping people's assumptions about coping with loss. Of course, many other types of models have been applied to the study of bereavement, including crisis models, illness and disease models, and the stress and coping approach (for reviews, see Kessler, Price, & Wortman, 1985; Osterweis et al., 1984; Raphael, 1983).

mourning was the gradual surrender of psychological attachment to the deceased. Freud believed that relinquishment of the love object involves an internal struggle, because the individual experiences intense yearning for the lost loved one yet is faced with the reality of the loved one's absence. This struggle is inevitably painful and involves turbulent emotions. Initially, the individual may deny that the loss has occurred, become preoccupied with thoughts of the deceased, and lose interest in the outside world. As thoughts and memories are reviewed, ties to the deceased person are gradually withdrawn. At the conclusion of the mourning period, the bereaved is said to have worked through the loss and to have freed him- or herself from an intense attachment to an unavailable person. When the process has been completed, according to Freud, the bereaved person regains sufficient emotional energy to invest in new relationships.

It was Freud who first advanced the idea that many psychiatric illnesses are expressions of pathological mourning. Freud argued that one of the most important preconditions leading to depression following bereavement was an "ambivalent" relationship with the deceased prior to death. Freud and his followers attributed a great deal of pathogenic significance to the early loss of a parent or to unhappy experiences during the early years of life. These theorists maintained that as a result of early loss experiences, some individuals become predisposed to form anxious and ambivalent attachments with others. Such individuals are thought to be extremely vulnerable to losses that occur later in life (see Abraham, 1924/1953; Freud, 1917/1957; Klein, 1935, 1940; and see Bowlby, 1980, for a review).

A second theoretical orientation that has been extremely important in current conceptions of reactions to loss is the attachment model of grief originally developed by Bowlby (1961, 1973, 1980). In developing his formulation, Bowlby drew heavily from psychodynamic thought, from the developmental literature on young children's reactions to separation, and from work on the mourning behavior of animals. Bowlby maintained that during the course of normal development, individuals develop affectional bonds or attachments, initially between child and parent and later between adult and adult. He regarded attachment behaviors as instinctive. Bowlby maintained that when such bonds are threatened, powerful attachment behaviors are activated, such as clinging, crying, and angry protest. He argued that bereavement could be conceptualized as an unwilling separation that can give rise to many forms of attachment behavior. Unlike Freud, Bowlby suggested that the biological function of this behavior is not withdrawal from the lost object, but rather, reunion. In short, he argued that the separation anxiety, pining, and restlessness—the behavior patterns that bind a child to its mother and spouses to each other—are critically important features of grief.

Drawing in part from these theoretical ideas and in part from available research, Bowlby (1980) identified four phases of mourning. According to Bowlby, individuals initially go through a phase of numbness or feeling stunned. He maintained that this initial phase is followed by a phase of yearning and searching, in which the bereaved may show manifestations of a strong urge to find, recover, and reunite with the lost person. During this period, the individual may experience anger at the loss as well as general restlessness and irritability. Bowlby argued that, over time, those behaviors aimed at reestablishing the attachment bond usually cease, and individuals enter the third phase of the mourning process. According to Bowlby, this phase is characterized by giving up the attempts to recover the deceased. The bereaved person typically experiences depression and feels a disinclination to look to the future. Eventually, individuals enter the final phase, in which they are able to break down their attachment to the lost loved one and start to establish new ties to others. In this phase of reorganization or recovery, there is a gradual return of former interests.

Other Stage Models

In both the bereavement and the physical disability literatures, several different theorists have proposed models which, like Bowlby's model, involve phases or stages of reaction to loss (see Silver & Wortman, 1980, for a review). An influential stage model of reaction to bereavement has been advanced by Horowitz and his associates (see Horowitz, 1976, 1985; Horowitz & Kaltreider, 1980). Horowitz has maintained that initially following a loss, a person will appear stunned and unable to process its meaning, responding with what is termed *outcry*—or a sense of feeling, "Oh no, it cannot be true." However, Horowitz suggested a tension between denial and intrusion of painful thoughts regarding the loss. Denial is characterized by numbness, and intrusion is characterized by the working through of the painful reality. Horowitz suggested that over time, an individual will experience oscillating periods of denial and intrusion. The loss is denied until reality begins to break through, and then the person experiences a period of intrusion. When that becomes too painful, the person will shift to denial again. Over time, these cycles are assumed to become less intense as the person successfully copes with the loss.

In the area of physical disability, stage models of emotional response have been advanced by several investigators (e.g., Bray, 1978; Cohn, 1961; Gunther, 1969; Guttmann, 1976; Hohmann, 1975; Siller, 1969). One of the most influential of such models was developed by Shontz (1965, 1975), who hypothesized a cyclical pattern similar to the one proposed by Horowitz. Shontz's first stage, shock, is characterized by a feeling of detachment, followed by an encounter phase in which the individual begins to experience helplessness, disorganization, and panic. During this period, reality may seem overwhelming, and individuals begin to manifest a type of avoidance that Shontz labeled *retreat*. Over time, the individual breaks down his or her defenses slowly in an attempt to deal with the painful reality piece by piece. According to Shontz, the adaptive sequence in coping with loss is characterized by a continual shifting between encounter and retreat from crisis. Each time an individual begins to face reality, feelings of anxiety, frustration, and depression may reoccur. Such feelings, in fact, are seen as necessary precursors to positive psychological growth. Eventually, the cycles are assumed to occur with less frequency until adaptation is complete.

Stage models of emotional response have been proposed by theorists or clinicians for many other types of losses, including miscarriage (Zahourek & Jensen, 1973), rape (Sutherland & Scherl, 1979), loss of a limb (Parkes, 1972), and life-threatening illness (Gullo, Cherico, & Shadick, 1974; Nighswonger, 1971). Perhaps the most well known of such models is the one proposed by Kübler-Ross in her highly influential book, *On Death and Dying* (1969). Although offered to explain dying patients' reactions to their own impending death, Kübler-Ross identified five stages of emotional response to anticipated loss: denial, anger, bargaining, depression, and, ultimately, acceptance. Each year, Kübler-Ross's stage models have been taught, in her estimation, in 125,000 courses in colleges, seminaries, medical schools, hospitals, and social work institutions (Rosenbaum, 1982).

Over the past 2 decades, descriptions of stage models like Kübler-Ross's have also appeared in numerous textbooks and articles written for and by physicians, nurses, therapists, social workers, members of the clergy, and patients and their families (see Silver & Wortman, 1980, for a review). As a result, these models have become firmly entrenched among health care professionals. There is evidence that professionals sometimes use the stages as a kind of yardstick to assess progress and evaluate how a given individual is doing. For example, Pattison (1977) has reported that, as a result of the pervasive belief in Kübler-Ross's (1969) stages of dying, "dying persons who did not follow these stages were labeled 'deviant,' 'neurotic,' or 'pathological' diers. Clinical personnel became angry at patients who did not move from one stage to the next. . . . I began to observe professional personnel demand that the dying person 'die in the right way'" (p. 242).

As research has begun to accumulate, it has become clear that although stage models of response to loss are widely believed among health care professionals, there is little empirical evidence to support them (see Silver & Wortman, 1980, for a review). In fact, the Institute of Medicine, in a recently issued authoritative review of bereavement research, cautioned against the use of the word *stages*, noting that this "might lead people to expect the bereaved to proceed from one clearly identifiable reaction to another in a more orderly fashion than usually occurs. It might also result in . . . hasty assessments of where individuals are or ought to be in the grieving process" (Osterweis et al., 1984, p. 48). They concluded that although individuals do not go through discrete stages in an orderly fashion, grief can be understood as a series of overlapping clusters of reactions or phases over time. It was acknowledged that individuals differ in the specific manifestations of grief and in the speed with which they move through the process. Nonetheless, it was assumed in this report that virtually all individuals who experience an important loss go through the grief process, beginning with a phase of intense distress and followed by ultimate recovery over time as the person comes to terms with the loss. (See also Donovon & Girton, 1984, and Jette, 1983, for recent comparable views of the grief process.)

Assumptions About Reactions to Loss

There are notable differences in the models of reaction to loss that were reviewed in the previous section. Despite these differences, however, these models share some common assumptions about the process of coping with loss. As is discussed more fully in the following section, in these models it is assumed that when a major loss is experienced, a phase of distress or depression is inevitable. Although not explicitly discussed by the theorists, by focusing on distress, they suggest that positive emotions are relatively absent during the early period following loss. In these models, it is assumed that failure to experience depression or distress is indicative of pathology, and that those who go through a phase of depression will make a better adjustment to the loss than those who continue to deny or repress their feelings. It is further assumed in these models that over time, individuals work through their feelings about the loss and break down their attachments to the lost object. Finally, all of the models are based on the assumption that, in time, the person who has undergone loss will achieve a state of recovery and return to normal role functioning. These assumptions about the grief process are not only prevalent in the most influential theories in the area, but they are also espoused by health care professionals and are reflected in cultural beliefs about coping with loss (see Silver & Wortman, 1980).

In our judgment, gaining a full understanding of the assumptions that are held by those who come into contact with individuals who have encountered loss, and by these individuals themselves, is of the utmost importance. People's assumptions about the grieving process can affect how they respond to others who have endured loss. Consider the following examples, which are from our own data:

1. A man whose wife died 6 months earlier exhibited little distress and mentioned that he is ready for remarriage.

2. A woman whose child has died seemed to be enjoying herself with friends a few days after the funeral.

3. A woman who lost her baby 2 months ago confessed that she believes her child might actually return.

4. A woman whose husband has been dead for 4 years said she still talks over problems with him and tries to behave as he would want her to.

5. A man who lost his son 7 years earlier still found himself reviewing the events leading up to the loss.

Because of their assumptions, people may evaluate or judge these individuals as reacting abnormally or inappropriately to their loss. In fact, such individuals may harshly evaluate their own responses and believe them to be indicative of underlying problems or pathology.

Because of the probable role played by these assumptions in evaluating reactions to loss, it is important to identify those assumptions that are most prevalent in our culture and to consider systematically the available research data in support of each one. In the following section, we focus on seven assumptions that we believe to be most prevalent in the theoretical and empirical literature on grief and loss. In each case, we will examine how these assumptions fare against the empirical evidence on the topic. We will then describe how the assumptions people hold about the coping process may lead them to respond to those who have endured loss in ways that are unhelpful and may only add to their difficulties.

1. Distress or Depression Is Inevitable

In theoretical statements, as well as in our culture, it is widely assumed that when a major loss is experienced, the normal way to react is with intense distress or depression. Virtually all of the stage models described earlier are based on the assumption that, at some point, individuals will confront the reality of their loss and go through a period of intense distress or depression. In fact, there is thought to be a "near-universal occurrence of intense emotional distress following bereavement, with features similar in nature and intensity to those of clinical depression" (Osterweis et al., 1984, p. 18). Similarly, depression has been the foremost reaction reported and discussed in the literature on spinal cord injury (see Bracken & Shepard, 1980; Deegan, 1977; Gunther, 1971). For example, Knorr and Bull (1970), drawing from their clinical experience, maintained that all spinal cord injury patients experience a period of depression that lasts from 2 to 4 months.

As empirical evidence has begun to accumulate, however, it is clear that the assumption of intense universal distress following a major loss such as bereavement or spinal cord injury may be unwarranted. It is true that in the bereavement literature, some studies have reported that feelings of sadness or depressed mood are fairly common. For example, Glick, Weiss, and Parkes (1974) have noted that 88% of the widows in their study experienced depressed moods (see also Clayton, Halikas, & Maurice, 1971). However, in those investigations that have included a more systematic and rigorous assessment of depression or distress, it is clear that such a reaction is by no means universal. In one study, Clayton,

Halikas, and Maurice (1972) interviewed widows who had lost their spouses within the previous 30 days. Using strict diagnostic criteria to assess depression, these investigators were able to classify only a minority of respondents (35%) as definitely or probably depressed.

Using the General Health Questionnaire, a self-administered screening test used to detect nonpsychotic psychiatric disorders, Vachon, Rogers, et al. (1982) found that 1 month after the loss, 30% of the widows they studied scored below 5—a score considered insufficient to warrant further psychiatric assessment. Similarly, Lund, Caserta, and Dimond (1986) administered the Zung Self-Rating Depression Scale to a sample of primarily Mormon elderly bereaved individuals. They reported that, at 3 weeks after the loss, only 14.6% of the men and 19.2% of the women they studied had "at least mild" depression. Therefore, the majority of their respondents were not experiencing a significant level of distress at this time point. These investigators collected information from respondents at six different points in time, ranging from 3 to 4 weeks to 2 years after the loss. In fact, they reported that only between 12.5% and 20% of the participants they studied had depression scores exceeding the cut-off score delineated as indicating depression at any of the six time periods.

Examination of empirical data in the spinal cord injury literature reveals a similar pattern. For example, Howell, Fullerton, Harvey, and Klein (1981) conducted a careful assessment of 22 patients who had been injured during the previous 6 months. Each patient completed the Beck Depression Inventory (BDI) weekly, and those with elevated BDI scores were given the Schedule of Affective Disorders and Schizophrenia to assess depression. They found that a minority of patients (22.7%) experienced a depressive disorder at some point in the study. Fullerton, Harvey, Klein, and Howell (1981) expanded the sample of this study to 30 and similarly found that only a minority of patients experienced significant depression (about 30%). Frank et al. (in press) conducted a study with 32 spinal cord injury patients who were evaluated for depression using DSM-III (American Psychiatric Association, 1980) criteria. Less than half of the respondents (44%) met the criteria for a depressive episode.

Using a longitudinal approach, Lawson (1976) studied 10 patients 5 days a week for the entire length of their rehabilitative hospital stay. Using a multimethod assessment of depression, including self-report, professional ratings, a behavioral measure, and a psychoendocrine measure of urinary output, he found no clear period of at least a week in which the depression measures were consistently in the depressive range for any patient. Finally, Malec and Neimeyer (1983) administered the BDI to 28 spinal cord injury patients on admission to an inpatient rehabilitation program. They reported that 57% of the sample appeared to be not depressed (BDI scores of 0–9), 25% appeared to be experiencing mild depression (BDI scores of 10–20), and only 18% obtained scores suggesting moderate or moderately severe depression (BDI scores of 21–32).

Thus available research that has examined the issue systematically has failed to demonstrate the inevitability of depression following loss.

2. Positive Emotions Are Absent

An important assumption underlying the stage models reviewed earlier is that loss will be met with intense distress—be it anger, disorganization, or depression. Positive emotions, such as happiness, implicitly are assumed to be absent. Each of the theories described earlier focuses solely on negative emotions; none has considered the possibility that positive feelings may be present following loss.

While at Northwestern University in the 1970s, we had the opportunity to discuss the possible role that positive emotions might play in the coping process with Philip Brickman, who had written several papers on happiness (see Brickman, Coates, & Janoff-Bulman, 1978). As a result of these conversations, we began to wonder whether individuals might experience moments of happiness or joy relatively soon after experiencing a significant loss. If such positive emotions were experienced, we became curious about whether they could sustain hope, and perhaps facilitate adjustment, among individuals who had encountered loss. We conducted a review of the literature in order to examine the impact of positive emotions on the coping process, but with notable exceptions (e.g., Brickman et al., 1978; Lazarus, Kanner, & Folkman, 1980) few researchers had examined the issue.

We therefore decided to measure positive as well as negative emotions in a study on coping with spinal cord injury that we were planning at the time. In this study (Silver, 1982; and see Silver & Wortman, 1987, for a more detailed discussion), we conducted interviews with approximately 125 individuals from Northwestern Memorial Hospital who became physically disabled as a result of a sudden, traumatic accident. Interestingly, we encountered extreme resistance among the hospital staff, who felt it was "ridiculous" to ask respondents about positive emotions. In addition, our own interviewers were quite reluctant to question respondents about positive feelings. As one of our interviewers expressed it, "If you think I'm going to go in there and ask that quadriplegic how many times he's felt happy in the past week, you're crazy." It took considerable effort and some careful pilot work to convince the staff and our own interviewers that the project was feasible, ethical, and worthwhile.

Respondents were injured in many different kinds of accidents, including motor vehicle accidents, sporting accidents, falls, and violent crimes. The subjects also varied in terms of the severity and permanence of their injuries. Two-thirds of the respondents experienced injuries to the spinal cord, with approximately one-half of those suffering permanent loss of sensation and function and the other half sustaining injuries for which the outcome was unclear. The group that had spinal cord injuries was also composed of approximately equal numbers of paraplegics or quadriplegics. The final one-third of the sample had broken their backs but suffered no spinal cord injury. The majority of our respondents were between the ages of 21 and 25, approximately 80% of our respondents were men, and about 80% were White.

Subjects were interviewed 1, 3, and 8 weeks following their accidents. To measure affect, respondents were asked to report how often in the previous week they had experienced four different emotional states: anxiety, depression, anger, and happiness. As illustrated in Figure 1, positive emotions at all three time points were more predominant than had been anticipated. By the second time point, which was 3 weeks after the accident had occurred, subjects reported happiness more frequently than anxiety, depression, or anger. Surprisingly, there was no effect for severity or permanence of injury. Individuals who were quadriplegic were no less likely to report happiness than were individuals who would eventually go home with no permanent disability.

When asked what had triggered their feelings of happiness, subjects reported that the most common source of positive emotion was social contacts (see Silver & Wortman, 1987, for a more detailed discussion). For example, one respondent said, "I was surprised by some letters and calls I got from people who I thought wouldn't care." The second most common source of happiness was some sort of physical improvement. For example, one respondent indicated that it made him feel happy when the weights were taken off his head.

One obvious way of accounting for these data is to attribute them to denial. In order to shed some light on this issue, respondents were asked a number of questions about their future expectations concerning their physical limitations. Patients' expectations did become more realistic, that is, more in line with their actual prognosis, over the course of the study (Silver, 1982). Yet negative affect was highest at 1 week and decreased significantly over time. Because feelings of happiness did not coexist with unrealistic expectations, the happiness data do not appear to be merely a function of denial.

Although our respondents reported more happiness than we or others might have expected (Silver & Wortman, 1987), it is important to note that patients were not always cheerful following the accidents that left many permanently paralyzed. In fact, a few patients were quite distraught and mentioned thoughts of suicide in the interview. As shown in the frequency data in Figure 1, at 3 and 8 weeks after their accident, most respondents reported feeling happy "sometimes" during the previous week. In addition, compared to a normative sample of nondisabled individuals who were approximately the same age as the disabled group, patients reported significantly less happiness than the norms at 1 and 3 weeks postinjury. However, while the disabled sample was less happy than the normative sample at the interview at 8 weeks, they were not

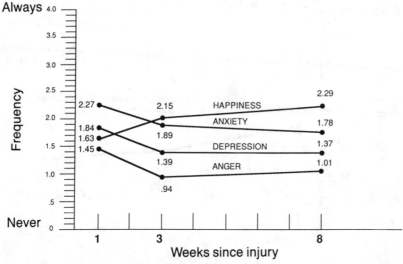

Figure 1. Frequency of positive and negative affect of a study sample of physically disabled persons. Adapted from Silver and Wortman (1987) by permission.

significantly so. Nonetheless, subjects appeared to experience happiness either as frequently or more frequently than feelings that are expected to be more common during the early weeks after the loss, such as anxiety, depression, and anger.

Because these results were unexpected, a replication was attempted in our research on how parents cope with the loss of an infant to the Sudden Infant Death Syndrome (SIDS; see Silver & Wortman, 1987). SIDS is the most common cause of death among infants under the age of 1 (Beckwith, 1977). SIDS is diagnosed in those cases where the death is unexpected and where a postmortem examination fails to reveal any pathology. In most cases, the parents find the baby dead in his or her crib and have had no prior warning that the death might occur (Beckwith, 1970).

In this study, approximately 125 parents in Wayne County, Michigan, and Cook County, Illinois, who had lost an infant to SIDS were interviewed at 3 weeks, 3 months, and 18 months after the death had occurred. The parents in the sample were relatively young (the average age was 25), about 70% were women, and about 60% were Black. In this study, we included a more extensive measure of how frequently respondents experienced positive and negative emotions. All respondents were asked to complete the 40-item Affects Balance Scale (Derogatis, 1975), which includes five adjectives designed to measure each of four different positive and four different negative affective states.

The results of this study are portrayed in Figures 2 and 3. As shown in

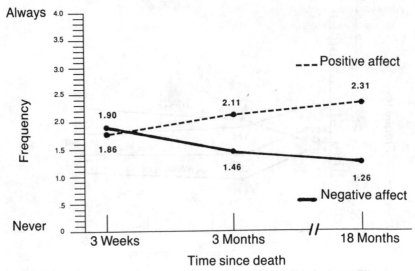

Figure 2. Frequency of positive and negative affect of SIDS parents. Adapted from Silver and Wortman (1987) by permission.

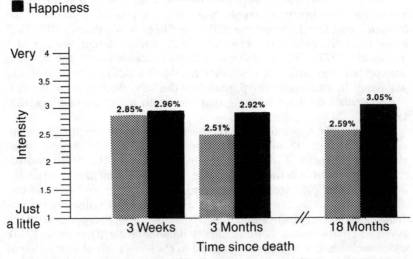

Figure 3. Intensity of positive and negative affect of SIDS parents. Adapted from Silver and Wortman (1987) by permission.

Figure 2, the data on frequency of emotion are highly similar to the findings from our study of patients with physical disabilities. By the second interview, conducted 3 months after the infants' deaths, positive affect was more prevalent than negative affect, and this continued to be the case at the third interview, 18 months after the loss.

One question that might be raised concerning these results is whether negative affect, although less frequent than positive emotions, may simply be more intense. In order to determine whether this was the case, SIDS parents were asked questions designed to probe the intensity of their feelings (see Silver & Wortman, 1987). If respondents said that they had felt happy or sad during the previous week, they were asked to indicate how intense these feelings were. In Figure 3, the same pattern of results is shown for the intensity measure as for the frequency measure. At all three interviews, feelings of happiness were at least as intense as feelings of sadness for all of the respondents. At the second and third interviews, respondents reported that their feelings of happiness were significantly more intense than their feelings of sadness. Taken together, these studies provide converging evidence that although people do experience distress following a loss, they experience positive emotions as well.

3. Distress Is Necessary, and Failure to Experience Distress Is Indicative of Pathology

In the clinical literature on reactions to loss, it is commonly assumed not only that distress will be experienced, but also that it is necessary to go through a period of distress. Failure to experience distress is universally regarded as indicative of a problem. In one of the earliest statements on the matter, Deutsch (1937) maintained "first, that the death of a beloved person *must* produce reactive expression of feeling in the normal course of events; second, that omission of such reactive responses is to be considered just as much a variation from the normal as excess in time and intensity" (p. 13). Bowlby (1980) has identified "prolonged absence of conscious grieving" (p. 138) as one of two types of disordered mourning, along with chronic mourning. Similarly, Marris (1958) has argued that "grieving is a process which 'must work itself out' . . . if the process is aborted from too hasty a readjustment . . . the bereaved may never recover" (p. 33).

In the recent authoritative report on bereavement published by the Institute of Medicine, "absent grief" was also classified as one of two types of "pathologic" mourning (Osterweis et al., 1984, p. 65). Osterweis et al. emphasized that it is commonly assumed, particularly by clinicians, "that the absence of grieving phenomena following bereavement represents some form of personality pathology" (p. 18). Although Osterweis et al. noted that there is little empirical evidence in support of this assumption, they nonetheless concluded that "professional help may be warranted for persons who show no evidence of having begun grieving" (p. 65).

The assumption that distress or depression is a necessary part of the grieving process is also quite prevalent in the literature on spinal cord injury (e.g., Karney, 1976; Kerr & Thompson, 1972; Nemiah, 1957; and see Trieschmann, 1978, 1980, for a review). Researchers have maintained that depression is therapeutic, because it signals that the person is beginning to confront the realities of his or her situation (see Nemiah, 1957). Failure to experience distress or depression is therefore viewed as a problem. As Siller (1969) has put it, "occasionally a newly disabled person does not seem to be particularly depressed, and this should be a matter of concern. In almost all instances something inappropriate is taking place. A person should be depressed because something significant has happened, and not to respond as such is denial. Such obvious denial is rare except in the case of a retarded person or in the very young" (p. 292). Cook (1976) and Dinardo (1971) have also commented that such denial is generally assumed to slow down the rehabilitation process.

In summary, in the literature on both bereavement and spinal cord injury, it is widely assumed that a stage of depression is necessary in order to achieve successful resolution or adaptation to the loss. An important component of this view is that if individuals fail to experience distress shortly after the loss, problems or symptoms of distress will erupt at a later point. As Bowlby (1980) has maintained, individuals who have failed to mourn may suddenly, inexplicably become acutely depressed. Marris (1958) has commented that "much later, in response to a less important or trivial loss, the death of a more distant relative, a pet—the bereaved person is overwhelmed by intense grief" (p. 27). Rando (1984) has likened grief to a wound, and if it "is not appropriately cleaned and tended to, time will not be helpful. It will only mark the progress of festering infection" (p. 114). According to Rando, "There is no way to go over, around, or under grief—we must go through it. Grievers must be helped to understand that grief cannot be delayed indefinitely, for it will erupt in some way, directly or indirectly" (pp. 97–98).

It is also widely believed that the failure to grieve will result in subsequent health problems. Bowlby (1980) has suggested that those who fail to grieve are apt to be afflicted with a variety of physiological ills. In the Institute of Medicine report, Osterweis et al. (1984) reviewed the work of several investigators who have suggested that those who fail to grieve may unconsciously become depressed and that this depression may be masked by a variety of physical symptoms.

As is discussed in more detail in a later section, the assumption that depression is necessary, and that lack of depression is a problem, has important therapeutic implications. Such assumptions may lead professionals to make judgments about who is coping well and who is coping poorly. Thus it becomes necessary to undertake a careful examination of the evidence in support of these ideas. In the following section we first

Table 1
Is a Phase of Depression Necessary for Adjustment
at 18 Months Following SIDS Loss?

Adjustment at 18 months post-loss	Depressed at first or second interview	Not depressed at first or second interview	p
Emotional resolution	2.31	1.67	< .005
Affects Balance Scale	.89	1.51	< .01
Symptom Checklist	.78	.36	< .001

Note. Higher scores = less emotional resolution, more positive affect balance, and more symptoms.

review evidence relevant to the idea that a stage of depression is necessary. Next we review evidence bearing on the idea that if individuals fail to go through a period of depression or distress, subsequent problems are likely to emerge.

If depression is necessary, those people who experience a period of depression should adapt to irrevocable losses more successfully than do those who do not become depressed. In our own research, we have not found this to be the case (Silver & Wortman, 1987). As noted previously, we interviewed parents who had lost an infant to SIDS at 3 weeks, 3 months, and 18 months after the loss. Parents were classified as having experienced a period of depression if they scored one standard deviation above the norm on the depression scale of the Symptom Check List (SCL-90) at either of the first two interviews (Derogatis, 1977). Using data from the interview at 18 months, these subjects were then compared to those who had not scored in the depressed range at either interview. As shown in Table 1, those who had gone through a period of depression were significantly less likely to have emotionally resolved the loss and reported experiencing more symptoms and more emotional distress 18 months after the loss than did those who did not experience an earlier period of distress.[2]

Similar results have been obtained by other investigators in the area of bereavement. Bornstein, Clayton, Halikas, Maurice, and Robins (1973) reported that among the conjugally bereaved, those depressed at 1 month had a significantly higher risk of being depressed at 13 months than did those subjects not depressed at 1 month. Similarly, Vachon, Rogers, et al. (1982) found that among the 162 widows they studied, scores on the General Health Questionnaire (a measure of distress and social functioning) at 1 month after the loss were the most powerful

---

[2] A possible alternative explanation for these findings centers around differences in subjects' willingness to report symptomology to researchers. Potential methodological solutions to this problem are considered in greater detail in a later section.

predictor of high distress at 24 months after the loss. Parkes and Weiss (1983) also found the experience of distress at 1 month post-loss to be predictive of long-term difficulties among the young widows and widowers they studied. Similarly, in a study of the elderly bereaved, Lund, Dimond, et al. (1985–86) found that those widows and widowers who reported feeling confused, helpless and alone, and wanting to die 1 month post-loss were most likely to have difficulties coping with their spouse's death 2 years later. In contrast, those who reported feeling amazed at their strength, proud of the way they were doing, and confident 1 month after their loss were likely to be doing well 2 years later.

Comparable findings suggesting that the absence of depression is not necessarily indicative of pathology have been obtained by investigators working in the spinal cord injury area. In a cross-sectional study of 53 male patients with spinal cord injuries, Dinardo (1971) assessed depressed mood by having subjects rate themselves on several evaluative scales and obtained adjustment ratings for each patient from physical therapists, occupational therapists, and nurses. He found that the absence of depression was associated with higher self-concepts and with staff ratings of successful adjustment to the disability, leading him to conclude that "those individuals who react to spinal cord injury with depression are less well adjusted at any given point in their rehabilitation than the individuals who do not react with depression" (p. 52). Similarly, Malec and Neimeyer (1983) used several well-validated scales to assess depression among a sample of 28 spinal cord injury patients upon admission to an inpatient rehabilitation program. They reported that the more distressed patients "tended to require longer rehabilitation and show lower levels of desirable self-care behaviors at discharge" (p. 361; see also Lawson, 1976).

In sum, there is little empirical support for the widely held assumption that a period of depression is necessary for successful resolution of grief. Interestingly, those showing early evidence of depression may be less likely, rather than more likely, to recover satisfactorily from their loss. Of course, this does not necessarily imply that it is detrimental to go through a period of depression following loss. Undoubtedly, some of the people who are most depressed after a loss may be those who have endured psychological difficulties that were, in fact, present prior to the loss. In the research that has been conducted to date, it is not possible to discriminate among those respondents who become depressed primarily as a result of their loss, and those who have a lifelong history of psychological disturbance. Only prospective designs, which assess such confounding variables prior to the loss, can help to shed light on this issue. Because most loss events are relatively infrequent, prospective studies are prohibitively costly and thus have rarely been attempted.

Earlier, we reviewed evidence suggesting that early displays of intense distress or depression will not necessarily lead to a successful adjustment to loss. As noted previously, however, it is widely assumed not only that expression of depression is valuable, but also that failure to express distress is likely to result in subsequent problems. What is the evidence in support of this belief?

Testing this idea requires a longitudinal study in which individuals who show little distress immediately after a loss are followed over time. According to those holding the widely assumed view, such individuals would be expected to become depressed at a later point or to evidence somatic health problems. We are not aware of any studies in the spinal cord injury area that would permit this kind of analysis. However, there are several bereavement studies conducted by other researchers, as well as our own study on reactions to SIDS loss, that allow us to examine what happens to people who fail to exhibit distress or depression shortly after their loss.

In the study by Bornstein et al. (1973) discussed earlier, interviews were conducted with 109 widows and widowers at 1 month, 4 months, and 13 months after their loss. As noted previously, approximately 35% of the respondents manifested enough symptoms at 1 month to be classified as either definitely or probably depressed. Of the 71 respondents who were not classified as depressed at 1 month, only 3 became depressed by the interview at 4 months. Moreover, only 1 evidenced depression for the first time at the interview at 13 months, leading the investigators to conclude that "delayed" grief is relatively rare.

Similar findings were obtained in a study by Vachon, Sheldon, et al. (1982). These investigators conducted interviews with 99 widows at 1 month after the loss and again 2 years later. As noted earlier, 32 of these women were classified as having "low distress" by virtue of their scores on the General Health Questionnaire at the 1 month interview. Of these women, 30 continued to evidence low distress at the interview at 2 years. Only 2 women in the study had low distress scores at 1 month and high distress scores at 2 years; the majority of those initially showing no distress appeared not to experience subsequent problems over time. Interestingly, Vachon, Sheldon, et al. (1982) found some evidence that those women with enduring low distress were more likely to demonstrate certain personality characteristics, such as emotional stability and conscientiousness. These findings led the investigators to conclude that "the enduring low distress for 30 women can perhaps best be understood not as the absence of mourning but as the presence of personality characteristics which promote adaptation into a new role" (p. 787).

We obtained a very similar pattern of findings in our study of coping with SIDS loss. Parents were classified as exhibiting low or high distress at the initial interview on the basis of their scores on the depression subscale of the SCL-90 (Derogatis, 1977). As in the studies described earlier, the vast majority of the respondents who showed low distress at 3 weeks also showed low distress at 18 months. Only three respondents, or 2.5% of the sample, moved from low to high distress. It is noteworthy that those parents who were evidencing the least amount of distress shortly after their baby's death were also significantly less likely to report "trying to forget the whole thing," "refusing to believe what was happening," and "trying to keep busy" than were parents who reported high distress at the first interview. Parents who showed low distress shortly after the loss were also no more likely than those who reported increased distress to indicate that the pregnancy had been unplanned or difficult to accept. Furthermore, these groups did not differ in their evaluation of their babies as having been beautiful, intelligent, not cranky, and happy while alive. Thus, the data fail to support the notion that absence of distress is due to insufficient attachment to the lost loved one.

In summary, research to date provides no support for the widely held view that those who fail to exhibit early distress will show subsequent difficulties. The data clearly suggest that absent grief is not necessarily problematic, and, at least as it is assessed in the studies conducted to date, delayed grief is far less common than suggested in the clinical literature.

4. Working Through the Loss Is Important

As noted earlier, it is widely assumed that a period of depression will occur once the person confronts the reality of the loss. At this point, it is commonly believed that the person must work through what has happened in order to recover successfully (see Brown & Stoudemire, 1983; Doyle, 1980). Implicit in this assumption is the notion that individuals need to focus on and process what has happened and that attempts to deny the implications of the loss, or block feelings or thoughts about it, will ultimately be unproductive. As Bowlby (1980) wrote, "Only if the person can tolerate the pining, the more or less constant searching, the seemingly endless examination of how and why the loss occurred and the anger at anyone who might have been responsible, not sparing even the dead person, can he [or she] gradually come to recognize and accept that the loss is in truth permanent and that his [or her] life must be shaped anew" (p. 93). Similarly, Parkes and Weiss (1983) have argued that for a state of emotional acceptance to be reached, "there must be a repeated confrontation with every element of the loss until the intensity of the distress is diminished" (p. 157). Marris (1958) has maintained that "if the bereaved cannot work through this process of grieving they may suffer lasting emotional damage" (p. 29). Rando (1984) concurred with this assessment, stating that "for the griever who has not attended to [his or her] grief, the pain is as acute and fresh 10 years later as it was the day after" (p. 114).

On the basis of statements such as these, it might be expected that those who show evidence of working through their loss in the weeks or months following it will be more successful in resolving the loss than will those who do not. In the bereavement area, we have been able to locate two studies (i.e., Parkes & Weiss, 1983; Silver & Wortman, 1987) that have assessed working through and related its presence to long-term recovery.

In each case, contrary to expectation, those who show the most evidence of working through the loss are those who ultimately have the most difficulty in resolving what has happened.

In the previously mentioned study by Parkes and Weiss (1983), coders rated the respondent on yearning for the deceased during the first interview, which occurred 3 weeks after the loss. Parkes and Weiss divided their sample into a High Yearning group, comprising those respondents who appeared to yearn or pine constantly, frequently, or whenever inactive, and a Low Yearning group, who yearned never, seldom, or only when reminded of the loss. At the first interview, about one-third of their respondents fell into the Low Yearning group, and two-thirds fell into the High Yearning group. In fact, high yearning was found to be predictive of poor mental and physical health outcomes at 13 months after the loss. As Parkes and Weiss (1983) expressed, "we might suppose that people who avoid or repress grief are the most likely to become disturbed a year later, yet this is not the case" (p. 47). They wrote, "A high level of yearning was often an early indicator of a recovery process which was going badly" (p. 228). Interestingly, high initial yearning was associated with poor outcome even 2 to 4 years after the loss. Of all of the different predictors that Parkes and Weiss examined, high initial yearning was the second best predictor of poor outcome 2 to 4 years after the loss. (The best predictor was the summary assessment made by coders, who rated the bereaved person on 10 dimensions of functioning from tapes and transcripts of the interview.)

In our study on parents coping with loss of an infant to SIDS, we also examined the impact of early evidence of working through the loss on subsequent adjustment (Silver & Wortman, 1987). Working through was defined as active attempts by the parent to make sense of and process the death, including searching for an answer for why the baby had died, thinking of ways the death could have been avoided, and being preoccupied with thoughts about the loss. As shown in Table 2, the more parents were working through the death at 3 weeks, the more distressed they

Table 2
The Relation Between "Working Through the Loss" and Distress for SIDS Parents

Level of working	Distress	
through at 3 weeks	3 weeks[a]	18 months[b]
Low	.79	.59
Medium	.91	.52
High	1.74	.92

Note. Higher score = higher symptomatology.
[a]$F(2, 118) = 30.7, p < .0001$.
[b]$F(2, 118) = 6.72, p < .002$.

were, as measured by the SCL-90, 18 months following the loss. In addition, those subjects who showed the least evidence of emotional resolution 18 months after the death of their infant (measured by distress in thinking and talking about the baby, feeling bitterness about the loss, and being upset by reminders of the baby) were those most likely to be working through the loss shortly after the death.

As is illustrated in this brief review, there is relatively little empirical evidence relevant to the issue of working through. If behaviors such as yearning for the deceased or being preoccupied with thoughts about the loss are conceptualized as working through, however, the assumption that working through is necessarily adaptive is challenged by the available research. Like early evidence of intense distress, early signs of intense efforts to work through the loss may portend subsequent difficulties.

5. It Is Necessary to Break Down Attachments

An important element of working through a loss that has received considerable attention from clinicians is the importance of dealing with one's attachment to the lost object. According to Freud and other psychoanalytic writers, a central process during bereavement is the loosening of the affective bond to the deceased (cf. Freud, 1917/1957). This view contends that grief work is completed only when the bereaved individual withdraws energy from the lost person and frees him- or herself from intense attachment to an unavailable individual. According to this perspective, if this process fails to occur, individuals will be unable to invest their energy in living. As Rando (1984) wrote, "The single most crucial task in grief is 'untying the ties that bind' the griever to the deceased individual. This does not mean that the deceased is forgotten or not loved; rather, it means that the emotional energy that the mourner had invested in the deceased is modified to allow the mourner to turn it towards others for emotional satisfaction" (p. 19).

Given these beliefs, it is interesting to note that continued and persistent attachments to the lost object appear to be very common. Phantom sensations from missing or denervated limbs have been reported commonly among amputees (Parkes, 1972; Randall, Ewalt, & Blair, 1945) and those with spinal cord injuries (Bors, 1951; Hohmann, 1975). Among the bereaved, fully 8 weeks post-loss, Glick et al. (1974) found that more than one-half of the widows they interviewed, and about one-fifth of the widowers, reported believing that their spouse might actually return. A year after bereavement, 69% agreed with the statement, "I try to behave in ways he [or she] would have wanted me to, or I think as he [or she] would have wanted me to." After 2 to 4 years, this type of attachment was still very prevalent, especially when the loss was sudden. Eighty-three percent of people who had experienced the loss of their spouse suddenly continued to agree with the statement, as did almost half of the sample who had had forewarning about the loss. Similarly, Parkes and Weiss (1983) reported that 2 to 4 years after the loss, 61% of those who lost their spouse suddenly reported sensing the presence of the dead person occasionally or always, as did 20% of those who had had some forewarning concerning the loss.

Continued attachment between the grieving person and the lost object may take many forms, such as through continued affective involvement with the loss (Parkes, 1972; Rubin, 1981); through turning to the deceased for help with decision-making (Zisook & Shuchter, 1986); through various types of legacies, in which the wishes or commitments of the deceased are carried out by family members (Goin, Burgoyne, & Goin, 1979); through hallucinations or dreams (cf. Rees, 1971); or merely through a continued sense of presence of the lost object (Bors, 1951; Zisook, DeVaul, & Click, 1982; Zisook & Shuchter, 1985). Bowlby (1980) noted that some bereaved individuals experience the dead spouse as a companion who accompanies them everywhere; in other cases, he or she is experienced as located in a specific place, such as in the garden or in a particular chair.

Contrary to the suggestion that such continued attachments may inhibit adjustment or be disruptive, there is evidence that those who have encountered loss seem to find them comforting (see Goin et al., 1979). Drawing from their study of widows, Glick et al. (1974) have argued that such attachments are not necessarily incompatible with independent action. As they have indicated, "Often the widow's progress toward recovery was facilitated by inner conversations with her husband's presence" (p. 154). Glick et al. (1974) maintained that although widows knew their spouses were not there, they nonetheless found it comforting to be able to talk through a problem, with the "feeling" that their spouse was there to listen.

In summary, there is little empirical data to indicate whether continual attachments to the lost loved one are adaptive or maladaptive in the long run. However, the data that are available suggest that the display of behaviors indicative of attachment are surprisingly common and not necessarily detrimental.

6. Recovery Is Expected

It is generally assumed that although a person who experiences an irrevocable loss will go through a phase of intense distress, this should not last indefinitely. Over time, the person is expected to achieve a state of recovery and return to normal role functioning. Almost every stage model of coping with loss has a final stage of adaptation, which may be called *recovery* (Klinger, 1975, 1977), *acceptance* (Kübler-Ross, 1969), or *reorganization* (Bowlby, 1980). *Chronic grief,* or failure to recover, is identified as a major type of pathologic mourning in virtually every major treatise on the bereavement process (see Bowlby, 1980; Osterweis et al., 1984; Parkes & Weiss, 1983). Similarly, failure to accept the loss of one's abilities is felt to impede motivation and rehabilitation of the spinal cord injury patient (see Heijn & Granger, 1974).

In none of the theories is it postulated precisely how much time should elapse before recovery from an irrevocable loss. In the bereavement area, notions about the length of the recovery process have been shifting over the last four decades. In early studies of bereavement it has been suggested that its psychological impact was relatively transient. In fact, in his study of relatives of victims of Boston's Cocoanut Grove nightclub disaster, Lindemann (1944) painted an optimistic picture of the recovery process, noting that with appropriate psychiatric intervention, it was ordinarily possible to settle an uncomplicated grief reaction in 4 to 6 weeks. A similar conclusion was drawn by Clayton, Desmarais, and Winokur (1968), who conducted two interviews, both within the first few months of an individual's loss of a spouse, child, grandchild, or parent. Although a sizable minority (27% to 37%) of respondents continued to experience a variety of symptoms at the second interview, including sleep disturbance, difficulty concentrating, anxiety attacks, anorexia, and fatigue, the authors concluded from their data that "bereavement is a relatively mild reaction for most subjects" (p. 176).

However, researchers recently suggested that it may take considerably longer to recover from the loss of a loved one, especially when the loss is sudden and traumatic (see Silver & Wortman, 1980; Tait & Silver, 1987, for reviews). For example, Clayton, Halikas, and Maurice (1972) interviewed 109 widows and widowers at 1, 4, and 13 months following the death of their spouse. As noted earlier, these researchers used strict diagnostic criteria in order to classify respondents as depressed: Subjects had to report low mood, plus at least four of eight other symptoms, including loss of appetite, sleep, fatigue, loss of interest, and feelings of guilt. Despite the strict criteria that were used, 17% of respondents were classified as either definitely depressed (low mood plus five of eight symptoms) or probably depressed (low mood plus four of eight symptoms) at the end of the first year. In the previously discussed study by Vachon and her associates, 38% of the bereaved widows studied were experiencing a high level of distress after one year. At the end of 2 years, 26% of women were still classified as exhibiting high distress (Vachon, Rogers, et al., 1982; Vachon, Sheldon, et al., 1982). In a longitudinal study of bereaved widows and widowers conducted by Parkes and Weiss (1983), over 40% of the sample were rated by trained interviewers as showing moderate to severe anxiety 2 to 4 years after the loss. Feelings of depression, as well as problems in functioning, were also quite common at the interview at 2 to 4 years, particularly if the loss was sudden.

Elizur and Kaffman (1982, 1983) examined behavior changes over a 3½-year period among kibbutz children who had lost their fathers in war and found marked severity and prolonged course of the postbehavioral emotional reactions. Although none of these children evidenced unusual psychopathology prior to their loss, they were subsequently found to be at risk for a variety of problems. Almost 50% showed marked emotional disturbance in each phase of the study—6, 18, and 42 months after their father's death. More than two-thirds of the bereaved children reacted with severe psychological problems and impairment in diverse areas of functioning.

In a study of the long-term effects of the sudden, unexpected loss of a spouse or child 4 to 7 years earlier, interviews were conducted with 39 individuals who had lost a spouse and with 41 parents who had lost a child in a motor vehicle crash (Lehman, Wortman, & Williams, 1987). Bereaved respondents were matched with a control group of nonbereaved individuals on a case-by-case basis by sex, age, income, education, and number and ages of children. Significant differences between bereaved spouses and controls were revealed on several indicators of general functioning, including depression and other psychiatric symptoms, social functioning, psychological well-being, reactivity to good events, and future worries and concerns (see Table 3). For the most part, these differences persisted when variables such as present family income and present marital status were controlled statistically. Comparisons between bereaved parents and controls also revealed significant differences on some measures of general functioning (especially depression), but these were not as pervasive as the differences obtained among bereaved spouses.

In the spinal cord literature, there is a dearth of longitudinal studies that have followed individuals for very long after their injury. Nonetheless, there is some limited evidence to suggest that it may take individuals longer to accept their loss than is commonly assumed. In a cross-sectional study of patients disabled up to 38 years earlier, Shadish, Hickman, and Arrick (1981) reported that many of them still thought about the things they could not do since their injury and "really miss" these things almost weekly.

Even when individuals appear to have recovered from their loss, there is some limited evidence to suggest that feelings of grief may reemerge, for brief periods, at a later date. Lindemann (1944) maintained that such reactions often arise following "deliberate recall of circumstances surrounding the death or spontaneous occurrences in the patient's life" and may appear "after an interval which was not marked by any abnormal behavior or distress" (p. 144). Bornstein and Clayton (1972) found that 67% of the bereaved they interviewed reported a mild or severe anniversary reaction to the death of their spouse. Similarly, Wiener, Gerber, Battin, and Arkin (1975) reported that some bereavement symptoms "tend to recur at various times, precipitated by anniversaries, memories, meetings, geographical locale, etc." (p. 64). Parkes (1970) suggested that during these times, "all the feelings of acute pining and sadness return and the bereaved person goes through, in miniature, another bereavement" (p. 464).

Table 3
Means, Standard Deviations, and Reliabilities for
Outcome Measures for Those Losing a Spouse or
Child in a Motor Vehicle Crash

Construct	No. of items	N	Spouse study		
			Bereaved spouse	Control spouse	SD
CES-D	10	39	1.08**	0.56	0.98
SADS Depression/Suicide	6	38	2.59***	1.46	1.28
SCL-90-R total score (GSI)	90	39	0.98***	0.52	0.78
Somatization	12	39	0.75****	0.48	0.87
Obsessive-Compulsive	10	39	1.28***	0.74	0.95
Interpersonal Sensitivity	9	39	1.04**	0.58	0.86
Depression	13	39	1.32***	0.65	1.04
Anxiety	10	38	1.01**	0.49	0.98
Hostility	6	39	0.87****	0.59	0.96
Phobic Anxiety	7	39	0.54***	0.14	0.65
Paranoid Ideation	6	39	0.88*	0.52	0.96
Psychoticism	10	38	0.66**	0.30	0.78
Alcohol	6	28	1.52	1.30	0.94
Drug	8	38	1.66	1.57	1.24
Bradburn Affects Balance	9	39	2.94***	2.27	0.95
Worry	3	39	2.64**	2.16	1.10
Reactivity to Good Events	3	39	1.95*	1.69	0.80
General State of Life-Open-Ended	1	39	2.64**	1.51	1.10
Weissman total	39	22	2.00	1.76	0.78
Spare Time	11	39	2.24**	1.82	0.79
Relatives	8	32	1.65	1.60	0.76
Family	8	16	1.88	1.83	1.01
Work Satisfaction/Stress	6	13	1.42	1.38	0.56
Housework Satisfaction/Stress	6	31	2.04*	1.74	0.90
Spanier Dyadic Adjustment Scale	7	—	—	—	—
Pearlin & Schooler Stress (Partner)	6	—	—	—	—
Pearlin & Schooler Stress (Parent)	7	17	3.02**	2.04	1.32
Physical Health	4	39	2.09	1.88	0.90

Note. Higher scores represent more depression, greater distress, worse psychological well-being, and so on. CES-D = Center for Epidemiologic Studies-Depression scale. GSI = Global Severity Index. SADS = Schedule for Affective Disorders Scale. *$p < .05$, two-tailed. **$p < .01$, two-tailed. ***$p < .001$, two-tailed. ****$p < .10$, two-tailed. Adapted from Lehman, Wortman, and Williams (1987) by permission.

continued

Table 3, continued

		Parent study			
Construct	*N*	Bereaved parent	Control parent	*SD*	α
CES-D	41	0.77*	0.48	0.84	.87
SADS Depression/Suicide	40	2.55***	1.60	1.32	.76
SCL-90-R total score (GSI)	41	0.77	0.63	0.74	.98
Somatization	41	0.71	0.66	0.97	.88
Obsessive-Compulsive	41	1.00	0.90	0.98	.88
Interpersonal Sensitivity	41	0.74	0.73	0.80	.88
Depression	40	0.93	0.74	0.98	.92
Anxiety	41	0.77	0.63	0.87	.90
Hostility	41	0.73****	0.48	0.87	.83
Phobic Anxiety	41	0.46****	0.26	0.76	.77
Paranoid Ideation	41	0.67	0.59	0.79	.79
Psychoticism	40	0.51	0.44	0.73	.82
Alcohol	33	1.51	1.36	0.89	.85
Drug	40	1.50	1.49	0.91	.72
Bradburn Affects Balance	40	2.71****	2.43	0.92	.88
Worry	40	2.46****	2.15	1.11	.76
Reactivity to Good Events	41	1.98	2.02	0.94	.72
General State of Life-Open-Ended	41	1.76	1.63	1.13	—
Weissman total	18	1.91	1.71	0.82	—
Spare Time	41	1.93	1.92	0.73	.70
Relatives	39	1.72*	1.52	0.58	.63
Family	17	1.87	1.66	0.55	.76
Work Satisfaction/Stress	12	1.40	1.31	0.37	.58
Housework Satisfaction/Stress	23	1.88	1.86	0.52	.72
Spanier Dyadic Adjustment Scale	32	1.86	1.95	0.71	.82
Pearlin & Schooler Stress (Partner)	31	2.10****	1.74	1.06	.87
Pearlin & Schooler Stress (Parent)	27	2.52*	2.07	1.04	.91
Physical Health	11	2.13	1.93	1.13	.77

Note. Higher scores represent more depression, greater distress, worse psychological well-being, and so on. CES-D = Center for Epidemiologic Studies-Depression scale. GSI = Global Severity Index. SADS = Schedule for Affective Disorders Scale. *$p < .05$, two-tailed. **$p < .01$, two-tailed. ***$p < .001$, two-tailed. ****$p < .10$, two-tailed. Adapted from Lehman, Wortman, and Williams (1987) by permission.

Taken together, the aforementioned evidence suggests that prevailing notions of recovery deserve reconsideration. There is evidence that a substantial minority of individuals continue to exhibit distress for a much longer period of time than would commonly be assumed. There are also a number of indications that people may continually reexperience the loss for the rest of their lives.

7. A State of Resolution Must Be Reached

It is widely assumed that over time, as a result of working through their loss, individuals will achieve a state of resolution regarding what has happened. One important type of resolution involves accepting the loss intellectually. Parkes and Weiss (1983) argued that people must come up with a rationale for the loss; they must be able to understand what has happened and make sense of the loss (see also Moos & Schaefer, 1986). This theme has also played an important role in the work of Marris (1958), who has suggested that bereavement is painful, in large part, because it deprives one's life of meaning. Similarly, in her writings on the loss of a child, Craig (1977) has maintained that an essential part of griefwork is to resolve the meaninglessness of the crisis (see also Miles & Crandall, 1983). A second type of resolution involves accepting the loss emotionally. Emotional acceptance is thought to be reached when the person no longer feels the need to avoid reminders of the loss in order to function. The lost person can be recalled, and reminders of the loss can be confronted, without intense emotional pain (Parkes & Weiss, 1983). It is generally expected that much of the griefwork engaged in by the bereaved, such as reviewing the events of the death or the course of the illness or accident, will aid in resolution.

Although few studies have focused on the issue of resolution, the limited data that are available suggest that a state of resolution may not always be achieved. In the study by Parkes and Weiss (1983) described earlier, it was found that as long as 2 to 4 years after the loss, 61% of the respondents who had suddenly lost their spouse, and 29% of those who had forewarning, were still asking why the event had happened. Almost half of the sample who had suddenly lost a spouse agreed with the statement that "It's not real; I feel that I'll wake up and it won't be true," and 15% of the individuals with forewarning agreed with this statement.

Similar data were obtained in our study of coping with the loss of an infant to SIDS (Silver & Wortman, 1987). It is illustrated in Table 4 that in all three of the time points we studied (3 weeks, 3 months, and 18 months after the loss), the majority of respondents were unable to find any meaning in their baby's death, and were unable to answer the question, "Why me?" or "Why my baby?" (Wortman, Ellard, & Silver, 1987). A particularly intriguing feature of our data on coping with SIDS loss is that we found little evidence that resolution increases over time. Indeed, we found a significant increase in the number of individuals who were unable to find meaning in their baby's death between the first and second interviews. (See Wortman et al., 1987, for a more detailed discussion of this issue.)

Table 4
Cognitive Resolution of SIDS Parents Over Time

	3 weeks	3 months	18 months
Unable to find any meaning	65%	74%	75%
Unable to answer "why me?" or "why my baby?"	81%	88%	86%

Note. Adapted from Wortman, Ellard, and Silver (1987) by permission.

In a study of the long-term impact of losing a loved one in a motor vehicle accident (Lehman et al., 1987), described earlier, even after 4 to 7 years, most respondents have not achieved a state of resolution. As shown in Figure 4, almost half of the sample had reviewed events leading up to the accident in the last month. A majority of the respondents were unable to find any meaning in the loss, had had thoughts during the past month that the death was unfair, and had had painful memories of their spouse or child during the past month.

Considered together, these data provide convergent evidence that, contrary to popular belief, individuals are not always able to resolve their loss and come up with an explanation for the event that is satisfying to them. Particularly when the event is sudden, a majority of individuals appear to have great difficulty in coming to terms with what has happened.

Implications for Theory and Research

Previously, seven different assumptions were reviewed reflecting beliefs concerning the "normal" way to cope with an irrevocable loss. These assumptions are based in part on theories of grief and mourning, in part on clinical lore, and in part on the cultural understanding of how people

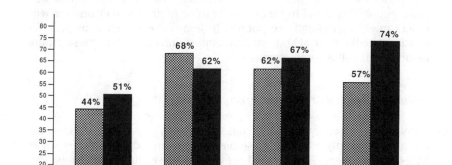

Figure 4. Resolution following loss of a loved one in a motor vehicle accident 4–7 years earlier. Adapted from Lehman, Wortman, and Williams (1987) by permission.

should react to permanent loss. Although current researchers of grief no longer see it as a set of discrete stages, it is still seen as a process—a process beginning with a state of intense distress that dissipates over time. Alternate patterns are usually labeled pathological or deviant (Brown & Stoudemire, 1983; Osterweis et al., 1984; Simons, 1985). Supposedly, individuals are able to work through their grief, resolve their loss, and recover their earlier level of functioning. At present, there is awareness that this may not happen in the 4 to 6 weeks Lindemann (1944) originally suggested (but see Agee, 1980, for a similarly optimistic view). However, within a year or two after their loss, people are expected to be pretty much "back to normal" (Silver & Wortman, 1980).

In our analysis, we suggest that in contrast to this view, there are at least three different patterns of adaptation to loss, each of which is prevalent enough to be considered normal. Some individuals indeed seem to go through the expected pattern, moving from high to low distress over time. But others seem to continue in a state of high distress for much longer than would be expected according to the traditional view of normal grief. Still others appear not to show the intense distress that would be expected, either immediately after the loss or at subsequent intervals.

In our judgment, traditional views about what constitutes a "normal" reaction to loss are so strong that they appear to have hampered theoretical development in this area and have limited the scope of empirical inquiry. With their emphasis on a universal process of grief, past theoretical approaches have provided relatively little insight into explaining the variability in response to loss. Traditional theories of grief and loss are able to account for those who move from high to low distress and resolve their grief over time. But these theories offer little explanation of why some people might fail to recover or resolve their loss over time or why others might consistently respond with less distress than expected. We consider the theoretical and research implications of each of these groups in turn in the following section.

Failure to Resolve or Recover From the Loss

Because of the belief that individuals will be recovered from a loss within a year or two, only a handful of studies have been focused on the issue of long-term recovery. As indicated previously, these studies suggested that particularly when the loss is sudden, individuals may have difficulties from 2 to 4 years (Parkes & Weiss, 1983), and even from 4 to 7 years (Lehman et al., 1987), after the loss of a spouse or child. In fact, Tait and Silver (1987), in a study of senior citizens, found that 10, 15, or 20 years after negative life events, respondents still experience unpleasant memories of their loss and do not feel they have recovered from it.

Now that it is becoming clear that there is considerable variability in the length of time it takes to recover, and that some people do not seem to recover despite the passage of many years, there is increasing interest in identifying those mediating factors that may promote or impede psychosocial recovery (cf. Kessler et al., 1985; Silver & Wortman, 1980). Recently researchers have, in fact, identified factors that may enhance the likelihood that individuals will react to loss with intense and prolonged distress. These factors include the nature of the relationship with the deceased, circumstances surrounding the loss, the presence of concomitant stressors, and the availability of social support. (Although a full discussion of all risk factors that have been associated with increased distress among people who are bereaved or have physical disabilities is beyond the scope of this chapter, the interested reader is referred to Bowlby, 1980, Osterweis et al., 1984, or Raphael, 1983, in the area of bereavement; and Trieschmann, 1978, 1980, for a review of the spinal cord injury literature.)

The two relationship qualities that have been most carefully addressed in the literature on loss are ambivalence and dependence. Psychologists have generally assumed that relationships characterized by ambivalence or dependence have their roots in the early experiences of the individual during childhood. For example, Bowlby (1980) has maintained that, for a variety of reasons, some children come to feel insecure about the extent to which they can expect nurturance or protection from parents. As a result of these insecurities, they develop "working models" of themselves and others that influence their behavior in later relationships. Individuals who are predisposed to ambivalent relationships are primed to feel disappointment, betrayal, or abandonment by their loved ones and typically react to disappointments with intense hostility. For this reason, marriages in which one partner is ambivalent are generally characterized by considerable marital conflict (Bowlby, 1980). In fact, empirical support has been obtained for the hypothesis that those involved in ambivalent relationships will experience more long-term difficulties with bereavement than will those who do not, both among parents who lost adult children in traffic accidents (Shanfield & Swain, 1984) and among individuals following the death of their spouse (Parkes & Weiss, 1983).

Similarly, it has been suggested that as a result of anxiety concerning separation from one's parents, some children develop a tendency to form "clinging" relationships. Supposedly, such individuals carry this tendency into adulthood, in which they continue to react to real or threatened separation with fear or distress (Bowlby, 1980). Raphael (1983) has noted that such relationships are usually of the symbiotic kind and are reflected in such comments as "he was like a father to me" or "he did everything for me" (p. 222). Parkes and Weiss (1983) reported that those spouses who had been involved in highly dependent relationships were more likely to have difficulties in coming to terms with their loss over time. Such individuals were also likely to experience intense yearning for the bereaved person, as well as feelings of helplessness and indecisiveness shortly after the death.

A second risk factor that has received considerable attention is the circumstances surrounding the loss. Although the evidence is not entirely consistent (see Osterweis et al., 1984, for a review), several studies have suggested that sudden, unexpected, and untimely deaths, especially deaths of the young, are more likely to be associated with subsequent distress (see Lehman et al., 1987; Parkes, 1975; Parkes & Weiss, 1983). As Parkes and Weiss (1983) have written, such losses may have their impact through their "transformation of the world into a frightening place, a place in which disaster cannot be predicted and accustomed ways of thinking and behaving have proven unreliable and out of keeping with the actual world" (p. 245).

In our research on people with physical disabilities, we suggested that a similar process may also operate in reactions to spinal cord injury. Just as the unexpected loss of a spouse can transform the world into a frightening and unpredictable place, a sudden, traumatic injury may shatter a person's assumptions about the world. As Lilliston (1985) has indicated, "A suddenly disabled person who was the victim of accident or disease is given a horrifying and permanent reminder of the world's injustice. If the person formerly believed in a just world, he [or she] must somehow harmonize the dissonance between what he [or she] expected life to be, and what it now has revealed itself to be" (p. 8). In a study of 29 individuals who had received spinal cord injuries in a sudden, traumatic accident, those who blamed another for the accident, and who felt that the accident could have been avoided, were rated by social workers and nurses as coping worse with their paralysis (Bulman & Wortman, 1977). These findings have also been replicated in our larger study of spinal cord injury patients described earlier. Transcripts obtained from each patient's interview were coded by outside observers according to whether they thought the accident had been perpetrated by the respondent or by someone else. Again, those whose accidents were perpetrated by others reacted with greater distress than those whose accident stemmed from their own behavior (Ellard, Wortman, & Silver, 1986; Silver, 1982). Individuals whose accidents were perpetrated by others were also more likely to have thoughts that the accident was unfair and to be troubled by unpleasant thoughts concerning the accident. Interestingly, the circumstances surrounding the loss turned out to be a more important predictor of distress than the severity of the injury, that is, whether the respondent became paraplegic, quadriplegic, or did not suffer a spinal cord injury (Silver, 1982; and see Athelstan & Crewe, 1979, for a similar finding).

A third factor that has been mentioned consistently as likely to intensify distress following loss is the presence of concurrent crises (see Silver & Wortman, 1980, for a review). In some cases, these crises may represent problems that existed at the time of the loss, such as chronic health ailments. In other cases, such problems may stem directly from the loss itself—for example, a person may become injured or lose a child in an accident in which his or her spouse was killed. In two different studies, researchers have found a presence of other crises to be predictive of poor outcome among the bereaved (Parkes, 1975; Vachon, Rogers, et al., 1982).

Finally, among people who are bereaved or have physical disabilities, the lack of available social support may also hinder the recovery process (see Osterweis et al., 1984; Trieschmann, 1978, 1980, for reviews). Clayton et al. (1972) have reported that subjects who were depressed at 1 month after the death of their spouse had significantly fewer children in the geographical area whom they considered close and available to render support (see also Bornstein et al., 1973; Dimond, Lund, & Caserta, 1987, for comparable results over time). In several studies, researchers have provided evidence that those who express feelings of lack of support, such as "nobody understands or cares," or feel that there is no one available to talk to or lean on shortly after their spouse's death are more likely to report subsequent problems (see Maddison & Walker, 1967; Vachon, Rogers, et al., 1982). Among people with physical disabilities, support from friends and family similarly has been demonstrated to be of critical importance for successful long-term adjustment to one's limitations (see Kelman, Lowenthal, & Muller, 1966; Kemp & Vash, 1971; Schulz & Decker, 1985).

Despite research on the aforementioned risk factors, much basic information about the process of recovery from loss remains unexplored. For example, relatively little is known about how this process is influenced by sociodemographic variables such as age, race, and sex. To date, most of the available research has been conducted on White women in the area of bereavement, and White men in the area of physical disability. Similarly, because it is widely believed that individuals eventually resolve or come to terms with their loss, few studies have included questions designed to examine the resolution process over time. In the evidence reviewed earlier, we suggested that contrary to what might be expected, a significant percentage of respondents appear unable to resolve the loss, even after considerable periods of time.

Moreover, in our study of parents who have lost an infant to SIDS, we suggested that if individuals are going to come up with a meaningful account of why their loved one died, they are likely to do so within the first few weeks after the loss (Wortman et al., 1987). This raises a number of fascinating questions for further research. Are there indeed some individuals who can incorporate a tragic event into their understanding of the world and thus have no need or desire to understand why the event happened to them? What factors predict whether an individual will not feel it necessary to search for meaning (see Silver, Boon, & Stones, 1983), will search for meaning and ultimately come up with an explanation, or will stop focusing on the event, although no satisfactory explanation has been found? Under what circumstances will an individual benefit from continued attempts to work through or resolve the loss, either by thinking about it or talking about it with others? And under what circumstances will attempts to block thoughts about what happened, or avoid discussing them, be more functional (cf. Silver et al., 1983)?

In our judgment, an unfortunate consequence of the pervasive belief in recovery from loss is that attention has been deflected away from examining the possible mechanisms through which loss may produce subsequent mental or physical health problems. A number of different mechanisms have been suggested in the literature (see Jacobs & Douglas, 1979; Klerman & Izen, 1977; Osterweis et al., 1984; Stroebe & Stroebe, 1983, for a more extensive discussion). For example, depression may cause physiologic changes in endocrine functioning, leading to illness and death through cardiovascular disease, infectious disease, or general susceptibility to illness. Alternatively, loss may result in changes in health maintenance behavior, such as eating regular meals and getting exercise. Individuals who are grieving may neglect or fail to notice early signs of disease, or they may fail to engage in the proper management of health problems already present, such as hypertension or diabetes. The excessive use of injurious substances, such as alcohol and drugs, may also contribute to subsequent problems among the bereaved.

Widowhood may also be accompanied by increased role strains, such as having to manage financial affairs, take care of home maintenance, and make major decisions on one's own; such strains may exhaust an individual's coping capacity. Bereavement also leaves many people with loss of their major source of social support, and this may account for the pathogenic effects of the loss of a spouse. Finally, as noted previously, experiencing an irrevocable loss such as bereavement or spinal cord injury might alter the individual's view of the world. Indeed, in a study of the long-term effects of losing a loved one in a motor vehicle accident (Lehman et al., 1987), many of the respondents had come to see the world as a hostile place where things can be taken away in a moment. Such an altered worldview is likely to be associated with depression, passivity, and impaired motivation to engage in subsequent coping efforts.

To date, existing theories of coping with loss have devoted little attention to the identification of mechanisms that may link irrevocable losses to subsequent mental and physical health problems. Perhaps because of the lack of theoretical interest in this matter, there are few empirical studies designed specifically to examine the mechanisms delineated previously or to discriminate among them. Clearly, evidence concerning the precise mechanisms through which loss leads to long-term difficulties is essential not only for theoretical advancement but also to guide intervention efforts in the area of grief and loss.

Failure to Become Depressed

As noted earlier, because of the assumption that early distress is inevitable, there has been limited research to carefully examine the range of emotions that may occur in the first few weeks or months after a loss. Are there some respondents who show very little, if any, feelings of distress, or do virtually all people experience some feelings of sadness or anxiety (cf. Wright, 1983)? Are those individuals who show little distress also likely to show few signs of positive emotion (cf. Deutsch, 1937)? Among those who show very little distress, is this best understood as a shock or denial reaction, or is it a sign of coping strength or resilience? Research in which respondents are frequently assessed in the early weeks or months following a loss would help to address these questions (cf. Lawson, 1976, 1978). In such a study, researchers could examine whether those who show low distress at one point in time are likely to become more distressed later, presumably after the shock wears off. This type of process has been described by several writers (e.g., Parkes, 1970, 1972; Shuchter, 1986).

Despite the belief among those working in the fields of grief and loss that failure to show early distress is indicative of a problem, there is little evidence to suggest that those who initially show minimal distress following loss are likely to become significantly depressed at a later point. In subsequent studies, it will be important to look closely at people who show low levels of distress. Are such people more vulnerable to subsequent minor losses, as some theorists would lead us to expect? Are such individuals more likely to develop somatic symptoms or physical health problems (cf. Brown & Stoudemire, 1983) or problems in other areas of their lives, such as at work or in their interpersonal relationships? In the data reviewed earlier there is evidence that low initial distress may not signal pathology. But clearly, more systematic data are needed before the firmly entrenched view that absent grief is a cause for concern can be dismissed. In collecting such data, it will be important to go beyond the self-report methodology that is most commonly used to study reactions to loss. Individuals who indicate that they are not distressed immediately after a loss may also be unwilling to admit subsequent problems in other areas of their lives. Supplementing self-report data with more objective indicators of problems, such as health records or ratings of supervisors at work, might be helpful in resolving such ambiguities.

If results obtained from further studies are consistent with the results reviewed in this chapter, the possibility exists that a sizable minority of people may come through the bereavement process relatively unscathed. By assuming latent pathology among those who fail to show intense distress following a loss, attention appears to have been deflected away from identifying strengths or coping resources that may protect these people from distress. The data suggest that some people may have something in place beforehand—perhaps a religious or philosophical orientation or a personality disposition—that enables them to be less vulnerable to the effects of loss.

In recent years, there has been increasing interest in philosophical perspectives or assumptions about the world and the role they may play in the coping process (Janoff-Bulman, 1987; Janoff-Bulman & Frieze,

1983; Wortman, 1983). For example, a person who holds a firm belief that all things are part of God's larger plan may cope differently with the loss of a child than will a person who does not believe in God. Similarly, individuals who have the perspective that bad things can happen at any time and that suffering is part of life may find it easier to cope with sudden loss than do those individuals who believe that if they work hard and are good people, they will be protected from misfortune (cf. Janoff-Bulman & Frieze, 1983).

A number of intriguing questions regarding these various life perspectives remain unanswered. What assumptions or philosophical views are most adaptive for what types of outcomes? The assumption that the world is a cruel place may be helpful to a person trying to cope with the loss of a child but may hamper coping with daily tasks, such as finding a job. The assumption that people cannot be trusted may impair the development of close relationships that could provide social support. But such a view could be critical to survival if the person holding it encounters a rapist at the door who poses as a delivery person (cf. Wortman, 1983). Clearly, future research is necessary to examine the role that such worldviews may play in protecting people from the deleterious effects of loss.

Implications for Treatment

What are the treatment implications of the widespread assumption that successful adjustment to irrevocable loss necessitates a progression from initial distress to recovery over time? Unfortunately, any deviation from this pattern is seen as a cause for concern, and health care professionals are often reminded of the importance of recognizing a deviant grief pattern (Brown & Stoudemire, 1983; Doyle, 1980; Osterweis et al., 1984; Simons, 1985; Tucker, 1980). As noted earlier, the two main variants of abnormal grief that have been identified are a prolonged absence of grief, and chronic mourning (Bowlby, 1980; Raphael, 1983). The possible treatment implications of each of these will be considered in turn.

The assumption that distress should occur following loss is so powerful that a variety of negative attributions have been made by health care professionals concerning those who do not evidence it. First, because grieving is considered to be a sign of a healthy personality, the apparent lack of it is thought to signal psychopathology (see Doyle, 1980; Raphael, 1983). Second, the absence of distress (and similarly, the presence of positive emotion) is often dismissed as denial (see Shontz, 1975; Siller, 1969). Third, specifically regarding the loss of a loved one, the absence of depression is sometimes seen as a sign of lack of attachment to the deceased. As Raphael (1983) has written, "Perhaps some of the preexisting relationships were purely narcissistic with little recognition of the real person who was lost" (pp. 205–206; see also Doyle, 1980; Platt, 1977;

Rando, 1984). Another explanation for the absence of grief is that the loss may provide secondary gains for the individual, sometimes solving problems instead of creating them (cf. Shontz, 1975).

Rather than recognizing the absence of grief as a sign of possible strengths of the individual (cf. Gans, 1981), many authors recommend attempting to provoke distress by confronting the individual with the reality of his or her loss. Regarding spinal cord injury, Nemiah (1957) has written, "It is often necessary to confront the patient gently but firmly with the reality of his situation, and to force him into a period of depression while he works out his acceptance of his loss" (p. 146). When dealing with a patient who has lost a loved one, physicians are reminded to encourage the bereaved to express their distress and to bring "latent anger and guilt to a conscious level of awareness" (Brown & Stoudemire, 1983, p. 382).

In a manual for grief counselors, Doyle (1980) discouraged the use of tranquilizers or anti-depressants by the bereaved during the early stages of grief, because grief "needs to be felt in all its ramifications. To be sedated means to be limited in one's awareness of the hurt, the pain, the anger, and the anguish" (p. 15; see Rando, 1984, for a similar argument). Unfortunately, if intervention efforts are based on the assumption that distress following loss is inevitable, little attention may be paid to modifying social or environmental factors that might have been responsible for eliciting such a response (cf. Goldiamond, 1976). Also implicit in such an assumption is that the best and primary intervention strategy might be to wait out distress following loss. As Freud (1917/1957) suggested, "We rely on [mourning] being overcome after a certain lapse of time, and we look upon any interference with it as useless or even harmful" (p. 244).

Any violation of the assumption that distress following loss should abate with time has also tended to be met with a negative reaction by health care professionals. In general, individuals who do not recover within the prescribed time limits have been derogated in the literature. For example, Falek and Britton (1974) maintained that "It may be that an inability to progress after a period of time from one stage to another is the pattern of the psychotic individual" (p. 5). Although it has been acknowledged that the progression to adjustment may be unsteady, health care professionals are reminded to encourage movement forward. As Stewart (1977–78) has written, "To be blunt, a pat on the back and kick in the pants are often necessary" (p. 341).

Even if health care professionals were more sensitive to the possible range of normal responses to irrevocable loss, it is unlikely that the problems arising for those who deviate from the expected pattern of response would be eliminated. Most people who suffer loss do not seek professional help for their difficulties (Cowen, 1982; Veroff, Douvan, & Kulka, 1981). Instead, these individuals typically turn to informal support systems, such as their friends, families, and neighbors, for support, advice, and validation of their feelings. Unfortunately, in their writings, professionals tend to reflect as well as influence general societal attitudes toward those who have encountered loss (Wright, 1983). The popular press is another likely source of the perpetuation of the myths surrounding adjustment to loss (see Gaylin, 1985; Mackey, 1983; Span, 1984). Thus laypersons are also likely to hold unrealistically narrow views of what constitutes a normal grief response. Like the assumptions shared by theorists and clinicians, the common assumption of society is that individuals will respond to a loss with intense distress that will dissipate over time.

For example, there is a fair amount of evidence, although mostly anecdotal, suggesting that shortly after loss, individuals are expected by their social network to respond with a significant amount of negative affect. During the initial months following a loss, expressions of happiness or enjoyment are not well tolerated. Members of peer support groups for the recently bereaved have told us that only within the confines of the support group walls were they free to laugh without risking censure from members of their social environment. Friedman, Chodoff, Mason, and Hamburg (1963) reported that parents of a dying child were expected to appear grief stricken all the time. They wrote, "Parents were not expected to take part in normal social activities or be interested in any form of entertainment" (p. 619). A mother who planned a birthday party for another one of her children was challenged by relatives who "could not understand how my family could have a party at a time like this" (p. 619).

In the early period following loss, social expectations regarding issues such as respect for and loyalty to one's dead spouse make it difficult for the bereaved to seek new partners (see Glick et al., 1974; Raphael, 1983; Wright, 1983). Despite this fact, Zisook and Shuchter (1986) noted that approximately one-half of the widows they studied "were aware of and admitted interest in dating as early as one month after their spouse's death, and over one-fifth had dated within weeks of the death" (p. 291).

In addition to the censure that arises from early expressions of positive affect, there is perhaps even less tolerance from the social network for displays of distress following loss beyond a relatively brief period of time (cf. Coates, Wortman, & Abbey, 1979; Walker, MacBride, & Vachon, 1977). Although there may be recognition of possible long-term difficulties following loss in the hypothetical case (see Lehman, Ellard, & Wortman, 1986), outsiders are likely to underestimate the likelihood of those close to them experiencing persistent loss-related difficulties and distress (Tait & Silver, 1987). In fact, evidence suggests that it may even be those individuals closest in the support network who are the least tolerant of expressions of distress (see Wortman & Lehman, 1985). The press reports many examples of this behavior among friends and relatives of the bereaved. For example, the fact that a widow turned down an invitation to a 25th wedding anniversary party 6 months after her own husband died of cancer was met with a son's worry that his mother was severely disturbed and in need of psychiatric help (Jacoby, 1984). As the son reported, "After all, it's been 6 months since dad died. It's time for mom to get on with her life" (p. 38). Because individuals tend to be held responsible for their responses to negative life events (cf. Brickman, Rabinowitz, et al., 1982), the continued presence of symptomatology is likely to be interpreted by others as a sign of coping failure.

It should also be noted that even individuals who share the same loss may bring different assumptions concerning the grief process into their interactions. In fact, lack of recognition of the variability in response to loss may be even more pronounced when such a loss is mutual. Following the death of an infant, several authors have reported that difficulties have arisen between parents when the mother's and father's patterns of grieving are not synchronous (see Cornwell, Nurcombe, & Stevens, 1977; Helmrath & Steinitz, 1978). In such cases, one person cannot comprehend or support the other's prolonged grief reaction, whereas the partner cannot understand the other's apparent indifference over the loss.

In recent years, many researchers have examined the perceived effectiveness of social responses to individuals who have encountered loss (see Davidowitz & Myrick, 1984; Helmrath & Steinitz, 1978; Lehman et al., 1986; Maddison & Walker, 1967). In general, these researchers have demonstrated that outsiders' attempts to cheer the person up in the short run, or to encourage recovery over time, are repeatedly seen by the person as unhelpful and distressing. By encouraging the person to look on the bright side, implicitly minimizing the loss, reminding the person that things are not really as bad as they seem, or encouraging movement forward, others subtly convey that the person's feelings are inappropriate (cf. Wortman & Lehman, 1985). In contrast, comments and support attempts that are accepting and nonjudgmental and allow the person to go through the loss experience in his or her own way consistently are seen as helpful by individuals who have endured loss. It is important that members of an individual's social network are made aware of the variability that exists in response to loss. In our own research with SIDS parents, we suggest that inappropriate social reactions to expressions of grief may actually exacerbate the distress over time (DeLongis, Silver, & Wortman, 1987).

Conclusion

As reviewed previously, assumptions about the process of coping with loss are generally unsupported, and in some cases contradicted, by available empirical work on the topic. Nonetheless, they tend to be held widely by health care professionals, laypersons, and undoubtedly by individuals who encounter loss themselves. Why might such beliefs continue in the absence of validating data and in the presence of contradictory data that indicate extreme variability of response to loss?

As we (Silver & Wortman, 1980) discussed, even if they are not supported by the data, widespread assumptions about the coping process are particularly resistant to disconfirming evidence. Social psychology researchers have demonstrated repeatedly that "people tend to seek out, recall, and interpret evidence in a manner that sustains beliefs" (Nisbett & Ross, 1980, p. 192). Thus the interpretation of data tends to be strongly biased by the expectations that researchers, clinicians, and laypersons may hold (Nisbett & Ross, 1980; see also Goldiamond, 1975; Wright, 1983), and these errors in information processing lead people's implicit theories to be "almost impervious to data" (Nisbett & Ross, 1980, p. 169).

As noted earlier, the assumption that distress is inevitable shortly after a loss has resulted in its absence being treated as pathological, even if there is no objective reason to assume this to be true. Failure to find problems resulting from the absence of grief may be dismissed for not looking long enough, not looking closely enough, or not asking the correct questions (cf. Volkan, 1966). Such insistence on distress following loss has been labeled the "requirement of mourning" (Dembo, Leviton, & Wright, 1956; Wright, 1983). In this hypothesis, outsiders need to "insist that the person they consider unfortunate is suffering (even when that person seems not to be suffering) or devaluate the unfortunate person because he or she ought to suffer" (Dembo et al., 1956, p. 21). Wright (1983) suggested that this phenomenon may be due to a number of possible factors, including outsiders imagining how they themselves would feel, imagining distress, and then projecting this onto the other person; and the outsider's need to preserve and elevate his or her own superior status. This requirement of mourning may explain why health care professionals tend to assume the presence of significantly more distress following loss than individuals report experiencing themselves (Baluk & O'Neill, 1980; Gans, 1981; Klas, 1970; Mason & Muhlenkamp, 1976; Schoenberg, Carr, Peretz, & Kutscher, 1969; Taylor, 1967; Wikler, Wasow, & Hatfield, 1981).

A series of complementary processes might explain the perpetuation of the assumption that the presence of long-term distress is abnormal. We (Silver & Wortman, 1980) have argued that outsiders may minimize the length of time a loss will affect an individual who encounters it, because they may be unaware that, in addition to the loss itself, the individual must also contend with the simultaneous destruction of future hopes and plans that were vitiated by the loss. Outsiders may also be unaware of the possible alterations in the individual's views of the world that may occur as a result of a loss (Silver & Wortman, 1980). Some psychologists have suggested that the fact that individuals who have experienced loss are often implored to control their expressions of grief and to stop "dwelling on their problems" (Glick et al., 1974; Maddison & Walker, 1967) means that outsiders also believe that the distressed could behave more appropriately if he or she wished. In fact, as Wright (1983) maintained, society frowns upon open displays of distress and has a "requirement of cheerfulness" that in fact contradicts its simultaneous requirement of mourning. It is likely that this subtle yet sometimes explicit message discourages the person who has encountered loss from expressing distress to others at all (DeLongis et al., 1987).

This process may become even more intensified over time. Perhaps so as to maintain harmonious social relations and not to be perceived as abnormal, the individual may hide the true degree of his or her distress or the nature of existing long-term difficulties from members of the social network (Tait & Silver, 1987). Thus the stigma that is associated with persistent distress following loss may result in self-presentational strategies that are in line with societal expectations, resulting in a discrepancy between private experience and public expressions of ongoing distress (Tait & Silver, 1987). The very act of concealing common aspects of the loss experience is likely to perpetuate the misconception that grief is time-limited for all but the few whose reactions are deemed pathological.

In conclusion, we maintain that a complex mixture of biased input and interpretation of data by outsiders, their own personal needs, as well as limited opportunity for open communication between parties has led to a perpetuation of unrealistic assumptions about the normal process of coping with loss. It is likely that this has restricted further theory and research on the topic. In addition, unrealistic assumptions held by health care professionals and the social network may also unnecessarily exacerbate feelings of distress among those who encounter loss and lead to a self-perception that their own responses are inappropriate (cf. Silver & Wortman, 1980) and abnormal under the circumstances.

Of course, the ability to identify pathological responses to loss would enable health care professionals to target those individuals who may be in need of professional assistance (Bracken & Shepard, 1980; Falek & Britton, 1974; Silver & Wortman, 1980). Perhaps this goal has overridden acceptance of alternatives to the current views regarding adjustment to loss. As Zisook and Shuchter (1986) have written in a recent journal of continuing education for psychiatrists, at the present time "there is no prescription for how to grieve properly for a lost spouse, and no research-validated guideposts for what is normal vs. deviant mourning. . . . We are *just beginning* to realize the full range of what may be considered 'normal' grieving" (p. 288, italics added). Recognition of this variability is crucial in order that those who experience loss are treated nonjudgmentally and with the respect, sensitivity, and empathy they deserve.

References

Abraham, K. (1953). A short study of the development of the libido, viewed in the light of mental disorders. In D. Bryan & A. Strachey (Eds. and Trans.), *Selected papers of Karl Abraham* (pp. 418–501). New York: Basic Books. (Original work published 1924)

Agee, J. M. (1980). Grief and the process of aging. In J. A. Werner-Beland (Ed.),

Grief responses to long-term illness and disability: Manifestations and nursing interventions (pp. 133–166). Reston, VA: Reston Publishing Co.

American Psychiatric Association. (1980). *Diagnostic and statistical manual of mental disorders* (3rd ed.). Washington, DC: Author.

Athelstan, G. T., & Crewe, N. M. (1979). Psychological adjustment to spinal cord injury as related to manner of onset of disability. *Rehabilitation Counseling Bulletin, 22*(4), 311–319.

Baluk, U., & O'Neill, P. (1980). Health professionals' perceptions of the psychological consequences of abortion. *American Journal of Community Psychology, 8*(1), 67–75.

Beckwith, J. B. (1970). Observations on the pathological anatomy of Sudden Infant Death Syndrome. In A. Bergman, J. Beckwith, & C. Ray (Eds.), *Sudden Infant Death Syndrome: Proceedings of the Second International Conference on Causes of Sudden Death in Infants* (pp. 83–101). Seattle: University of Washington Press.

Beckwith, J. B. (1977). *The Sudden Infant Death Syndrome.* Washington, DC: U.S. Department of Health, Education, and Welfare.

Bornstein, P. E., & Clayton, P. J. (1972). The anniversary reaction. *Diseases of the Nervous System, 33,* 470–472.

Bornstein, P. E., Clayton, P. J., Halikas, J. A., Maurice, W. L., & Robins, E. (1973). The depression of widowhood after thirteen months. *British Journal of Psychiatry, 122,* 561–566.

Bors, E. (1951). Phantom limbs of patients with spinal cord injury. *Archives of Neurology and Psychiatry, 66,* 610–631.

Bowlby, J. (1961). Processes of mourning. *International Journal of Psycho-Analysis, 42,* 317–340.

Bowlby, J. (1973). *Attachment and loss: Vol. 2. Separation: Anxiety and anger.* New York: Basic Books.

Bowlby, J. (1980). *Attachment and loss: Vol. 3. Loss: Sadness and depression.* New York: Basic Books.

Bracken, M. B., & Shepard, M. J. (1980). Coping and adaptation following acute spinal cord injury: A theoretical analysis. *Paraplegia, 18,* 74–85.

Bray, G. P. (1978). Rehabilitation of spinal cord injured: A family approach. *Journal of Applied Rehabilitation Counseling, 9,* 70–78.

Brickman, P., Coates, D., & Janoff-Bulman, R. (1978). Lottery winners and accident victims: Is happiness relative? *Journal of Personality and Social Psychology, 36*(3), 917–927.

Brickman, P., Rabinowitz, V. C., Karuza, J., Jr., Coates, D., Cohn, E., & Kidder, L. (1982). Models of helping and coping. *American Psychologist, 37*(4), 368–384.

Brown, J. T., & Stoudemire, G. A. (1983). Normal and pathological grief. *Journal of the American Medical Association, 250*(3), 378–382.

Bulman, R. J., & Wortman, C. B. (1977). Attributions of blame and coping in the "real world": Severe accident victims react to their lot. *Journal of Personality and Social Psychology, 35,* 351–363.

Clayton, P. J., Desmarais, L., & Winokur, G. (1968). A study of normal bereavement. *American Journal of Psychiatry, 125,* 168–178.

Clayton, P. J., Halikas, J. A., & Maurice, W. L. (1971). The bereavement of the widowed. *Diseases of the Nervous System, 32,* 597–604.

Clayton, P. J., Halikas, J. A., & Maurice, W. L. (1972). The depression of widowhood. *British Journal of Psychiatry, 120,* 71–78.

Coates, D., Wortman, C. B., & Abbey, A. (1979). Reactions to victims. In I. H. Freize, D. Bar-Tal, & J. S. Carroll (Eds.), *New approaches to social problems* (pp. 21–52). San Francisco: Jossey-Bass.

Cohn, N. K. (1961). Understanding the process of adjustment to disability. *Journal of Rehabilitation, 27,* 16–18.

Cook, D. W. (1976). Psychological aspects of spinal cord injury. *Rehabilitation Counseling Bulletin, 19,* 535–543.

Cornwell, J., Nurcombe, B., & Stevens, L. (1977). Family response to loss of a child by Sudden Infant Death Syndrome. *The Medical Journal of Australia, 1,* 656–658.

Cowen, E. L. (1982). Help is where you find it: Four informal helping groups. *American Psychologist, 37,* 385–395.

Craig, Y. (1977). The bereavement of parents and their search for meaning. *British Journal of Social Work, 7*(1), 41–54.

Davidowitz, M., & Myrick, R. D. (1984). Responding to the bereaved: An analysis of "helping" statements. *Research Record, 1,* 35–42.

Deegan, M. J. (1977). Depression and physical rehabilitation. *Journal of Sociology and Social Welfare, 4*(6), 945–954.

DeLongis, A., Silver, R. C., & Wortman, C. B. (1987). *Coping with the loss of a child: The role of the response of others in the recovery process.* Unpublished manuscript, University of Michigan, Ann Arbor.

Dembo, T., Leviton, G. L., & Wright, B. A. (1956). Adjustment to misfortune: A problem of social–psychological rehabilitation. *Artificial Limbs, 3,* 4–62.

Derogatis, L. R. (1975). *The Affects Balance Scale.* Baltimore: Clinical Psychometric Research.

Derogatis, L. R. (1977). *SCL-90: Administration, scoring and procedures manual—I.* Baltimore: Johns Hopkins University, School of Medicine.

Deutsch, H. (1937). Absence of grief. *Psychoanalytic Quarterly, 6,* 12–22.

Dimond, M., Lund, D. A., & Caserta, M. S. (1987). *The role of social support in the first two years of bereavement in an elderly sample.* Unpublished manuscript, University of Utah.

Dinardo, Q. (1971). *Psychological adjustment to spinal cord injury.* Unpublished doctoral dissertation, University of Houston.

Donovon, M. I., & Girton, S. E. (1984). *Cancer care nursing.* Norwalk, CT: Appleton-Century-Crofts.

Doyle, P. (1980). *Grief counseling and sudden death: A manual and guide.* Springfield, IL: Charles C Thomas.

Elizur, E., & Kaffman, M. (1982). Children's bereavement reactions following death of the father: II. *Journal of the American Academy of Child Psychiatry, 21*(5), 474–480.

Elizur, E., & Kaffman, M. (1983). Factors influencing the severity of childhood bereavement reactions. *American Journal of Orthopsychiatry, 53*(4), 668–676.

Ellard, J. H., Wortman, C. B., & Silver, R. L. (1986, August). *Coping with tragedy: Coming to terms with shattered assumptions about the world.* Paper presented at the annual convention of the American Psychological Association, Washington, DC.

Falek, A., & Britton, S. (1974). Phases in coping: The hypothesis and its implications. *Social Biology, 21,* 1–7.

Frank, R. G., Umlauf, R. L., Wonderlich, S. A., Askanazi, G. S., Buckelew, S. P., &

Elliott, T. R. (in press). Differences in coping style among persons with spinal cord injury: A cluster analytic approach. *Journal of Consulting and Clinical Psychology.*

Freud, S. (1957). Mourning and melancholia. In J. Strachey (Ed. and Trans.), *The standard edition of the complete original works of Sigmund Freud* (Vol. 14, pp. 152–170). London: Hogarth Press. (Original work published 1917)

Friedman, S. B., Chodoff, P., Mason, J. W., & Hamburg, D. A. (1963). Behavioral observations on parents anticipating the death of a child. *Pediatrics, 32,* 610–625.

Fullerton, D. T., Harvey, R. F., Klein, M. H., & Howell, T. (1981). Psychiatric disorders in patients with spinal cord injury. *Archives of General Psychiatry, 38,* 1369–1371.

Gans, J. S. (1981). Depression diagnosis in a rehabilitation hospital. *Archives of Physical Medicine and Rehabilitation, 62,* 386–389.

Gaylin, J. (1985, February). When a child dies. *Parents,* pp. 80–86.

Glick, I. O., Weiss, R. S., & Parkes, C. M. (1974). *The first year of bereavement.* New York: Wiley.

Goin, M. K., Burgoyne, R. W., & Goin, J. M. (1979). Timeless attachment to a dead relative. *American Journal of Psychiatry, 136,* 988–989.

Goldiamond, I. (1975). Insider–outsider problems: A constructional approach. *Rehabilitation Psychology, 22,* 103–116.

Goldiamond, I. (1976). Coping and adaptive behaviors of the disabled. In G. L. Albrecht (Ed.), *The sociology of physical disability and rehabilitation* (pp. 97–138). Pittsburgh: University of Pittsburgh Press.

Gullo, S. V., Cherico, D. J., & Shadick, R. (1974). Suggested stages and response styles in life-threatening illness: A focus on the cancer patient. In B. Schoenberg, A. C. Carr, A. H. Kutscher, D. Peretz, & I. K. Goldberg (Eds.), *Anticipatory grief* (pp. 53–78). New York: Columbia University Press.

Gunther, M. S. (1969). Emotional aspects. In D. Ruge (Ed.), *Spinal cord injuries* (pp. 93–108). Springfield, IL: Charles C Thomas.

Gunther, M. S. (1971). Psychiatric consultation in a rehabilitation hospital: A regression hypothesis. *Comprehensive Psychiatry, 12,* 572–582.

Guttmann, L. (1976). *Spinal cord injuries: Comprehensive management and research* (2nd ed.). Oxford, England: Blackwell Scientific Publications.

Heijn, C., & Granger, G. (1974). Understanding motivational patterns—Early identification aids rehabilitation. *Journal of Rehabilitation, 40,* 26–28.

Helmrath, T. A., & Steinitz, E. M. (1978). Death of an infant: Parental grieving and the failure of social support. *Journal of Family Practice, 6,* 785–790.

Hohmann, G. W. (1975). Psychological aspects of treatment and rehabilitation of the spinal cord injured person. *Clinical Orthopedics and Related Research, 112,* 81–88.

Horowitz, M. J. (1976). *Stress response syndromes.* New York: Aronson.

Horowitz, M. J. (1985). Disasters and psychological responses to stress. *Psychiatric Annals, 15*(3), 161–167.

Horowitz, M. J., & Kaltreider, N. B. (1980). Brief psychotherapy of stress response syndromes. In T. Karasu & L. Bellak (Eds.), *Specialized techniques in individual psychotherapy* (pp. 162–183). New York: Brunner/Mazel.

Howell, T., Fullerton, D. T., Harvey, R. F., & Klein, M. (1981). Depression in spinal cord injured patients. *Paraplegia, 19,* 284–288.

Jacobs, S., & Douglas, L. (1979). Grief: A mediating process between a loss and illness. *Comprehensive Psychiatry, 20*(2), 165–176.

Jacoby, S. (1984, February). You'll be your old self again soon. *McCalls*, pp. 38–43.
Janoff-Bulman, R. (1987). *Exploring people's assumptive worlds*. Unpublished manuscript, University of Massachusetts at Amherst.
Janoff-Bulman, R., & Frieze, I. H. (1983). A theoretical perspective for understanding reactions to victimization. *Journal of Social Issues, 39*(2), 1–17.
Jette, S. H. (1983). Nursing the person with loss. In J. Lindbergh, M. Hunter, & A. Kruszewski (Eds.), *Introduction to person-centered nursing* (pp. 641–657). Philadelphia: Lippincott.
Karney, R. J. (1976). Psychosocial aspects of the spinal cord injured: The psychologist's approach. In W. M. Jenkins, R. M. Anderson, & W. L. Dietrich (Eds.), *Rehabilitation of the severely disabled* (pp. 201–205). Dubuque, IA: Kendall/Hunt.
Kelman, H. R., Lowenthal, M., & Muller, J. N. (1966). Community status of discharged rehabilitation patients: Results of a longitudinal study. *Archives of Physical Medicine and Rehabilitation, 47*, 670–675.
Kemp, B. J., & Vash, C. L. (1971). Productivity after injury in a sample of spinal cord injured persons: A pilot study. *Journal of Chronic Disease, 24*, 259–275.
Kerr, W., & Thompson, M. (1972). Acceptance of disability of sudden onset in paraplegia. *Paraplegia, 10*, 94–102.
Kessler, R. C., Price, R. H., & Wortman, C. B. (1985). Social factors in psychopathology: Stress, social support, and coping processes. *Annual Review of Psychology, 36*, 531–572.
Klas, L. D. (1970). *A study of the relationship between depression and factors in the rehabilitation process of the hospitalized spinal cord injured patient*. Unpublished doctoral dissertation, University of Utah.
Klein, M. (1935). A contribution to the psychogenesis of manic-depressive states. In *Love, guilt and reparation: and other works, 1921–1945* (pp. 262–289). London: Hogarth.
Klein, M. (1940). Mourning and its relation to manic-depressive states. In *Love, guilt and reparation: and other works, 1921–1945* (pp. 344–369). London: Hogarth.
Klerman, G. L., & Izen, J. E. (1977). The effects of bereavement and grief on physical health and general well-being. *Advances in Psychosomatic Medicine, 9*, 63–104.
Klinger, E. (1975). Consequences of commitment to and disengagement from incentives. *Psychological Review, 82*, 1–25.
Klinger, E. (1977). *Meaning and void: Inner experience and the incentives in people's lives*. Minneapolis: University of Minnesota Press.
Knorr, N. J., & Bull, J. C. (1970). Spinal cord injury: Psychiatric considerations. *Maryland State Medical Journal, 19*, 105–108.
Kübler-Ross, E. (1969). *On death and dying*. New York: Macmillan.
Lawson, N. C. (1976). *Depression after spinal cord injury: A multimeasure longitudinal study*. Unpublished doctoral dissertation, University of Houston.
Lawson, N. C. (1978). Significant events in the rehabilitation process: The spinal cord patient's point of view. *Archives of Physical Medicine and Rehabilitation, 59*, 573–579.
Lazarus, R. S., & Folkman, S. (1984). *Stress, appraisal, and coping*. New York: Springer Publishing.
Lazarus, R. S., Kanner, A. D., & Folkman, S. (1980). Emotions: A cognitive–phenomenological analysis. In R. Plutchik & H. Kellerman (Eds.), *Theories of emotion* (pp. 189–218). New York: Academic Press.

Lehman, D. R., Ellard, J. H., & Wortman, C. B. (1986). Social support for the bereaved: Recipients' and providers' perspectives on what is helpful. *Journal of Consulting and Clinical Psychology, 54*(4), 438–446.

Lehman, D. R., Wortman, C. B., & Williams, A. F. (1987). Long-term effects of losing a spouse or child in a motor vehicle crash. *Journal of Personality and Social Psychology, 52,* 218–231.

Lilliston, B. A. (1985). Psychosocial responses to traumatic physical disability. *Social Work in Health Care, 10*(4), 1–13.

Lindemann, E. (1944). The symptomatology and management of acute grief. *American Journal of Psychiatry, 101,* 141–148.

Lund, D. A., Caserta, M. S., & Dimond, M. F. (1986). Gender differences through two years of bereavement among the elderly. *The Gerontologist, 26*(3), 314–319.

Lund, D. A., Dimond, M. F., Caserta, M. S., Johnson, R. J., Poulton, J. L., & Connelly, J. R. (1985–86). Identifying elderly with coping difficulties after two years of bereavement. *Omega, 16*(3), 213–224.

Mackey, A. (1983, March). Dealing with death: Living with loss. *Teen,* pp. 14–19, 80.

Maddison, D., & Walker, W. L. (1967). Factors affecting the outcome of conjugal bereavement. *British Journal of Psychiatry, 113,* 1057–1067.

Malec, J., & Neimeyer, R. (1983). Psychological prediction of duration of inpatient spinal cord injury rehabilitation and performance of self-care. *Archives of Physical Medicine and Rehabilitation, 64,* 359–363.

Marris, P. (1958). *Widows and their families.* London: Routledge & Kegan Paul.

Mason, L., & Muhlenkamp, A. (1976). Patients' self-reported affective states following loss and caregivers' expectations of patients' affective states. *Rehabilitation Psychology, 23*(3), 72–76.

Miles, M. S., & Crandall, E. K. B. (1983). The search for meaning and its potential for affecting growth in bereaved parents. *Health Values: Achieving High Level Wellness, 7*(1), 19–23.

Moos, R. H., & Schaefer, J. A. (1986). Life transitions and crises: A conceptual overview. In R. H. Moos (Ed.), *Coping with life crisis: An integrated approach* (pp. 3–28). New York: Plenum Press.

Nemiah, J. C. (1957). The psychiatrist and rehabilitation. *Archives of Physical Medicine and Rehabilitation, 38,* 143–147.

Nighswonger, C. A. (1971). Ministry to the dying as a learning encounter. *Journal of Thanatology, 1,* 101–108.

Nisbett, R. E., & Ross, L. D. (1980). *Human inference: Strategies and shortcomings of social judgment.* Englewood Cliffs, NJ: Prentice-Hall.

Osterweis, M., Solomon, F., & Green, M. (Eds.). (1984). *Bereavement: Reactions, consequences, and care.* Washington, DC: National Academy Press.

Parkes, C. M. (1970). The first year of bereavement: A longitudinal study of the reactions of London widows to the death of their husbands. *Psychiatry, 33,* 444–467.

Parkes, C. M. (1972). Components of the reaction to loss of a limb, spouse or home. *Journal of Psychosomatic Research, 16,* 343–349.

Parkes, C. M. (1975). Unexpected and untimely bereavement: A statistical study of young Boston widows and widowers. In B. Schoenberg, I. Gerber, A. Wiener, A. H. Kutscher, D. Peretz, & A. C. Carr (Eds.), *Bereavement: Its psychosocial aspects* (pp. 119–138). New York: Columbia University Press.

Parkes, C. M., & Weiss, R. S. (1983). *Recovery from bereavement.* New York: Basic Books.

Pattison, E. M. (1977). *The experience of dying.* Englewood Cliffs, NJ: Prentice-Hall.

Platt, N. V. D. (1977). What will happen to the flowers when winter comes? *Journal of Religion and Health, 16*(4), 326–332.

Randall, G. C., Ewalt, J. R., & Blair, H. (1945). Psychiatric reaction to amputation. *Journal of the American Medical Association, 128,* 645–652.

Rando, T. A. (1984). *Grief, dying and death: Clinical interventions for caregivers.* Champaign, IL: Research Press Co.

Raphael, B. (1983). *The anatomy of bereavement.* New York: Basic Books.

Rees, W. D. (1971). The hallucinations of widowhood. *British Medical Journal, 4,* 37–41.

Rosenbaum, R. (1982, July). Turn on, tune in, drop dead. *Harpers,* pp. 32–42.

Rubin, S. (1981). A two-track model of bereavement: Theory and application in research. *American Journal of Orthopsychiatry, 51*(1), 101–109.

Schoenberg, B. B., Carr, A. C., Peretz, D., & Kutscher, A. H. (1969). Physicians and the bereaved. *General Practitioner, 40,* 105–108.

Schulz, R., & Decker, S. (1985). Long-term adjustment to physical disability: The role of social support, perceived control, and self-blame. *Journal of Personality and Social Psychology, 48*(5), 1162–1172.

Shadish, W. R., Hickman, D., & Arrick, M. C. (1981). Psychological problems of spinal cord injury patients: Emotional distress as a function of time and locus of control. *Journal of Consulting and Clinical Psychology, 49,* 297.

Shanfield, S. B., & Swain, B. J. (1984). Death of adult children in traffic accidents. *Journal of Nervous and Mental Disease, 172*(9), 533–538.

Shontz, F. C. (1965). Reactions to crisis. *Volta Review, 67,* 364–370.

Shontz, F. C. (1975). *The psychological aspects of physical illness and disability.* New York: Macmillan.

Shuchter, S. R. (1986). *Dimensions of grief: Adjusting to the death of a spouse.* San Francisco: Jossey-Bass.

Siller, J. (1969). Psychological situation of the disabled with spinal cord injuries. *Rehabilitation Literature, 30,* 290–296.

Silver, R. L. (1982). *Coping with an undesirable life event: A study of early reactions to physical disability.* Unpublished doctoral dissertation, Northwestern University, Evanston, IL.

Silver, R. L., Boon, C., & Stones, M. H. (1983). Searching for meaning in misfortune: Making sense of incest. *Journal of Social Issues, 39*(2), 81–102.

Silver, R. L., & Wortman, C. B. (1980). Coping with undesirable life events. In J. Garber & M. E. P. Seligman (Eds.), *Human helplessness: Theory and applications* (pp. 279–340). New York: Academic Press.

Silver, R. C., & Wortman, C. B. (1987). *The role of positive emotions in the coping process.* Unpublished manuscript, University of Waterloo, Waterloo, Canada.

Simons, R. C. (Ed.). (1985). *Understanding human behavior in health and illness* (3rd ed.). Baltimore: Williams & Wilkins.

Span, P. (1984, November). When a child dies. *Glamour,* pp. 292–293, 333.

Stewart, T. D. (1977–78). Coping behaviour and the moratorium following spinal cord injury. *Paraplegia, 15,* 338–342.

Stroebe, M., & Stroebe, W. (1983). Who suffers more? Sex differences in health risks of the widowed. *Psychological Bulletin, 93,* 297–301.

Sutherland, S., & Scherl, D. (1970). Patterns of response among victims of rape. *American Journal of Orthopsychiatry, 40,* 503–511.

Tait, R., & Silver, R. C. (1987). *Coming to terms with major negative events: Long-term psychological impact and recovery.* Unpublished manuscript, University of Waterloo, Waterloo, Canada.

Taylor, G. P. (1967). *Predicted versus actual response to spinal cord injury: A psychological study.* Unpublished doctoral dissertation, University of Minnesota.

Trieschmann, R. B. (1978). *The psychological, social, and vocational adjustment in spinal cord injury: A strategy for future research* (Final Report No. 13-P-59011/9-01). Washington, DC: Rehabilitation Services Administration.

Trieschmann, R. B. (1980). *Spinal cord injuries: Psychological, social and vocational adjustment.* New York: Pergamon Press.

Tucker, S. J. (1980). The psychology of spinal cord injury: Patient–staff interaction. *Rehabilitation Literature, 41,* 114–121, 160.

Vachon, M. L. S., Rogers, J., Lyall, W. A. L., Lancee, W. J., Sheldon, A. R., & Freeman, S. J. J. (1982). Predictors and correlates of adaptation to conjugal bereavement. *American Journal of Psychiatry, 139*(8), 998–1002.

Vachon, M. L. S., Sheldon, A. R., Lancee, W. J., Lyall, W. A. L., Rogers, J., & Freeman, F. J. J. (1982). Correlates of enduring stress patterns following bereavement: Social network, life situation and personality. *Psychological Medicine, 12,* 783–788.

Veroff, J., Douvan, E., & Kulka, R. A. (1981). *The inner American: A self-portrait from 1957–1976.* New York: Basic Books.

Viorst, J. (1986). *Necessary losses.* Central Point, OR: Simon & Schuster.

Volkan, V. (1966). Normal and pathological grief reactions: A guide for the family physician. *Virginia Medical Monthly, 93,* 651–656.

Walker, K. N., MacBride, A., & Vachon, M. L. S. (1977). Social support networks and the crisis of bereavement. *Social Science and Medicine, 11,* 35–41.

Wiener, A., Gerber, I., Battin, D., & Arkin, A. M. (1975). The process and phenomenology of bereavement. In B. Schoenberg, I. Gerber, A. Wiener, A. H. Kutscher, D. Peretz, & A. C. Carr (Eds.), *Bereavement: Its psychosocial aspects* (pp. 53–65). New York: Columbia University Press.

Wikler, L., Wasow, M., & Hatfield, E. (1981). Chronic sorrow revisited: Parent vs. professional depiction of the adjustment of parents of mentally retarded children. *American Journal of Orthopsychiatry, 51*(1), 63–70.

Wortman, C. B. (1983). Coping with victimization: Conclusions and implications for future research. *Journal of Social Issues, 39*(2), 197–223.

Wortman, C. B., Ellard, J. H., & Silver, R. C. (1987). *Reaching a state of resolution following loss.* Unpublished manuscript, University of Michigan, Ann Arbor, Michigan.

Wortman, C. B., & Lehman, D. R. (1985). Reactions to victims of life crises: Support attempts that fail. In I. G. Sarason & B. R. Sarason (Eds.), *Social support: Theory, research and applications* (pp. 463–489). Dordrecht, The Netherlands: Martinus Nijhoff.

Wright, B. A. (1983). *Physical disability—A psychosocial approach* (2nd ed.). New York: Harper & Row.

Zahourek, R., & Jensen, J. S. (1973). Grieving and the loss of the newborn. *American Journal of Nursing, 73,* 836–839.

Zisook, S., DeVaul, R. A., & Click, M. A. (1982). Measuring symptoms of grief and bereavement. *American Journal of Psychiatry, 139,* 1590–1593.

Zisook, S., & Shuchter, S. R. (1985). Time course of spousal bereavement. *General Hospital Psychiatry, 7,* 95–100.

Zisook, S., & Shuchter, S. R. (1986). The first four years of widowhood. *Psychiatric Annals, 15,* 288–294.